Richard.
I hope you enjoy this book
Love Sue

First published in 2019
Quentin Wilson Publishing
105 Moncks Spur Road
Christchurch 8081
New Zealand
quentin@quentinwilsonpublishing.com
www.quentinwilsonpublishing.com

Text copyright Michael Willis © 2019
Unless otherwise attributed, all photographs copyright Michael Willis © 2019

The moral rights of the author have been asserted.

978-0-9951053-4-8

A catalogue record for this book is available from the National Library of New Zealand.

This book is copyright. Except for the purpose of fair review, no part may be stored or transmitted in any form or by any means, electronic or mechanical, including recording or storage in any information retrieval system, without permission in writing from the publishers. No reproduction may be made, whether by photocopying or by any other means, unless a licence has been obtained from the publisher or its agent.

Edited by: Anna Rogers

Front cover design concept:
Burton Silver & Quentin Wilson

Book & cover design & page layout:
Quentin Wilson, Quentin Wilson Publishing
quentin@quentinwilsonpublishing.com

Printed in Taiwan ROC by CHOICE Printing Inc.

Frontispiece and full title page: Michael Willis (right) with Adam Henson of BBC *Countryfile*, on Arapawa Island in 2017.

CONTENTS

Foreword by Lawrence Alderson CBE — 9

Acknowledgements — 13

Introduction — 15

1. Against the Tide — 19
2. The Call of Arapawa — 37
3. A Cat – Or Less — 49
4. Katch Me a Kune Kune — 63
5. When is a Camel Not a Camel — 81
6. Ode to an Otter — 97
7. A Country Fit for Horses — 111
8. A Change of Life — 129
9. The End of the Rabbit — 143
10. Chasing Rainbows — 161
11. The Seaweed-Eating Cow — 175
12. If Only Noah Knew — 189
13. Can Do Kiwi — 199
14. A Pig of an Idea — 217
15. Hair of the Dog — 233
16. A Donkey Debacle — 243
17. Oz Odyssey — 261
18. The Way of the Future — 275

It has been said that humans made to animals the offer of a partnership. Some accepted and became domesticated; others refused, remained wild and always will be. My question would be: Have we honoured the partnership?

This book is dedicated to partners of every kind, especially mine.

FOREWORD

There was a moment in the mid-twentieth century when realisation dawned on some members of the human species – a realisation that something was not right, that breeds which had been a familiar sight in pastures and farmyards were no longer to be seen. It was not an issue of significance for governments and business leaders who were interested primarily in maximising business efficiency and profits, but the kernel of concern felt by others was real and slowly it germinated. The movement to conserve the genetic diversity of our planet was born.

The motivation to save endangered breeds demands passion. It may be directed by pragmatic reasoning, but the heart is its driving force – an in-built compulsion to undertake action that often may seem inexplicable to an uninvolved observer. There are passionate movements for many causes, saving wildlife, saving forests, saving fertile soil, saving the atmosphere, and yet poachers still decimate wildlife, illegal logging fells forests, monoculture crops denude soils, and global warming exposes us to cosmic radiation. In the midst of this dark scenario a guiding torch still shines. The visionary torch-bearers who saw the need to save our breeds of domestic livestock and their feral relatives began a movement which has gathered force and stemmed the rush towards extinction.

It began in small pockets of local activity in widely separated areas – Whipsnade in England, Massachusetts in North America, Hortobágy in Hungary – but gradually the passion spread and linked into an international defence of the global livestock heritage. National groups of activists extended

Opposite: Back from extinction – the takahē.

their expertise and developed projects under the umbrella of Rare Breeds International. Improved global communications during the twentieth century enabled more rapid movement of breeding stock allowing popular breeds to displace local breeds. At the same time scientists applied genetics to increase the intensity of selection and advances in reproductive technology accelerated even more the speed of change. The result is that 750 breeds of livestock now are listed by the Food and Agriculture Organisation of the United Nations as extinct and a further 1000 are at risk of extinction; each is an irretrievable loss and devastating reduction in genetic global diversity. The situation was dire and the arrival of the torch-bearers, although too late for some breeds, was the turning point.

The torch-bearer in New Zealand fits closely the description of a passionate visionary. Michael Willis' childhood ambition to have a zoo changed when he discovered that native New Zealand creatures were threatened with extinction, and he opened Willowbank Wildlife Reserve to the public in 1974. It is a New Zealand-themed park which is visited each year by more than 185,000 national and international visitors to hear the story of the national natural heritage. He is a trend-setter who is not afraid of innovation and relishes pioneering opportunities. His visitors are able to enjoy a direct interactive experience with the animals in a natural environment. Willowbank Farm is associated with the reserve and focuses on breeding programmes for many rare heritage breeds of New Zealand as well as native and endangered species of wildlife. His pre-eminence in his chosen field of work was recognised in 2015 by the award of the prestigious MNZM (Member of the New Zealand Order of Merit) for services to conservation.

Michael also founded the Rare Breeds Conservation Society of New Zealand and was a director of Rare Breeds International, but time has not dimmed his enthusiasm or exuberance. His rescue missions have taken him over rough seas and rocky shores to remote islands to capture and relocate feral breeds, many descended from animals put ashore by Captain Cook and threatened with extermination by governmental policy. Auckland Island pigs, Arapawa Island sheep, and Enderby Island rabbits all owe their continued existence to his determination and courage. In some cases he is at the cutting edge of conservation, vying with the scientists at the Roslin Institute in Edinburgh to be the first to achieve successful cloning of farm animals with the Enderby cow in 1996.

Not only is he a visionary and a man of passion, but he pens prose of unpretentious fluency with a flowing matter-of-fact style which yet transmits to the reader the immediacy of his feelings of excitement (even danger) and

FOREWORD

Bonzo, a beautiful scarlet macaw. As for so many species, including homo sapiens, the very existence of macaws is threatened by environmental issues such as climate change.

humour experienced on many of his missions which encapsulate his pioneering spirit. Michael is a powerful advocate for his cause of saving endangered breeds. His style of writing and the details of his crusading missions serve only to reinforce his message. The man, the book and the manner of his story-telling deserve to recruit many adherents to the causes he has espoused.

Lawrence Alderson CBE BA MA(Cantab) CBiol FRAgS FRBI MRSB
Founder President of Rare Breeds International

ACKNOWLEDGEMENTS

One of the most difficult parts in compiling the final version of this manuscript was having to leave things out. This applied especially to mentioning the names of the many people who have contributed to the stories, or helped to make things happen. This army has my heartfelt thanks: without their involvement and support in so many different ways, we could never have achieved what we have.

I am fortunate to have the support of Lawrence Alderson, who contributed the foreword. In many ways he is the David Attenborough of international rare breed conservation and his work and writing have been a guiding light to so many people and organisations throughout the world.

The tribute by Adam Henson is also appreciated. A staunch supporter of rare breed conservation and director of Cotswold Farm Park, he is also recognised as the presenter of the BBC series, *Countryfile*, which is shown in many countries throughout the world.

My thanks also to Anna Rogers, who for the second time has edited a book for me, creating, from the raw material, a much more polished and finished article. Orchestrating the book's design and production has been Quentin Wilson, whose guidance and expertise have been invaluable.

Opposite: The kaka, a friend to save.

INTRODUCTION

The morning sun rose slowly over the trees, the light filtering through the tips and dancing on the ripples of water on the lake created by a small group of scaup or black teal and their babies. I've always loved these plump little ducks with their orange eyes. Swimming not far away from them were four grey teal, who had also nested there. Tall willows wept down into the far side, and gliding like gondolas through the overhanging branches were a pair of black swan, serene and graceful. In the branches of the trees above them, I could see twelve or so haphazard basket piles of sticks, each containing a pair of pied cormorants, for this was their nesting tree. I had placed nesting platforms and painted plywood cut-outs of the birds in the tree in order to attract them, and hours could be spent just watching the comings and goings of the little colony. This was springtime, but in the autumn the air over the water would be filled with clouds of brilliant coloured swallows, waiting to migrate.

As Sue and I ate our breakfast a pair of Californian quail jumped up onto the rail about 3 metres from our dining room windows, while underneath strolled Mr Amhurst, a beautifully coloured male pheasant who visited every morning. A few months ago a white heron had sat on a post only metres away. We may not have a lot of material possessions, but it's hard to put a value on some of the simple things in life. When the dogs are released from their runs, their enthusiastic greeting is always the same, no matter how much money you owe, or what the weather. While Sue feeds the horses and donkeys, I wander over to the aviaries and start feeding the parrots and cockatoos.

Opposite: My partner Sue with an African Grey friend.

Macaws are beautiful and smart.

Many of these birds are highly intelligent, and if you ignore them and don't ask personal questions like 'How was your night?', they will get grumpy and pull your hair in retaliation. The Cochin chooks will get the remains of the parrot food, and having finished the morning chores I'll climb into the Land Cruiser truck, and head off to work at the Willowbank Wildlife Reserve in Christchurch.

It takes a while to get down the driveway, and it's an excuse to check the different breeds of sheep and cattle stock in the paddocks, and on the half-hour drive from our home property to the park, I always have plenty of planning to occupy my thoughts. When I pull into the carpark, it's generally full of cars and buses. Too many people, and I scurry around like a scared rabbit, hoping nobody will see me. It's not that I don't like people, and I certainly enjoy them visiting the park. Some of my work is highly public, and that goes with the territory, but I started Willowbank because I'm comfortable in the unjudgemental company of animals, and never fully relaxed around people. I've always loved working with animals and birds, backing breeding programmes and creating an environment that encourages their natural behaviour and shows them off to the visiting public in a way that allows for a personal connection between people and creatures.

Catching up with the staff and getting an update on what's happening is always a pleasure. When you have such a committed, talented and enthusiastic team, all these qualities seem to rub off and the word 'work' is forgotten. Unfortunately the world is changing faster than we can keep up with it, and few really care beyond their allotted lifetime. Climate change alone will create a global battle, because there are no frontiers, and nowhere in the world you can hide, immune from its effects. We can all, however, make a small difference that cumulatively may effect an outcome, and I would like to think that places such as Willowbank will help to create some of that positive change.

Driving back home at the end of the day I cannot but think how fortunate I have been. Sure, there have been some bad times, but when I settle back in my chair and watch the cormorants feeding their babies while an unwanted rabbit bounces on the front lawn, I'm grateful to be where I am, and to live in such a wonderful country.

Note: This book is a collection of stories brought together over a number of years. Some readers may recognise one or two anecdotes from my earlier book, *Some of My Best Friends are Animals*, but I'm sure their reappearance will be forgiven.

CHAPTER ONE

AGAINST THE TIDE

'This would have to be the worst bit of land that I have ever seen in my life.' My father stood grimly on a bank and surveyed his surroundings with ill-concealed disdain.

Following his gaze, I saw a weed-choked drain bounded by wide marshy areas rising back into poor grasslands of indeterminate parentage. We were on a 3-metre-high shingle bank that ran the length of the property, and edged half of its available usage. A forest of broom and gorse waved gently in the breeze, a riot of sweet-smelling yellow flowers and twisting black seed pods, crisping in the sun and popping like a packet of Kellogg's rice bubbles, as they shot yet another generation of noxious seeds into the substrate below. Not even any road access, just a bumpy track through the next-door neighbour's property. No one in their right mind would buy it.

I had to admit that Dad had a pretty good point but, pretending not to have heard, I half closed my eyes, let my mind relax, and looked again at the land I was proposing to buy. Under the floating weed was a beautiful creek welling with springs coming from subterranean depths, and rich with trout, eels and other wildlife. The marsh edges were in fact a soft velvet carpet festooned with golden flowers that were buzzing with insects, while the grassland wastes became paddocks of verdant green grass mixed with wild flowers.

It was hard to visualise, past a massive shingle bank that came with its own consented gravel rights. Remove the gorse and broom, and you had left a vast dry pad that must be useful for something, but however you looked at it,

Opposite: A Bren gun carrier, used by all the family, was part of my mountain upbringing.

it was an irregularly shaped piece of disused Waimakariri riverbed, unloved and unwanted. Again my mind wandered off, and I could see a road running along the far boundary, and an access driveway winding across the lower reaches, across the creek, and up to a cottage perched on top of the bank. A cosy little cottage, isolated and private, with trees and shrubs helping it to nestle into the surroundings so it became part of the overall landscape.

As we turned and left the property by climbing over the neighbour's fence, there was little discussion on the merits of the land. I knew that my father was essentially right. For most purposes it had few redeeming features, but he was unable to see my mental picture of what it might be. This block of discarded real estate had all the quirky attributes that I needed to start a zoo in Christchurch, an idea that I had had since early childhood, and one that I was determined to turn into a reality.

I had come from a large and boisterous family of six children, and two committed parents. I was fourth in line with two older brothers, John and Paul, and an older sister, Ann. Below me were two younger sisters, Robyn and Susan. I was too young to be of any interest to my brothers except as a potential pea gun target or hostage, too old to play dress-up with Ann, and my younger sisters, in my eyes, were too young and femininely orientated to be capable of doing good boyish things. So my life was reasonably solitary and I pursued my own interests, which revolved largely around an imaginary world of wildlife and adventure. City retail may have developed into the lifeblood of the family, but our parents also had a strong attachment to the high country, where my father had established a family cottage in the Craigieburn Valley of the Southern Alps. In many ways that combination of lifestyles provided an exciting balance. Almost every weekend we would climb into the old Chevrolet, and make our way up to what was known as 'the hut'.

I spent a lot of time on my own in the mountains, growing up in an environment where obstacles were overcome by necessity, should you wish to get home again. It was a childhood that is now seldom possible in the constraints of today's world. I grew up with a butterfly net in one hand and a rifle in the other. Firearms were a tool, and their size and calibre were governed not by your age but by your strength to hold and fire them. The back country shaped my life, and in many ways I went on to become a professional hunter and trapper. Cyanide I purchased from the local chemist in large lumps, enough, if dropped into the water system, to kill half a town. I used it to kill insects for my collection, and would also crush it on rocks in riverbeds to make a powder form to kill opossums. If your legs were long enough to reach the pedals then you could drive a vehicle, even if it meant sitting on a cushion to be able to

CHAPTER ONE **AGAINST THE TIDE**

My father, Alan, was a man of the mountains. He, Roger Chester and Bill Mirams were the first to climb Mount Whitcombe by the original route in December 1931. On his eighty-fifth birthday my brother John (right) and I arranged a chopper flight for him back to the peak they had conquered.

see out the windscreen, and drinking alcohol was a family affair governed by the simple rules of hospitality and manners derived from association and example. There were huge family parties where all the old uncles and aunts would gather to drink and dance the night away. Early dawn would see them stepping unsteadily into the old Morris 8 or Austin 7, and wandering off down the road in the direction of home. Maximum horsepower was about 27, and top speed was around 50 kph, and I can't recall any accidents or disasters taking place.

My love for the mountains was also coloured by my avid reading of tales of exploration and settlement and, occasionally, traumatic accounts of survival (or otherwise). People such as Ernest Shackleton, Mr Explorer (Charlie) Douglas and the characters in Jack London's books were all grist to the mill for a highly impressionable youngster. Freedom, space, being at one with nature, lives that seemed so uncomplicated, clear and purposeful. Clean snow, clean air, bulging sledges of warm furs. Even the bad tales romanticised the actuality. Antarctic explorer Captain Robert Falcon Scott was an icon of fortitude and duty, on the side of God. His dying words were read to men

Hunting was a part of my life growing up.

going into battle, to reinforce the notion that whatever happened, their lives would never be lost in vain. I dreamed of and longed for such a world and on weekends in the mountains, I would live to some extent the life I imagined.

One Christmas I was given Gerald Durrell's book, *The Bafut Beagles*, a present that was supposed to appease the ambitions of a frustrated ten-year-old animal collector, big game hunter and intrepid explorer of jungle and desert. The pleasure that I derived from that book was out of all proportion

CHAPTER ONE AGAINST THE TIDE

Kea were just one of the many creatures I kept as a young lad.

to its undoubted literary merit, and what for me had previously been a little world of fantasy was now given an element of realism. That passion for wildlife only grew and gained momentum as I grew older, especially as I was exposed to books written by such great men as Durrell, David Attenborough, Konrad Lorenz and Carl Hagenbeck. Like other readers throughout the world, I just loved their stories and the life they breathed into their wildlife exploits, along with the laughter, humanity and rich kaleidoscope of characters they met along the way. What their work also showed to me was that it could be done: if I really wanted to work with animals and own a zoo, then anything was possible.

In the meantime I kept as many pets as the confines of suburban Christchurch, an indulgent mother and a father struggling to understand his animal-mad son would allow. I had all the usual cage birds, rabbits, guinea pigs and mice, along with frogs and lizards, interspersed with kea, opossums, hawks and other reluctant captives. I worked part-time for a veterinarian, but the course of my life was shaped: I wanted to create a zoo.

Typically I met my future wife Kathy while skiing in the mountains. It was a childhood romance that led to us getting married several years later, and like many young colonials, boarding a ship bound for Europe, and our great OE experience. Unlike most tourists, however, we didn't travel from cathedral to cathedral, but rather from zoo to zoo. I soaked up everything

RESCUE ONE NEW ZEALANDER'S CRUSADE TO SAVE ENDANGERED ANIMALS

Mak the capuchin monkey and his friend, Horrible the rescue kitten, tucked up in bed in the hot water cylinder cupboard of our house in Kent.

I saw, and when we returned to England, took on the role of managing an animal rescue centre in Kent. Those were the days when you could walk into Harrods and buy a lion cub for a few pounds, or visit any dealer for a range of other exotic species. We did just that and in addition kept a Capuchin monkey in the house for a year or so, before donating it to another zoo when we left Britain. It was the first of many animals in the house, ranging from bush babies to foxes. Great fun but a bit of a reality check in the difficulties of retaining any normal social life when your co-lodgers do not enjoy the same etiquette standards, and also in accepting the responsibility for their future.

My overseas experience and travels back through Africa cemented my desire to start my own animal park. While I was away, my grandmother had died and left me a small amount of money. Within a month of being back in Christchurch I began looking for land, and it was during a casual conversation while buying eggs from a farmer that I found out about some that had been for sale for quite a while, just up the road.

In my view it was on the right side of town. It was near the main route going from north to south and close to the airport. It appeared to be unlikely to be built around, and it had all the physical characteristics that I needed. Best of all, it was in my price bracket, and before long I was the proud owner of 12 acres of second-hand Waimakariri riverbed, and had reinforced my father's view that I had inherited little business acumen from my ancestors.

Purchasing the land took all the money I had available, and although it was a giant step forward, we still had a long way to go. I was offered a position in Te Anau as conservator of wildlife for an American businessman who had built, up a secluded valley, a hospitality complex that catered mainly for wealthy sportsmen. In reality it was a jack of all trades position, with a lot of time acting as a hunting and fishing guide. Te Anau was buzzing with energy. There was a massive hydro-electric scheme being developed by the government, which was also flat out developing and settling farmers onto blocks that were being carved out of the surrounding scrublands. The export of wild deer, shot either on foot or from helicopters, was in full swing, as was the start of deer farming and the live capture of wild animals. It was a true wild west town, with its own rules and the improbable happened with almost impossible regularity.

Two years later, and with a bit more money in the bank, we loaded up the van with as many of our possessions as we could, along with three dogs and a new baby boy named Mark, and headed back to Christchurch. At long last we were in a position to put a stick in the ground, and begin the journey to fulfil a lifelong ambition.

First we needed a house to live in, and I chose an interlocking timber design, that allowed me to do as much of the building as possible. The roofing material was a heavy-duty bitumen felt, weighed down by 10 tonnes of river gravel. Cheap, practical and always changing as the shadows danced across the irregularities of the stones, it always looked right to me, perched on that dominant shingle bank. We were back to having no money, but had made yet another big step forward.

As a qualified radiographer, Kathy easily found work at the hospital. That left me with a baby son, and a lot of work to do during the day. At nights I worked as a commercial cleaner, and so we passed like ships in the night, handing Mark between us. Slowly the shingle bank was cleared of broom and gorse, and for the first time we could actually see what was underneath it. Painfully it relented enough to have postholes dug, and slowly some paddocks were established that gave some form of control, and the property lost its wild look, and became more managed, which had both good and bad effects.

We now had a few grazing cattle, sheep and goats, which kept things vaguely under control. As happens to most small block owners with enthusiasm but no money, our fencing budget stretched to what may have looked okay, but effectively was not. Goats are great animals for quality control work – they find every shortcoming there is to be found – and I painfully learnt the necessity for good fencing.

We needed aviaries, but how to find and build some? My father would never buy new if he could fabricate something using second-hand materials, and that part of the genetic influence proved strong. Demolition and recycling yards were scoured for anything useful, as were the 'for sale' columns in any publications. There isn't much call for used aviaries, and in fact many people were pleased to have them removed, and so slowly a higgledy-piggledy collection of enclosures gradually came together. Wooden pallets were a great source of timber, especially the hardwood ones in which Toyota brought their vehicles out from Asia. These were meticulously pulled apart and hundreds of nails straightened for reuse.

I gave up commercial cleaning and started a pet shop in the city. Toilet cleaning was not my forte, and I was pleased to be back into something that I enjoyed. It was not a particularly profitable business, but it did help to build up a list of breeders and other animal contacts that would be useful for the future. It also provided access to a range of stock, some of which I could siphon off into the embryonic collection that we were now gathering. We were given the loan of a donkey if we bought her foal and, best of all, we managed to get hold of a llama.

Because, in those days, llamas were strictly allowed to be kept only by a registered zoo, getting that registration and our first exotic animal was a big step forward, if you overlooked the slight drawback that he was a gift from the Nelson City Council, who wanted him gone because he spat green globules of sticky saliva over anyone who was unwise enough to get within his range. He was surprisingly accurate, and seemed to enjoy the effect he had on people. It was a habit I tried several methods to try and stop, including throwing a bucket of water at him when he spat, on the theory that he would realise that I could spit bigger spits than him, but that just seemed to further infuriate him. He came with considerable notoriety, and gained more with us. He had been called Larry the Llama in Nelson, but for some reason we rechristened him Sammy, possibly hoping that a name change might have a beneficial effect. Any publicity was reckoned to be good publicity, and so he became a star attraction for all of the wrong reasons.

Animals are always a tie. Once you have one, your life becomes restricted and the responsibility grows. As you get more animals, that responsibility increases, until a normal life becomes increasingly difficult. There's no such thing as having a day off, as everything still needs cleaning and feeding. Nor is there such a thing as being too sick to work. So it was a routine of working seven days a week, for months leading into years. I was too focused to consider that that was any hardship – it just became normal for me – but

CHAPTER ONE **AGAINST THE TIDE**

family life was probably the biggest casualty. Money was tight, and eventually I judged that we had gone as far as we could go. We had scraped the bottom of the barrel clean, and there was nothing to be gained by delaying opening any longer. So on Labour Weekend 1974 we decided to take the plunge and open the gates to visitors.

There was no ticket box, just an old Land Rover with a cardboard box on the front seat. At least the vehicle could be locked, and it gave me a chance to do some other jobs between customers. Fortunately a gravel road had by now been put past the property. The fact that it didn't go anywhere and was really just an improved farm track was irrelevant. At least it had a name, and I could nail up a sign on the lamp post at the beginning of it. We charged 50 cents for an adult, 20 cents for a child, and over that first weekend a small trickle of people did come. It was an exciting time as we meticulously counted our takings. It was only a small amount of money, but it helped to stem the financial tide, and all of it was allocated to next week's projects.

It was never enough. Nothing was ever wasted: we were like scavenging seagulls grabbing at any useful offerings and using them to create a facade of pretence. Our living requirements were nominal and even spartan, but I was too engrossed to worry about that. We were committed and every dollar had to be turned into three, every bargain seized. Things were made to happen, and I learnt early on there was no such thing as it can't be done. There was always a way, you just had to find it. Used and salvaged materials were the norm, and in a strange way their use began to give the park an identity. The old adage, that one person's rubbish was someone else's treasure, became very pertinent. It wasn't what you had and did that mattered, it was what you did with what was available that was important. If it was built honestly and well, with a certain amount of imagination, then the very nature of the salvaged materials often gave character that new materials couldn't provide.

The weeks and months went by, and we were still there. It was a hand-to-mouth existence, but miraculously we survived the first year. The parked Land Rover was replaced with a shelter that looked a bit like a telephone box, and my father relented enough to donate money for a large wooden carved sign above the gates that proudly stated 'WILLOWBANK'.

A building firm closing down in town had two large buildings they wanted to get rid of. A visit to the bank manager and $4000 later they were on site. One became the new entrance building and shop, while the other became the feed store, kitchen etc. They were substantial purchases for us but were invaluable additions. My neighbour dumped an old house on his property, in the hope that the council would give approval for it to be put in

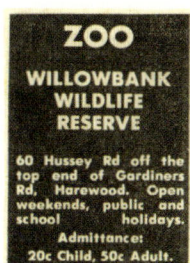

The advertisement for the opening of Willowbank Wildlife Reserve – 50 cents for an adult, 20 cents for a child.

We were very proud of the sign at the gate.

permanently. They didn't, and I got permission from the neighbour to pull it to pieces and remove the materials. After weeks of work I had demolished the house, straightened all the nails and transported everything up to where I wanted to put a farmyard. These materials allowed for a central building to be put up, and the farmyard became an important and popular addition to the reserve.

It was always interesting to survey people and see what they enjoyed most during their visit to the park. Almost without exception the answer would surprise you with its simplicity. 'I liked the bantam with the chicks or the duck with the ducklings. I liked feeding the lamb. I liked touching the

Kathy and I with some of the Willowbank residents.

CHAPTER ONE **AGAINST THE TIDE**

It was always interesting watching visitors interacting with the animals.

The farmyard has always been a popular exhibit, especially the Clydesdales.

horse's nose.' Our most popular exhibit became what we called the contact area, a small fenced-off part with a stile for people to climb over, and filled with rabbits, guinea pigs and other miscellaneous bits and pieces. There was a central edifice that people could sit on, and the animals could hide underneath, and everyone could have as much interaction as they desired. But although the farmyard was popular, it was not what people expected when they visited a zoo. We needed something more exotic than that, and monkeys were by far our preferred choice. So how to find a monkey?

There were then two main zoos in New Zealand, one in Auckland and the other in Wellington. We had developed good relationships with the management of Wellington Zoo in particular, and to my delight they were happy to offer me two monkeys that were surplus to their requirements. One was a South American Capuchin, which to me was one of the loveliest species and one of which we had already had experience. Capuchins, normally a light brown in colour with a long dark tail, are named for the black patch on the top of their heads which resembles the skull caps worn by Capuchin monks. The other monkey was a delightful little Talapoin monkey, an African breed,

CHAPTER ONE **AGAINST THE TIDE**

The enclosure we built for the monkeys.

named Martin. Both were said to be male, in good health and available when we were ready. First, of course, we had to build a suitable enclosure.

I made a large artificial rock, a bit like a concrete boat turned upside down. It was a great way of using up old pieces of chicken wire, bits of steel and odds of mesh, all tied together and plastered over. Most of that was done by hand, and by the time I'd finished the lime had taken so much skin off the tips of my fingers that they burst and bled like ripe tomatoes if knocked. Eventually, however, the construction, which became affectionately known as the bun, was finished. It had five rooms with a central corridor, and was designed to be able to be used by a range of different species. Off it were built two large runs, one of which was designated for the monkeys.

Finally the great day arrived when the two animals were flown down to us in their crates. Little Martin was the first out, and bounced around the cage like a jumping flea. He was an attractive little animal with an olive coat, a pale face with whiskers and a long dark tail. Inherently nervous, he had an extremely mobile and expressive face, spent most of his time chattering with excitement at every new thing he saw and opted for an active but rather

In 1975 Willowbank went to town to take part in New Zealand's first Telethon, which raised money for St John Ambulance.

stressful life. The Capuchin was a little bit more stolid, and although very active, was a much more thoughtful animal, whose explorations were more considered. As a species, Capuchin monkeys are recognised as being one of the more intelligent creatures; some have been trained to assist tetraplegics with domestic tasks. In the old days, when organ grinders used to roam the cities of Europe and America, like early buskers, grinding out tunes on their organs, several kept Capuchins on leads, and would let them run up drainpipes and into bedrooms to steal the jewellery of the rich.

They were sent down as two males, but after a while I became a bit suspicious about the little Capuchin, who once a month became extremely loving and affectionate towards me. He would throw himself at me and clutch my arm, hugging with all his strength and gazing up with devoted deep brown eyes, full of what could only be interpreted as lust. It didn't take me too long to work out that he was actually a she, an easy enough mistake to make with some monkeys. In spite of the chemistry between us, it was obvious now that nothing was going to happen, and we needed to find a boy for her. As luck would have it, Auckland Zoo had a spare old male named Sundance. He had been wild caught in South America, gone to London Zoo, and from there to Auckland. I thought he was handsome, with heavily muscled shoulders, glossy coat and an aura of confidence. Our little female, now called Cappy, obviously thought so too, and Sundance consummated their union immediately, and with aplomb, while nonchalantly eating a banana at the same time.

CHAPTER ONE AGAINST THE TIDE

Obtaining stock for the fledgling park was always an ongoing quest. In most cases you would be following up leads about animals that you had heard about all over New Zealand, and then taking the first opportunity to go and track them down. Events seldom turned out the way that you planned it, something that I discovered very quickly on one of the earlier trips.

I arrived in the North Island in the ancient old Land Rover with a horse float behind. Auckland Zoo had offered us a llama and to save time I had organised a horse transporter to pick it up in Auckland and deliver it to the sale yards in Masterton where I had arranged to meet them. I waited for hours in the pouring rain and no truck turned up. Eventually I got hold of the driver and after a rather terse conversation found that he had no intention of picking up the animal after all. I could stick it up my backside, spit, gurgle and all, and if I wanted it that badly, I could go and get it myself. Lesson number one: You can't always rely on other people.

It was two long days before I was back again with the llama on board, and starting to assemble everything at Staglands, the wildlife park in the Akatarawas north of Wellington owned by our friends John and Carole Simister, ready for the trip home. The Simisters, who were English and had travelled overland to New Zealand, had established Staglands two years before I opened Willowbank to the public. John, who had been brought up as a huntsman, had always wanted a wildlife park, and set about creating one of the best and most skilfully designed. His love of simple detail, which helps to create a perfect picture, was a hallmark of Staglands. There were many synergies between us – no money, passion, and wanting to create something unique for both wildlife and visitors – and we developed a very close friendship.

It was with some consternation that I noticed that over the last few days the animal total had increased somewhat. One llama, three Shetland pony mares and a stallion called Quasar, two goats, half a dozen fantail pigeons, two Chinese roosters, a couple of piglets and more. When someone pointed out that, on the ferry, I would have to pay for each individual animal and bird as well as the Land Rover and the horse float, an astronomical amount, I rang New Zealand Railways. 'Yes sir,' was the reply, 'that is correct.' When I protested that I wouldn't be taking up any more room than when I had driven up empty, I was told that this made no difference and that each animal cost the same going rate, regardless of its size. Lesson number two: Even the government will try and rip you off.

I was stuck between a rock and a hard place, but the animals had to be taken across. The solution to this price gouging came to me later in the day when I was dumping some rubbish.

There was a pile of cardboard cartons that had contained some product such as meat, which the Ministry of Agriculture and Fisheries, better known as MAF, had probably condemned and plastered with very official-looking seals and other impressive logos. Perfect, I thought. After an hour's soaking in water I had the seals off. We made a timber and ply shutter for the float that completely covered the gap above the door, so that no one could see inside, but there was still plenty of air flow for the animals. At the last possible moment we packed in all the animals, then shut and padlocked the back and side doors. I covered everything with the seals so the whole thing looked impressive and impregnable.

As the animals started to grasp who their fellow bedfellows were the float began to rock and emit strange noises and the situation didn't improve down on the dock. By the time I reached the official at the ferry terminal desk, the float looked as if it was in a heavy sea and he wasn't impressed by my request to pay for a Land Rover and horse float to travel to Picton. 'You and who else?' he asked. Lesson number three: A half-truth is technically not a lie. Airily I explained that it was a llama and very endangered.

'What's a llama?' the man asked.

I replied, 'It's like a miniature camel without the hump and the Arab.'

But his rule book yielded no mention of camels so I suggested calling it a sheep. Just then Quasar gave a piercing whinny.

'Sounds more like a horse to me.'

I insisted that a goat would be more like it and, on cue, one of the goats bleated.

The suspicious, and humourless, official was now walking around the float, but he couldn't see inside. The seals certainly impressed him, as did the sheaf of documents I waved in front of him. I added that the float could only be opened under government supervision at the zoo, because of foot and mouth, which llamas were at high risk of transferring because they spat on people. It was all getting too much for him. He reluctantly accepted my compromise of calling it a calf and charging accordingly. But then he said that commercial rates would apply to the whole shipment. I protested that Willowbank was a private zoo and all the animals, including the llama, were pets. By now there was a long and impatient queue behind me. Unable to locate anyone more senior, he finally let me go, especially when I threatened to call the SPCA. Lesson number four: Officious officials are always scared of more officialdom.

CHAPTER ONE **AGAINST THE TIDE**

Above: Animals have always been part of my children's lives: Mark makes friends with Stella the donkey. Press

Above right: Kathy and an opossum get close.

The ferry crew were wonderful and allowed me to visit the animals during the voyage, and once in Picton I was able to offload some into the back of the Land Rover to give more room, and we all made it successfully down to Willowbank. It was like opening a huge Christmas stocking to let everyone out into the paddocks and enclosures to meet their new friends. All of this was a massive step forward in the establishment of a zoo, and the fulfilment of a dream.

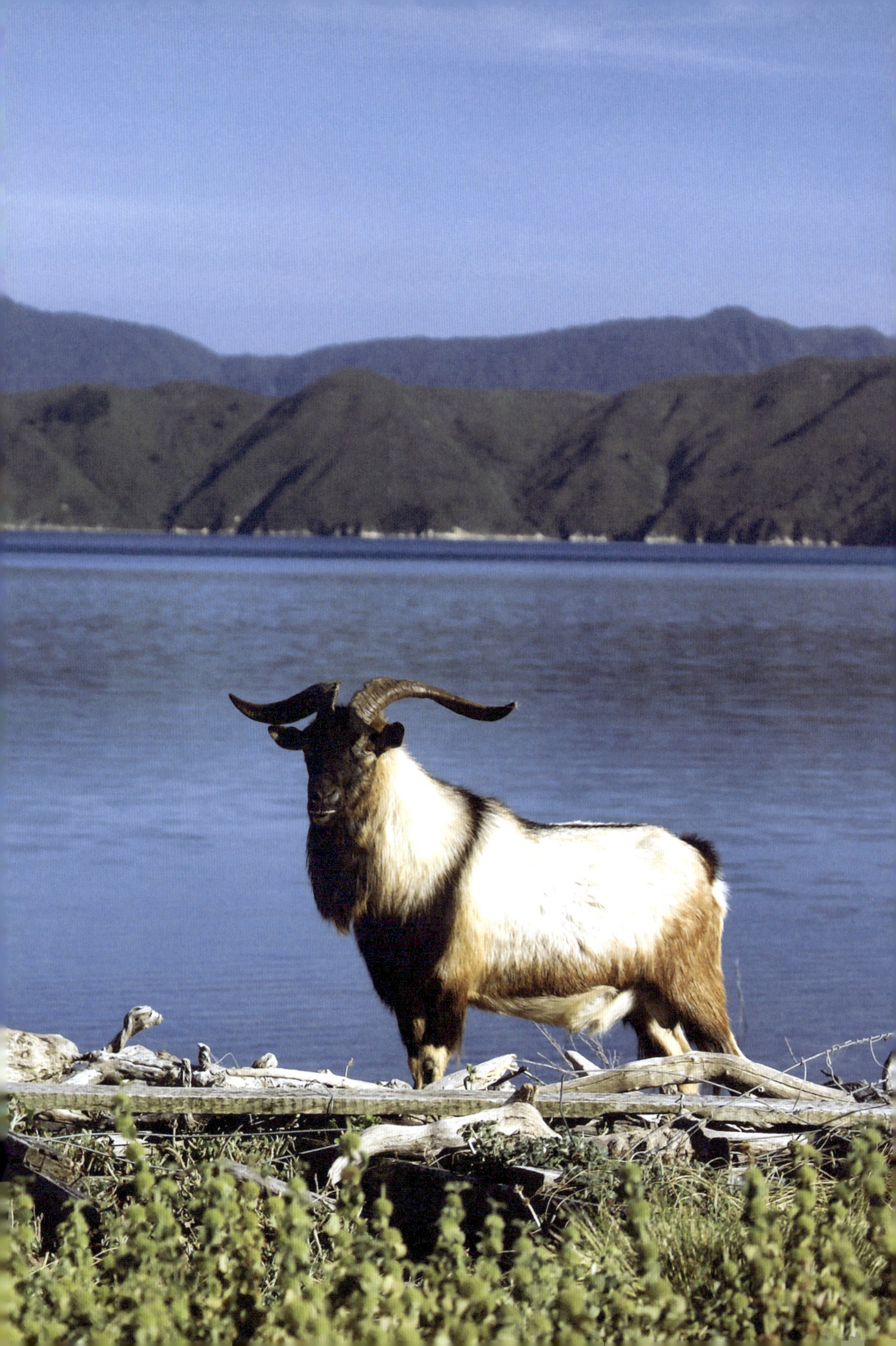

CHAPTER TWO

THE CALL OF ARAPAWA

As the farmyard component of Willowbank grew, I became increasingly aware of the value of the animals involved. Here, too, was a conservation field of immense significance, both for its historical importance and genetic impact. Many of these livestock breeds and introduced species were as rare, if not rarer, than much of our endangered wildlife. Conservation should begin at home, but did we even know what we had?

It is astonishing what mammals and birds were brought into New Zealand over the years. Governor George Grey, for example, had both zebras and kookaburras on Kawau Island and there are still kookaburras in the wild in this country. There was once an emu farm in the middle of what is now the Christchurch CBD and squirrels were released into Hagley Park for a few years during the First World War. The acclimatisation societies were totally focused on liberating anything they could, especially if it meant they could be shot later. Farmers imported livestock breeds, many of which disappeared into the bush, or ended up being kept by isolated communities in remote areas. New Zealand became a kaleidoscope of breeds and species, waxing and waning in their struggle for survival and recognition. Some were right under our noses, like the French Houdan fowls from Kaikoura, but some were further afield, such as the sheep on Pitt Island in the Chathams.

Sometime in the past an ancient mariner had dropped off on the shores of Pitt some sheep, which had bred up to become a wild flock that lived mainly on the exposed coastal reserve. No one knew their origin, or even if they had changed with the passage of time. They were, in the main, black,

Opposite: A fine Arapawa billy goat with an impressive horn span.
Photo: Michael Trotter

upstanding sheep, with pencil-thin legs and hard, shiny hooves. The rams had spectacular curling horns with wide, heavy bosses. A friend of mine who had been bulldozing tracks on the island had filled his spare time by catching and rearing some of the lambs, which he then brought back to New Zealand where he established a small flock at Pleasant Point in South Canterbury. I was offered some for Willowbank and brought them home in a crate on the back of the truck.

I almost went off the road several times while watching them in the rear-vision mirror. Fascinated with everything around them, they acted for all the world like a bunch of kids in a new playground. They would run up to the front of the truck and watch intently until something took their fancy. As it passed they would follow it with their heads and then run back for a better look as it receded into the distance. As one of my friends put it, if you wanted something to attest to the strength and effectiveness of a fence, they were perfect. Anything even slightly sub-standard was eyed with great interest, and if found wanting was soon a mechanism for a mass breakout. The rams viewed fenceposts as a measure of their virility and they would compete to see who could snap off the biggest. They would back up 10 to 15 metres and hurl themselves at any unsuspecting post, bouncing off it with a resounding crash. They were quite happy to do this for some time until they eventually found a weak one, which was cracked off at ground level.

Some years later I put a ram in with the deer, in an enclosure made with good solid posts, opposite the main building. He looked stunning among the deer, and I was pleased with the effect. What I hadn't counted on was the reflection from the huge floor-to-ceiling windows on three sides of the building. When the sun hit the right spot and the ram saw his reflection, he charged through the plate glass and barrelled across the restaurant and into the cafeteria, before exiting through the windows on the far side. We never tried that again.

I was surprised to see what appeared to be replicas of my Pitt Island sheep in the photos that accompanied a handwritten letter I opened while sitting at the kitchen table on a warm sunny morning in November 1976. It was from a woman called Betty Rowe, who lived on Arapawa Island in the Marlborough Sounds. 'We have here animals,' she wrote, 'that I believe have a history. Captain Cook is said to have liberated pigs, goats and sheep here in about 1777. It is assumed that the sheep died, but we have here black feral sheep, as yet unidentified. We also have some beautiful wild goats and pigs.' The Department of Scientific and Industrial Research was planning the complete extermination of the goats and pigs on the island and she wanted

CHAPTER TWO **THE CALL OF ARAPAWA**

to find homes for as many as possible. I was both puzzled and fascinated as to why there should be two groups of sheep so far apart, resembling each other, and yet each with an unknown history.

At the first opportunity I was in the old Land Rover and heading for Picton and the two-and-a-half-hour boat journey to Arapawa. After turning into East Bay we chugged sedately into lovely Te Aroha Bay, where I was met on the jetty by Betty, her husband Walt and their son Mitch. We had met only on paper, but this did not matter at all. They were Americans, who had decided to abandon the rat race for a saner and more peaceful life in New Zealand. They produced the vast majority of food themselves, relying very little on modern amenities. There was an abundance of food from the garden, and an apparently unending supply of superb and powerful home brew.

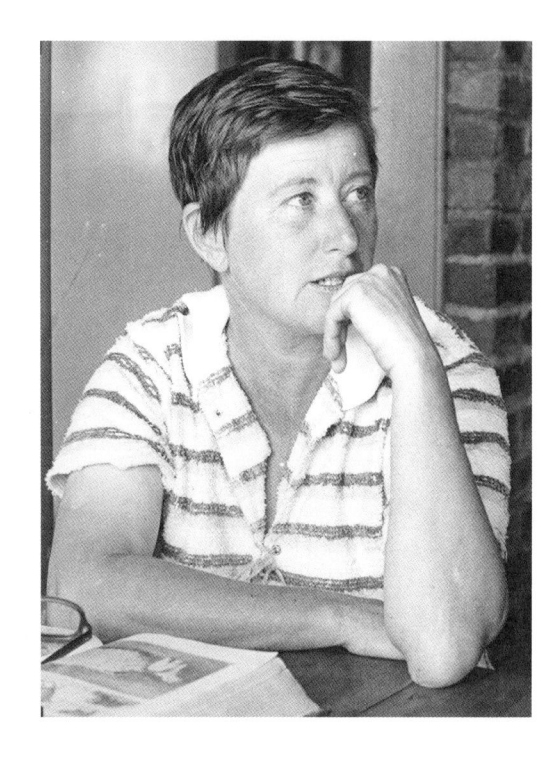

Right: Betty Rowe.

It was easy to fit in, and I even looked like one of the family, as Mitch and I were very similar in age and appearance. Walt was a big man, happy in his own space, who dealt with life deliberately, and with generous good humour. Betty, or 'The Mouth' as Walt affectionately called her, was small and energetic, with an as yet undimmed trust and faith in people.

My first task was to get acquainted with the problem, and so I spent several hours sitting in the little lounge with Betty, going through cartons of documents and listening to her side of the argument, for there was no doubt there was an argument. The problem lay on the other side of the island. It was very steep, faced the violent weather coming from the southern oceans off Cook Strait and was precariously covered with native bush, with slow regeneration capabilities. The Parks Board quite rightly wanted to protect that area, and with some justification considered the goats a threat to its survival. Accordingly they had asked for government shooters to be brought in to control the goats. Betty, on the other hand, considered that the goats had been there 150-odd years and had not destroyed the bush yet. In fact they had achieved a balance and so had a right to be there. The parties were poles apart. Both presented valid points but no way would they meet in the middle. From my point of view I tried to keep it as simple as I could. The animals were unique and we needed to find out more about them. They were under threat of extermination, and so we needed to try and remove some from the island and establish breeding groups.

Rick Denton and John Simister were among the mates who made trips with me to Arapawa.

It was time to see the animals for myself. Armed with some high-powered binoculars, I headed off around the foreshore and up a spur. The going wasn't difficult but I was soon stripped to the waist in the burning sun. Very soon I found myself high up in wild goat and sheep country. As I rounded a ridge I could see up the valley and there were clusters of goats dotted all over the faces ahead: family groups and bachelor herds, some playing and frolicking among the scrub. I was surrounded by the bleating of kids, the answering calls of nannies, and the grunting of billies. Most extraordinary, though, was the obvious similarity of type that they all showed. Other herds of feral goats I had seen throughout New Zealand were always a mixture of colours and shapes, but these all had the same clean physical lines, and showed a coat

CHAPTER TWO **THE CALL OF ARAPAWA**

Above: Men, dogs and goats on an island beach.

Right: I load a captured goat into a boat that will then take it out to a supporting vessel.

pattern that was consistent across the herd. Their ancestors must surely have been reasonably genetically pure.

As I ascended it grew colder and I was hit by freezing blasts of wind

41

coming straight off the Southern Oceans. It was in this bleak, harsh area that I encountered the first of the wild sheep, all with their heads down in stunted bushes, unaware of my presence. Their fleeces, dark brown on the tips and black underneath, were long and unkempt. Their tails all had a white tip. As I approached they noticed me and pulled their heads out like startled rabbits. The rams had some impressive curling horns, and many of them had a white skull cap or even a bit of a blaze down the nose. They were remarkably similar to the Pitt Island sheep, probably not as rangy in the body, but it was hard not to feel there must be a close relationship. It was dark when I returned to the warm cottage tired, but excited. A glass or two of Walt's home brew rounded off an interesting day.

I had hoped to take some animals back with me, and had brought up a tranquilliser gun for that purpose. It wasn't very accurate over any great distance, but I had used it often, and I had plenty of time and cover to stalk to within good range. So the next afternoon I was off, back up the ridge and into the scrubby gullies running off and up the faces beyond. But each of my three attempts failed and I got back to the homestead empty handed and disgusted. Walt and Betty had an explanation. Often when they tried to shoot a goat for the dogs, they had been prevented from doing so, and this happened so often that they decided it was the work of some protective entity they called the 'Goat God'. I found out later that when James Cook released the first goats, he was uneasy about their future, so the local Māori chief put a tapu on the animals, which was in effect a sacred protection order. I took the point but wasn't totally convinced. By the end of the next day, however, I had failed again. Obviously another approach was needed.

There was a small herd of goats on the hillside across the bay so, with one of the dogs, named Tipiwha, Mitch and I headed across in the little dinghy. We tried the gun yet again, but had no success. We had walked only a short part of the distance down to the boat when we looked back and saw three more goats standing on a bluff above the water. It was steep with few escape routes, and so this time we decided to use Tipiwha. After returning to the beach we got ourselves onto the easiest access point, and blocked off the main escape route. Mitch let the dog go and the goats bolted, following the steepest and prickliest possible route. There was one young billy we really wanted, and this time our luck held. While the others tore off up the hill, he darted into a rocky chimney that had no exit. The Goat God had relented at last.

When we saw the same mob next morning in almost the same place, Walt, Mitch and I, this time with four dogs, rowed back across the bay. This time we climbed high up the hill to get above them before letting the dogs go and the chase was on yet again. With little trouble we captured a lovely nanny and Betty also gave me an orphan nanny kid, who although still on the bottle, would help to complete a family group. I was also hoping to get some of the sheep and that, by comparison, was ridiculously easy. It became just a matter of mustering them in with a flock of domestic sheep, and then sorting out a ram and three ewes. Although we could muster them in this way, in the wild they never associated with the other sheep, and cross-breeding was unheard of. To the best of anyone's knowledge, the population had never risen above 100 animals, and often much fewer, so their future was by no means certain, especially as the rams were being continually hunted for their large and impressive horns.

The day we left the goats were sedated and loaded, but the sheep were just left to stand freely in the bottom of the boat. We felt it was probably better to have the goats quiet, especially the big billy. One of Cook's goats butted a Tahitian prince off the decks of the *Endeavour*, to everyone's consternation, and we had no wish for a repeat performance. The animals created a lot of interest when we docked at Picton, where some friendly fishermen gave us a hand to lift them into crates for the trip south. All except the little orphan, now named Daisy. To her delight, I had held her in my arms for the entire boat journey and she insisted on riding with me in the cab of the truck on the way home.

Back in Christchurch the animals were settled into enclosures around the park. They generated quite a bit of publicity and sparked a lot of interest. If they were goats originating from Cook's liberations, then they may well have been what were known as Old English goats, a breed functionally extinct in Britain, making these the sole survivors. Interest came from around New Zealand as well as overseas, making it imperative that we do something more to save them, though how best to achieve that was the big question.

By the time I had made five trips to the island, and organised three major ventures to catch and relocate Arapawa goats, the conservation issues surrounding them had became a catalyst for actions never before considered. Wildlife vigilantes and extremists were becoming involved, an aspect that I kept well away from. I've never really ever been a crusader, but you couldn't help but be influenced by the way people responded to the 'call', if it was made. Once people knew of the situation, they just kept coming out of the woodwork and volunteering their boats and services, or whatever else they had to offer. The authorities had certainly not anticipated this rag-tag army when they decided they were going to exterminate the goats.

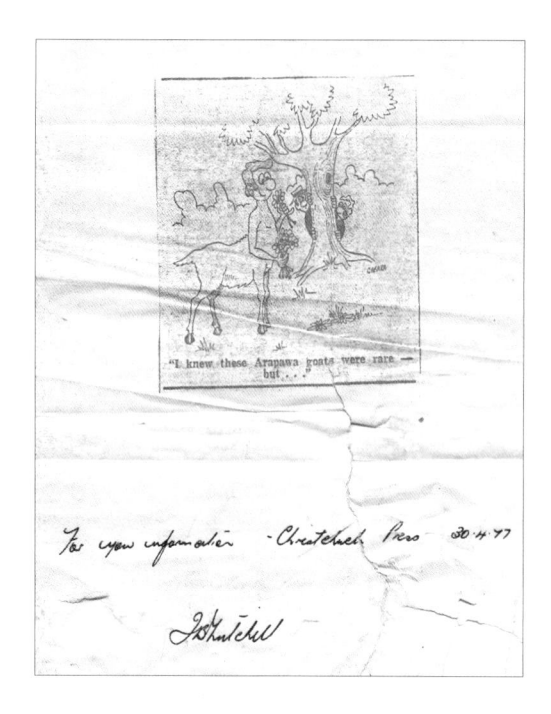

The publicity grew and with it the factions. Passions flared, and the goats were caught in the middle of an emotional barrage from both sides. Numerous meetings were held with government officials and the Parks Board, but the government cullers kept coming in. Frustration led to large numbers of people camping out on the hill and following the shooters from the time they awoke, and during their time trying to hunt on the hill. It was a crusade that made a point, but a temporary one, for the hunters just had to postpone their activities and wait until everyone went home. At one stage a compromise was found – to build a fence along the axial ridge, which would keep the goats and sheep out of the reserve. Those that breached the fence would be disposed of. It was a sensible solution, but the terrain was tough and the fence was continually compromised by tree fall and other environmental hazards. It was, however, an honest attempt at some form of wildlife management in a situation where it became increasingly difficult to achieve any kind of balance. The position of the pro-goat fraternity shifted from trying to save the breed to wanting to save all animals because they were God's living creatures. The knee-jerk reaction from the hunters was to then shoot everything.

Betty left the homestead and moved up the coast a bit to Lily Valley, a harsh little bay with a small cottage where she found some peace in solitude. Walt later joined her, and they had some contented years together and developed what became known as the Sanctuary and established the Arapawa Wildlife Trust. They fenced some paddocks off and provided shelters, and Betty had her beloved goats around her again until Walt's sudden and unexpected death. Over the intervening years, my relationship with Betty fluctuated. I wasn't into saving the life of every goat on the planet. I was happy to compromise if

Kim Gabara's cartoon in the *Press* on 30 April 1977 has fun with the Arapawa controversy.

CHAPTER TWO **THE CALL OF ARAPAWA**

Betty and Walt in later years.

it meant saving the breed as a whole. After Walt died, I spent a lovely few days with her at Lily Valley. We sat through the long sultry evenings on the verandah of the little cottage, watching the wildlife, enjoying a glass of refreshment, and just talking. Shortly after that Betty died, in May 2008, and I very much treasure that last time, and the peace it created.

Betty left the property as a sanctuary for the goats, but nothing worked out as she would have planned it. I've called into Lily Valley several times since, and on each visit the whole place looks more derelict. The fences are collapsing, the goat shelters and outbuildings slowly deteriorating, and the animals have gone. The scrub has slowly reclaimed most of the land, shading out the grasses and limiting its ability to hold any livestock. The trustees were unable to agree as to the future of the Sanctuary, and eventually it was put up for sale. I've seen this type of scenario so often: projects talked about and developed with an incredible amount of zeal and passion, but when the person who is the driving force runs out of energy, or can't carry on, the whole thing collapses. In Christchurch alone, I've been involved in the closure of two zoos, both of which became inoperable on the deaths of their owners. Few people want to work with the passion and dreams of pioneers. It was a lesson I noted well, and I was determined that Willowbank's future wouldn't depend on me alone, but would be based on sound business practices with a strong conservation ethic.

In 2017 I joined Adam Henson and the BBC on a filming trip to Arapawa for *Countryfile*, one of the best known and most watched programmes in Britain and around the world. They wanted to film the Arapawa story, mainly because of the ties back to England. Within a few minutes we had found some twenty sheep. They were just at the head of the bay, and may have been the last decent group of the breed. There's no provision to protect them: government and social hunters shoot them whenever they can. Off the island, most have been cross-bred with other stock. However, the BBC people were certainly excited, even if no one else in New Zealand was. Further along the coast, and rather to my amazement, we had a splendid view of a magnificent Arapawa pig. These animals are now recognised as having a special heritage status. I had been there a year or so before with a full team of people and dogs, trying to find some of those pigs to collect semen for a genebank operated by the Rare Breeds Conservation Society, which was started in 1988. We couldn't find a pig anywhere and now here was one virtually on parade, poking around in the scrub without a care in the world. As if it had been choreographed, we found a nanny goat, then another with kids, and then saw several groups. The crew shot some wonderful footage, and the Goat God excelled himself that day.

With us was Dr Alison Sutherland, who had just completed a book on the history of the Arapawa wildlife, and had come to a number of conclusions. The book, called *No Ordinary Goat*, was in many ways a breath of fresh air. Somewhere along the way you need some evidence to support whatever action you wish to take, and Alison's unbiased and professional research goes a long way towards providing that.

There was an interesting sequel in some goats that Betty had given to a friend, on the understanding that, should his circumstances change, they were to be returned to the island. Betty had died, his situation had altered, but he wished to honour the agreement. Knowing that I was going to the Arapawa to try and obtain pig genetics, he asked if I would transport the goats, which I was more than happy to do. At Betty's old homestead we were met by some of the Arapawa Wildlife trustees, who released the goats into paddocks that had previously been their home, but now opened out into the freedom of the farm.

About a month later I got a phone call from DOC, who said that it had been reported that I had liberated goats onto Arapawa Island, which was against the Wild Animal Control Act, and I was liable for prosecution. Thinking quickly, I said that these weren't wild animals but tagged domestic animals, and it was a farm-to-farm transfer. They grumbled but couldn't do much about it. Two weeks later, though, I got another phone call, this time from the SPCA in Nelson. It had now been reported that I had left domestic animals

CHAPTER TWO **THE CALL OF ARAPAWA**

My brother Paul watches as Dave Hughes and Greg McKay release goats into the sanctuary.

in a paddock on Arapawa Island without monitoring their future needs. As politely as I could I explained that I was only the transporter, they weren't my goats and they could annoy somebody else if they wished. Sometimes no matter how hard you try, you can't please everyone. Even after all these years, the issues are obviously still raw for some people.

It was undeniable that Arapawa affected my thinking on conservation matters within New Zealand. Here were some animals of fascinating heritage value, probably not replicated anywhere else in the world, and we were hell-bent on getting rid of them before we even understood why. The message, however, was taking a while to really take root in my brain. I was in denial. I had always wanted a zoo, and zoos didn't concentrate on goats and sheep, they had big stuff like monkeys and even big cats. Now that would be something. If I could only get some big cats, then surely we would attract heaps of people and surely we would be a success.

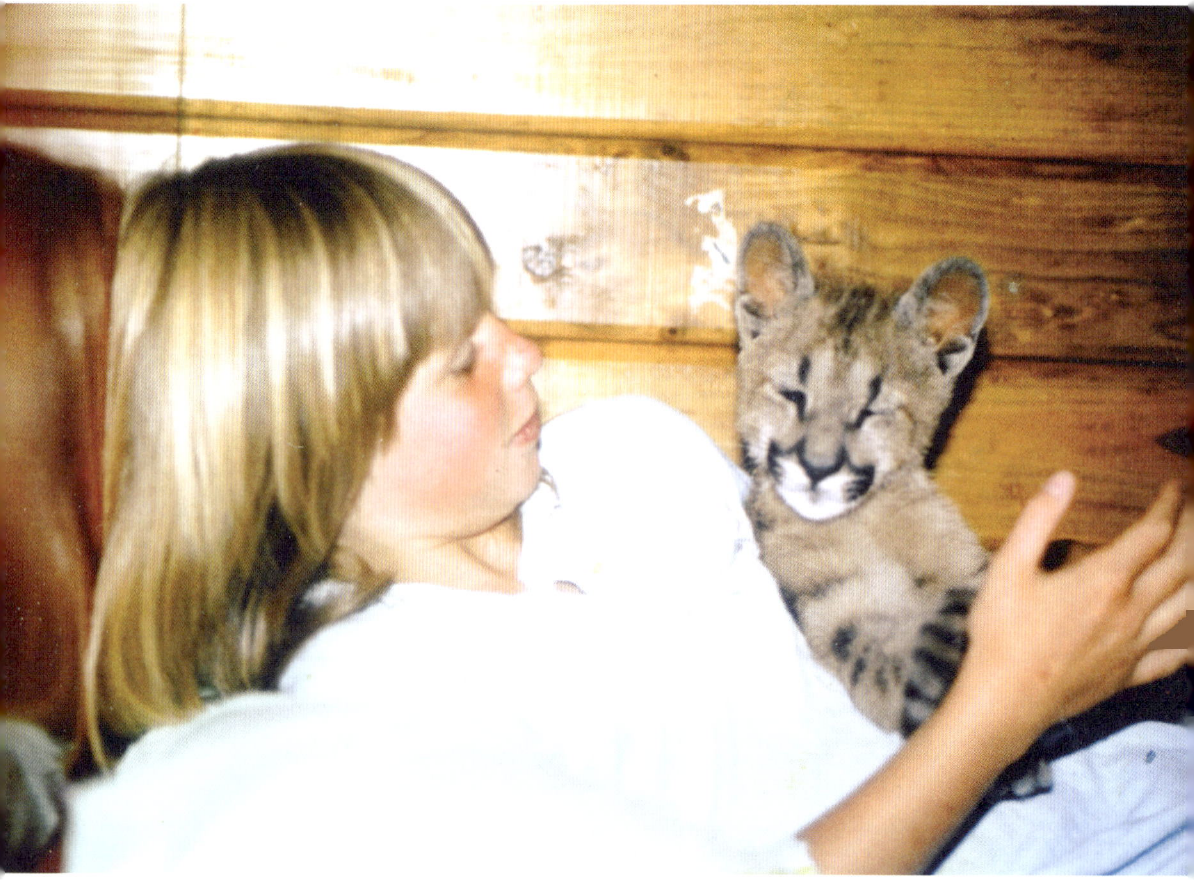

CHAPTER THREE

A CAT – OR LESS

Opposite: Kirsty with Louis the lion cub.

Armed with a shopping list, I went looking for big cats – and it was quite surprising what was out there. African lions were cheap as chips: you could buy four or five for the price of one cockatoo. They would certainly be a drawcard, but there was no market for any cubs that might be born, and they would probably have to be euthanised. This was a common practice and one that had no appeal for us. We were offered a pair of jaguars, and they were very appealing, but again many zoos were breeding them and there was no place for any surplus cubs. The two black leopards available at Auckland Zoo were breathtakingly beautiful, with their deep golden eyes and ebony coats shining like polished coal, and would have been popular, but the same cub problem applied.

It was difficult to understand why such rare and endangered animals had no future, but outside their country of origin, their value plummets until they have exhibit value only. When a big cat place, Zion Wildlife Park, was started in Northland, some years later, it attracted a large following. A TV series was made based around the antics of Craig Busch, the Lion Man. People donated large sums of money, and talked about what a wonderful job he was doing. I watched developments with apprehension, and shuddered when I was confronted with any publicity about the place – and there was a lot of it, which only helped to promote and develop a situation that was flawed from the beginning. It all started to unravel when a tiger mauled and killed keeper Dalu Mncube in 2009. The Ministry for Primary Industries got involved, and basically became the statutory managers. They wanted to close the whole operation, but there was nowhere for all the cats to go, and they included white lions, white tigers and other misfits of all descriptions. It would have been a promotional nightmare for MPI to put all the animals down, and to some extent the place was rescued by a group of locals, hoping to rebuild and create a new future for it.

This was all to come, but back then it was very obvious which way the future seemed to be heading, and that became part of our decision-making process. So in a roundabout way we settled on mountain lions as our cat of choice, for many reasons. They were big enough to be impressive, but small enough to fit into the scope of the place; they were very attractive cats; they were on the endangered list and, more importantly, they had a reasonably stable temperament and weren't too hard to work with, as big cats go.

With their almond-shaped eyes and lithe tawny bodies, they resemble huge Burmese cats. (A large male will measure some 3 metres from his nose to the tip of his tail.) The striking little white patch around their nose and under their chin makes them look as if they've just had a close encounter with a bucket of cream. They're very adaptable animals, with impressive capability: they can take on a bear or bring down a moose. They can leap over 10 metres and drop down from above over 13 metres. Newborn cubs have spots and look like little leopards, but gradually lose them until, around the age of six months, look like miniature adults.

I found two young females, sisters, in Auckland Zoo, who were coaxed into substantial steel-lined travelling cages, and flown to Christchurch. They arrived on a bitterly cold day with snow and hail but didn't seem to mind the change in temperature, and leapt around their new enclosure like young kittens. As a result of a mountain lion naming competition they were christened Cheena and Karu. Despite being full siblings, they looked and behaved completely differently. Cheena, playful and outgoing, would come to the netting and play tug of war with me using a stick, or would climb up the wire to take food from my hand. Karu, darker and bigger, was very nervous and more difficult to deal with. They were perfect for what we wanted, fitted in really well and were enjoyable to keep. It would be nice, however, to have a male to go with them, and I started to make some enquiries. As fate would have it, a major North Island zoo had a single cub available, and it was a male. 'Perfect,' I said, 'we'll take him.'

A few weeks later a small crate arrived by air. I took it home, put it in the living room, unscrewed the front and peered inside. Looking solemnly back at me were two dark eyes, a sharp white muzzle and the indistinct outlines of an overgrown kitten. He got up, stretched and peered sideways out the door, before boldly introducing himself. He was a beautiful little spotted cat about the size of a Cavalier spaniel but twice as athletic and with the naughtiness of innocent youth.

We had hardly met before the phone went. It was the curator of the zoo who had sent him.

'Hey Michael, has that cat arrived yet?'

'Yep, lovely wee animal, looking at him right now.'

'Well, for heaven's sake hide him under the bed or something and don't tell anyone you've got him. I forgot to get a transfer permit and at the moment he should not be there'.

'No worries, he can stay right where he is.'

Right: One of the family: Mark and Louis.

So for the first few weeks the mountain lion cub just became part of the family. He played around the house like any normal kitten, and especially enjoyed stalking and leaping on Kathy when she least expected it. She had a limited tolerance for his antics, and I think he enjoyed the violent response he got after a particularly good catch. By now our family had grown, as we also had a daughter, Kirsty. The cub loved the children, and would regularly climb into bed with Kirsty and lie snuggled up among the bed clothes. He was an exceptional animal and quickly became one of those creatures to whom you have a special attachment, just as you would to a special friend. He quickly became used to a collar, and we could go for walks together, although at times it was a bit debatable who was leading whom. He would stop and sniff the flowers, running his nose up and down the stems looking for signals left behind by the last, now forgotten passer-by. Then something else would take his interest, and he would crouch and stalk a duck or one of the park's unsuspecting inhabitants. I would regularly take him down to have lunch with the staff, and he was the surprise guest at one or two dinner parties.

I called him Louis, after a very close friend who was big, strong and greeted life with ebullience. Louis wasn't always pushing boundaries; he was often just a big pussy cat. During his sensitive moments he would put his head into my chest and push. The fur on the top of his head was short

Louis and I get to know each other.

and bristly, and I would run my hands over it and down round his neck and along his back. He would push harder, and I would rub harder, and the purr, which, among big cats, only mountain lions have, would start from the bottom of his stomach and resonate through his throat. You could feel the vibration in your hands. We would push and tumble together and generally be good mates, but I drew the line at play fighting, for it often ends up with someone becoming the loser, and I had no illusions as to what might happen should that line be crossed and who the loser would be.

When Louis had matured I was asked to do a commercial shoot with him in Riccarton Bush, a central city park. In those days it wasn't unusual to use exotic animals in filming commercials or in major productions. It gave them a point of difference and often gave us some much-needed funds. We filmed the commercial, everyone packed up and left and I took Louis for a walk and let him settle down before crating him and heading for home. He

CHAPTER THREE **A CAT – OR LESS**

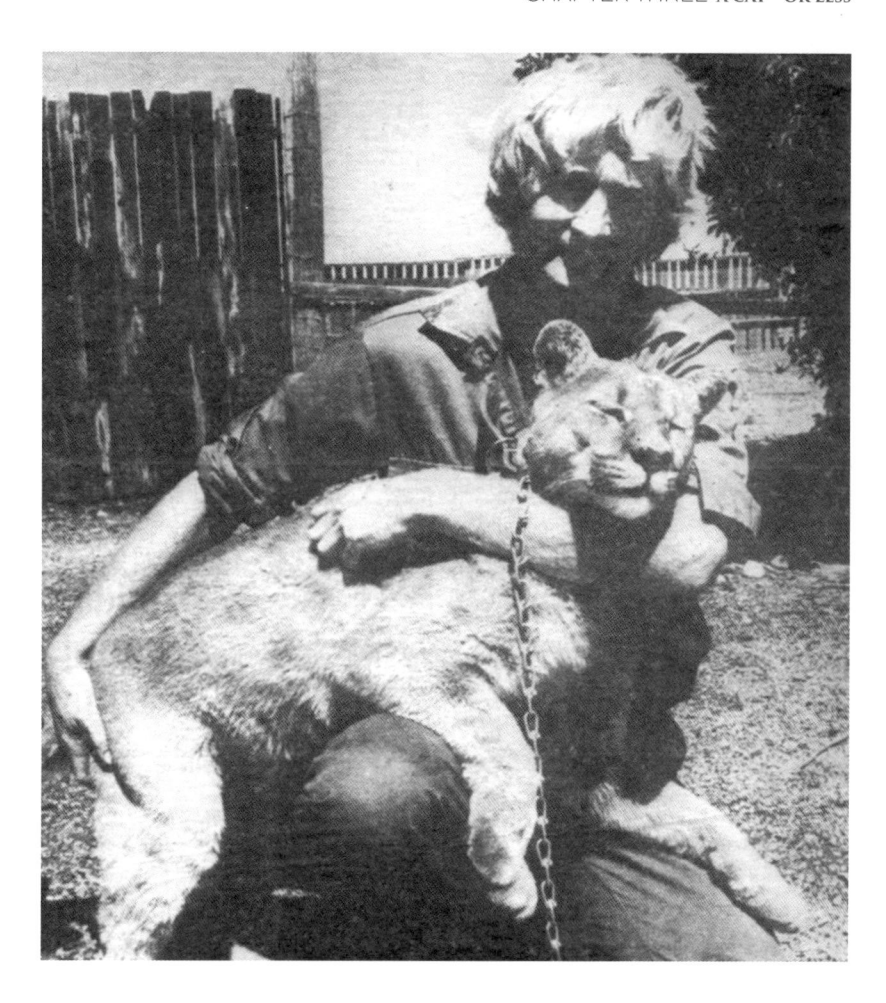

Louis and I make the papers.

loved the daffodils and thought acorns were quite fun. The cyclists riding past in the distance looked like something he should have been chasing, and his world had suddenly become larger and much more entertaining than he previously thought.

'Come on, Louis, time to go home. Back in your crate.'

That suggestion drew a big blank. He took one look at the door into his crate, and said, 'No thanks, much more fun here.'

The battle of wits began and he was winning every skirmish. I wanted to get home, and he wanted to stay. I pleaded, tried subterfuge, pretended I didn't care. Nothing worked. The street lights were starting to come on and I was stuck in Riccarton Bush on my own with an increasingly uncooperative mountain lion, and every chance of things going badly wrong. I would lead him up to the front of the crate, but he always pulled back and as his and my patience thinned, struck out at the lead with his front paws, claws out, pulling against the collar and baring his fangs in a spit and snarl, as only big cats can. If he slipped that collar, then I would be in big trouble, because by this stage he had massive neck muscles and a small head. This was the first time I had put myself in a situation that, in hindsight, was probably stupid. After all, nobody had told Louis what the script was.

There was no way I was going to allow this to develop into a civil defence exercise, and certainly no way was our fledgling zoo going to be compromised by the adverse publicity that could result if this situation got out of hand. Decision made, I took Louis for yet another walk and as we passed the front of the crate I grabbed the collar and the loose skin on his back, thrust him in and slammed the door down. To my huge relief, it worked, for there was going to be only one chance to play that game. Although he quickly spun around and bounced off the door, it was too late and we headed off home. For me it was a very good lesson. These animals may be pussy cats, but the veneer of customised behaviour is very thin. Cross that line at your peril, because these animals aren't used to accommodating their lives to yours.

I liked Louis too much to expose him to that scenario again, and he never did any more filming, to my relief but possibly not his, as he had rather enjoyed the change. However, our relationship was special, and it did make it easier to manage him. This showed up on another occasion that could also have ended badly.

I was walking Louis through Willowbank one day, when a kune kune piglet came trotting innocently along the track towards us. Louis crouched, tail swishing, and then leapt. Because I had hold of the leash and control of his head, he couldn't mouth the piglet, but instead held onto it with his front paws. I grabbed him from behind and picked him up and he lost his grip but as the little creature fell he caught it immediately with his back feet. The dexterity was incredible but eventually he lost his grip and the piglet ran away unscathed and with a story to tell. The tables, however, got turned later.

It was a busy Sunday, and people were flocking into the park. At the busiest time of the day a wild ferret decided to run through the mountain lion enclosure. This was much more fun than daffodils. Louis probably just wanted to play with the ferret but never made his intentions obvious. Ferrets are very quick, and this one was no exception. It latched onto Louis's nose and held on, knowing that it was probably the safest place to be and the best course of action until some other option turned up. I was called and by the time I arrived Louis was walking aimlessly around his enclosure, eyes crossed and watering as he tried to see what was attached to his nose, while the ferret hung on for grim death. Every now and then Louis would half-heartedly swipe at the beastly creature with his paw, but that only generated more pain and a tighter grip. After assessing the situation, I asked for a hose and gave it to my son Mark to hold. Normally water in a good spray is enough to defuse many situations, but because it was a busy day, toilets and other uses were siphoning off any excess, and barely a trickle came out.

The crowds had gathered, sensing a developing situation. After instructing Mark to try and spray the trickle if I got into trouble, I opened the gates into the enclosure. Louis wasn't cross, just sore and confused. I grabbed him by the scruff of the neck and with all my strength lifted his front feet off the ground and held him there. I then grabbed the ferret by the tail and held him out, not quite sure what would happen next and taking little comfort from the forlorn arc of water coming from Mark's hose. Mercifully the ferret let go after a moment or two, allowing me to drop Louis and, swinging the ferret by the tail, back carefully out the gate with as much dignity as I could muster. I was experiencing a whole range of emotions, from embarrassment and relief to gratitude for the relationship I had with Louis, even if we did have some bad days. That could have been a very bad day. The water trickled and spat from the hose, and I thought yet again that we must get a bigger and better pump when we could afford it.

Louis developed some growths on and around his nose, which we decided should be removed. When the vet arrived to sedate him, dressed in his sparkling white overalls, Louis took one look and disappeared back into his cage. Telling the vet to go away and hide, I took the syringe and a few minutes later Louis was asleep and being bundled into the old Land Rover and taken off to the clinic. There Chris Toovey, a park warden, and I carried him into the theatre, where the vet and his assistant were waiting in anticipation. Louis was stabilised and the procedure was carried out with little problem. It was a big moment for the medical team, and they were being ultra-efficient, trying to do everything as professionally as possible, but they were working on a knife edge of nerves. They descaled Louis's teeth, clipped his claws and were about to check his anal glands when the assistant unthinkingly made a remark to the vet that could have been interpreted the wrong way. Suddenly you could have cut the air with a scalpel. The assistant, realising the possible interpretation of what he had said, went white, fled out the door to his car and was gone. The vet left by another door, and a heavy silence prevailed. Chris and I looked at each other and waited, and waited. Eventually I left the surgery, looked around past the waiting and consulting rooms until finally I found the vet sitting out in the yard, with his head in his hands. I retreated, leaving him to his thoughts and returned to Chris. 'I

The magnificent Coruba.
Press

think we'd better just pack up and get Louis back to the park,' I suggested. 'I doubt we'll get much more done here.'

So we unhooked all the tubes, picked Louis up off the table and, laying him across the front seats of the vehicle, we headed back to Willowbank, with Chris driving. Louis's head was on my lap and periodically I would touch the corner of his eye to check for a response. To my alarm I started to get a twitch, and suggested to Chris he had better put his foot down and get there quickly. Animals coming out of anaesthesia can behave in some pretty unpredictable ways, and being locked in the cab with a panicked big cat didn't appeal. We had the old Land Rover fairly wound up on the highway before turning off and into a side street towards the park. Each tap on the corner of the eye was eliciting a very positive response now, and I knew we were running out of time. As we reached the gates, I said to Chris, 'Just open them and drive through. Don't bother about closing them, and don't slam the door.' We cruised as quietly as we could up the driveway and pulled up alongside the safety door of the pen. It was open and I fed Louis over my lap and he walked in, if rather shakily. I enjoyed a gin that night.

It wasn't a good day, the morning that I found Louis lying dead in his enclosure. Life and death with animals is something that you have to get used to, and can't avoid. The night before he was a happy chappy and there was no indication of anything being wrong. How quickly things can change. I mourned the loss of a companion who had taught me so much.

We looked for a replacement and found a magnificent male called Coruba. He was a massive animal, and although there was no close personal bond, he was without doubt a magnificent specimen. Sometime after his arrival we began an introduction to the two females who were still lying in waiting. A few days later, to my absolute dismay, I found Karu lying dead in her enclosure. It was obvious what had happened. When cats mate the male usually holds the female by the back of the neck, pinning her down, and the whole thing is accomplished with a lot of yowling and very little foreplay. The marks on Karu's neck showed that the foreplay, if any, had been inadequate, and the bite marks told their own story.

A friend offered to send some replacement animals out from the States, and pay for all costs. It was a tempting offer, but the whole experience had left me with a lot of confused feelings and I found it hard to commit myself to repeating the experience, even though it had meant so much. I loved the animals but maybe I loved them too much. It went into the too hard basket and signalled the end of a lifetime's desire to keep big cats.

When you keep working away at something, it is surprising how people just seem to turn up and offer to help. Two early key figures were Chris Paterson and Chris Bilizcka and their families. They turned up regularly weekend after weekend and contributed hugely to some early projects. At the same time we had a lot of fun and became close friends. They in turn brought friends, and that group morphed into what loosely became known as the Friends of Willowbank, a rather nebulous organisation without any real structure. Strangely enough it grew, and later, in 1980, became the Willowbank Wildlife Trust, whose aim was to support the conservation efforts that were being undertaken at the park, and become the guardian for any donations of material or money that might, and did, eventuate.

Another group that had a big impact, although often not quite how you wanted it, was the Justice Department's Periodic Detention Unit. They came out to see me one day and asked if I thought Willowbank would be workable for them. We walked around and I explained roughly the layout and the type of work that might be suitable. They were very happy and as they left the senior officer turned to the other and said, 'Frizzell's the man for this job. Just perfect for him', and so Don Frizzell became firmly entrenched in the park and in our lives. In real life Don was a pig farmer who worked as a prison warder in the weekends in order to feed a large and thriving family. He was a huge man in presence and stature, with a bellow on him that would cower the toughest miscreant. It was a rule that all of the men in the gangs had to address the officers as Mr so and so. Not with Don. 'My name's Don,' he would say, 'and it will stay that way unless you misbehave.' In spite of his extremely gruff exterior, he was a very compassionate guy, and looked after his men well. He established a shed for them to use, with a fire outside to cook on. He had them growing vegetables for their lunches, and it was probably the best feed many of them had had for days. Each week a cook would be delegated, and they would usually raid our pig drums, which came from supermarkets, for some extra food.

Some were harmless like 'Pinkie Boy', who was a drug addict and was just left sitting in the corner of the cookhouse talking to himself. Some were career criminals making the most of any opportunity, as happened when a couple slipped into our house and stole some wine and had themselves a party until their drunken behaviour brought the wrath of Don down on their heads. As a unit I called them the Beagle Boys after the comic book characters who always wore masks and striped clothes and got into trouble.

Don was also very practical and very clever. He always found ways of doing things, and enjoyed seeing the results as they slowly took place. For each week he planned an achievable goal, which over the months became a substantial input. In the main the Beagle Boys were kept away from the general public, but the Justice Department were also careful to send out people who were unlikely to cause too much problem in a public place. Sometimes it could not be avoided, however, and we occasionally had some fairly notorious criminals, and you always had to be on your guard. One day Don cut his hand badly and had to go to hospital to be stitched up. He rang his bosses and said that I would manage the gang until the bus came to pick them up. It was much more difficult than I ever dreamt it would be to manage a group of men with different backgrounds, and with confrontation always just bubbling under the surface. Put me in a pen of lions any day.

Don was there for about twelve years and I only once saw a situation escalate, when a detainee had a pick-axe handle and every intention of using it. Don could take good care of himself and had absolutely no fear. The bellow of rage in itself was enough to melt and defuse opposition. Most of the men loved him, and several would visit him and the park with their families for years afterwards. When he left the service Don became part of the Willowbank Wildlife Trust and went on to be its chairman.

I sometimes liken the park to a great big parasite – in other words it grows by feeding off people. Our strongest asset has always been our staff, and the commitment that they made to developing the place. At first we could only afford one staff member. That was Jenny Warmington, who started with me in the pet shop and has maintained a working relationship until the present day. Most of the early ones were women. We had Big and Little Lisa, named for obvious reasons, but more correctly known as Lisa McKeefry and Lisa Ross, and also Trish Hann. This seasoned core stayed as a group for years as the park struggled to get on its feet. The pig food we collected from supermarkets came in large drums that had to be loaded onto a trailer, and brought to the park, where it would be taken into a sawdust paddock inhabited by pigs and tipped out. It was then a race for the humans to beat the pigs to the best food, which was placed in buckets and later washed and cleaned for the monkeys and other animals. On a summer's day this task could be quite pleasant, but on a wet winter's day, it was a dispiriting job – just mud, slush, squealing pigs and shivering women. Creating the odd diversion could help. It might be as simple as tripping someone up so they fell into the mud, or, after rescuing a particularly ripe tomato from the mouth of a pig, throwing it at some unsuspecting person, who would usually retaliate in style. Everyone coming out of the paddock dripping with tomato juice was usually a sign that there had been a drum of rotten tomatoes on board. Some of the food was very good, and we had one member of staff who took the drums home first and took the best out for his house. We obviously did not pay him enough.

Shaun Maloney was another character who kept everyone on their toes. He had been an undercover police officer for many years, and as such had been exposed to a lot of drug taking. He had left the force and was working hard to reprogramme his brain. He was hard-working, with a great sense of humour, and we achieved an enormous amount together. Later came Shaun Horan, Jeremy Maguire and Aaron Webb, all larger than life characters who put their souls into their work. Lance Dartnall started as a schoolboy and spent years working for us. As a totally dedicated zoo professional, he went on to work and gain experience in other establishments before later returning to us.

RESCUE ONE NEW ZEALANDER'S CRUSADE TO SAVE ENDANGERED ANIMALS

Out and about in Christchurch with the lovely Sheba.

Laughter was a big component, and we all worked and played hard, with a total commitment to both. We have a continual influx of volunteers, some of whom have disabilities. Just as the staff nurture the animals, so they often go well out of their way to help such people, some of whom have later entered into full employment. One such person was John Pycroft, who was deaf and dumb, so for several nights after work the staff learnt sign language. Alister Wall, who has the mental age of a young child, and very limited ability to socialise, has now worked for us for over sixteen years. He has a name badge saying 'Compost Manager', which he proudly wears. Today our staff may exceed sixty to eighty people a year, depending on how you count them, but the driving force to help and achieve, is still the passion that so many of them put into their work.

Llamas are okay, but give me a camel any time. Ungainly and aloof, they're the epitome of an animal designed by a committee. When they run they have legs flying in all directions, probably not dissimilar to me. Their adaptations to survive are nothing short of impressive, and to look into their eyes would make your heart melt. Their eyelashes are seductively long and beautifully curled, and it is a shame to think that so much effort has gone into just keeping the sand out of your eyes.

Sheba, our first camel, came down in a horse float from Wellington Zoo. Because she had been wild caught and brought out from Australia, her age was unknown, but it mattered nothing. She was my camel and I loved her. Her paddock was on a small rise just above the house. By stretching her neck she could just reach the barbecue area, and was a regular feature at house parties. It was by no means uncommon to go down and have a ride on her in the early hours of the morning, although this never worked properly. She would put her head down and everyone would slide off. Few realised that to ride a camel you actually have to be on or behind the hump. As part of an international event arranged by CORSO in 1977 to raise money for projects in Nepal and West Africa, I took Sheba on a 'Walk for Water', across the Port Hills with Mayor Hamish Hay, the British actor Norman Bowler, a bunch of other dignitaries and 1500 people. She was the perfect ambassador, playing the part with dignity and aplomb.

I really wanted to get a baby camel, and so Sheba went off to the local lion park, which also had a male camel. After a couple of months of liaison, Sheba came back, and I treated her like royalty. Nothing was too good for my camel, and I spent hours holding my hands against her stomach, wanting to feel that first kick. It never came. Later we heard the bull had been gelded years before and no one had bothered to check.

A few years went by and the same park had acquired a new bull camel, and again it was offered to us to use. This had to be about the last chance and so we took Sheba out again for what we hoped would be her swan song. A few weeks later I got a phone call. Sheba had been found with two of her legs broken and had to be put down. These things do happen but I must admit I struggled with the concept of a male camel breaking the legs of a female. Some years later I was told that a rhinoceros had escaped and had attacked her. Again, that may be irrelevant but was the end of my desire to be involved in keeping camels without the ability to provide a better future for them

If I didn't have a dog handy and felt in need of someone to share my problems with, then I would often go into the farmyard in order to pat and talk to my pigs. Pigs are very understanding creatures with a high level of intelligence. In George Orwell's novel, *Animal Farm*, they lead the revolt. The little kune kune who had escaped Louis the mountain lion was none the worse for his adventure. He rolled on his side with his trotters in the air, giving every impression of ecstasy as I rubbed his stomach and pondered on his background. Mountain lions had been a blast, but the humble kune kune was hard to ignore. When you thought about it, it was strange that a pig had a much higher conservation value than a mountain lion, but then this was a different pig, a kune kune, a breed that had a huge effect on my personal life and on the development of the park.

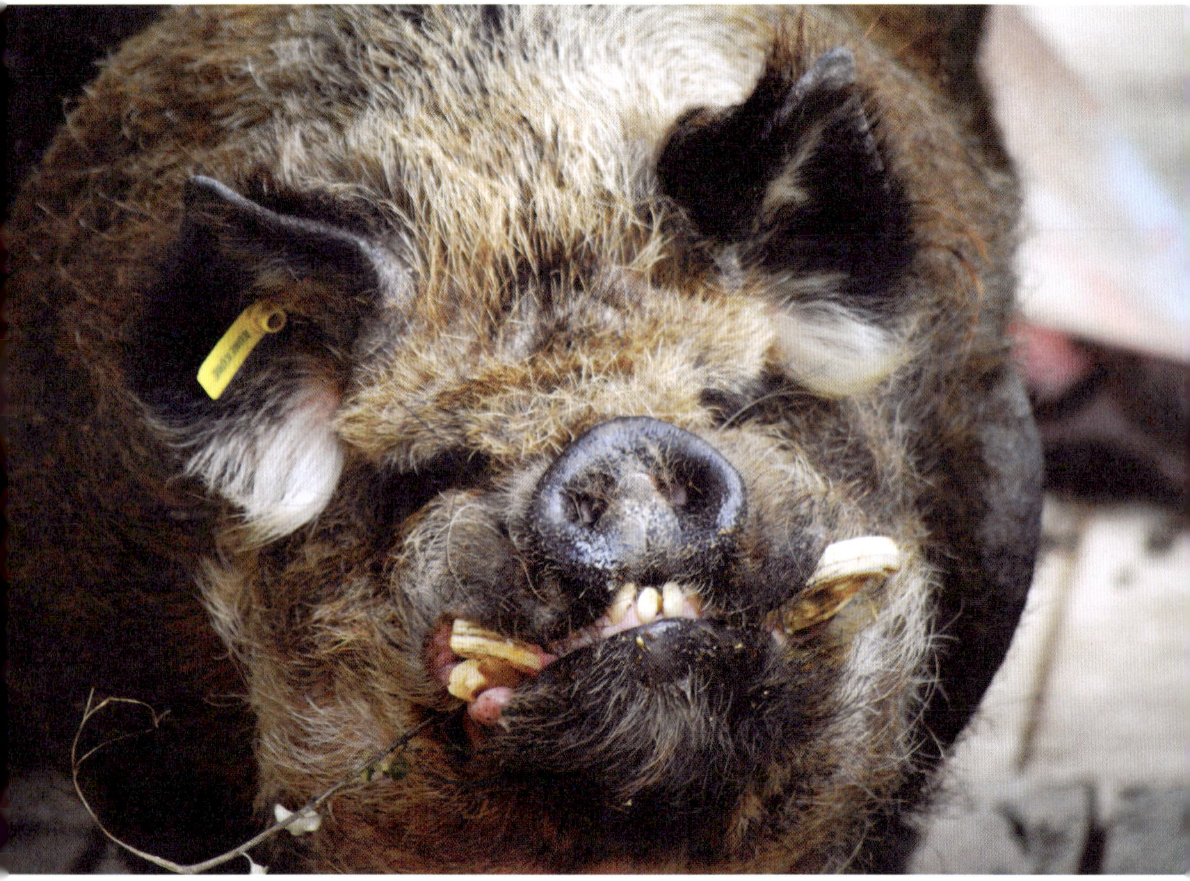

CHAPTER FOUR

KATCH ME A KUNE KUNE

It was about three o'clock in the morning, the world had a rosy glow and I was almost prepared to believe anything that my friend John Simister told me. But could there really be such a creature as a short, roly-poly fat pig, with little legs that just kept its tummy off the ground, and a nose so snub that its nostrils pointed skyward while it grazed (being unable to root up the ground)? The whole thing sounded more like a vertically challenged bulldog than a pig, and, what's more, according to John, the animal had tassels hanging under its chin, more like a goat.

Another few months would pass before I had an opportunity to take back my doubts, and in no uncertain terms, when John and I called into what was then known as Hilldale Zoo in Hamilton, where he maintained that he had seen a specimen of a kune kune. It was all true, and I instantly fell in love with the two strange little porcine creatures who trotted up and grunted to say hello. They had charisma, and they looked as though they could have walked straight out of a Walt Disney cartoon.

The people who had supplied Hilldale with the pigs didn't have any more and either couldn't or wouldn't give any information about other sources or availability. A year went by without any other information: it was as if the pigs never existed. Then one day I was rung by some bird breeders to whom I had mentioned the pigs when they passed through Willowbank. They in turn had asked around, and apparently a friend of theirs had managed to obtain a pair for me. This was our first real lead, and after a few hurried phone calls I was on the road, telling everyone that I would only be away for a few days.

Opposite: Ru the kune kune boar is used to smiling for the camera. He met Gandalf and the other celebrity actors when on set during the filming of *Lord of the Rings*. He was a favourite of Sir Peter Jackson, who often brought his family to visit between shoots.

Disney-cute kune kune piglets.

After a short stop at Staglands, John and I climbed into his ute and headed north up the west coast of the North Island. After several hours' driving we arrived at the nearest township to the location of the contact who, we hoped, had two kune kune pigs for me.

I had only a name but no address, and so it was a case of asking around. The girl behind the counter at the local store looked blank at first but after a few minutes said, 'Oh, you must mean Weasel. He lives just up the road.' As we arrived in a rundown back yard we looked around for a runty little fellow who might merit the name Weasel, but he turned out to be a genial hulk of a man. We introduced ourselves, and he took us over to a pen made of corrugated iron, where he proudly introduced the extremely rare and revered occupants.

Crouched in the corner amid the liquid slurry of mud, straw, potato peelings and all the other condiments that make up the typical environment of the everyday farm pig, and glaring at us, were a couple of white weaners with the odd blue patch. They appeared to be mainly domestic pig crossed with a Captain Cooker, which had bequeathed them long noses and skinny bodies. They were sporting three tassels between the two of them, the little boar having only one, but there any resemblance to kune kune began and ended. Weasel explained that they had been bred by an old hermit living in the bush, although he knew neither his name nor his location. Not wishing to be ungrateful for the effort that he had obviously gone to on our behalf, we paid him for the pigs, thanked him and went on our way. At least we had the tassels.

Enquiries around New Plymouth brought nothing but Awakino showed more promise. At the pub there we met an interesting character called Des Cox, who farmed nearby and had a deep interest in history and Māori culture. He had never heard of kune kune but went over to talk to a group of Māori standing around the pool table, who shot several dark looks in our direction. When Des came back, his expression was serious. Yes, the men knew about kune kune but they considered them to be Māori pigs: Pākehā should not have or keep them. Des, now rather intrigued, offered us a bed for the night.

The next morning, while John and I dug postholes in his yards in some recompense, Des spent time on the phone talking to most of the older local Māori families. About ten posts later, he eventually hit pay dirt with one Charlie Marshall, who apparently did have some kune kune and was happy to meet and talk to us. Putting down our shovels and crowbars with relief, we made our farewells and an hour or so later were pulling up outside Charlie's house.

A fine-looking man with a magnificent physique for his seventy-odd years, Charlie told us that he had brought the breed with him when he left Whanganui in 1926, and kept them ever since. He told us that kune meant fat or plump, and reiterated a story we had now heard a couple of times: that the pigs were in fact a Chinese breed, brought out by Chinese navigators or settlers, and looked after by Māori ever since. They were supposedly an ideal food source on long sea voyages when space was at a premium. They were fed up until their skin was almost splitting, then loaded into whatever vessel was being used. Living on a diet of water and a pinch of food, the pigs could survive such voyages with very little harm, and after a couple of months would be just coming back into their prime.

When I looked into Charlie's pen, I had some difficulty in not laughing as I asked if anyone had purchased any pigs off him recently. It seemed that a big fellow had driven up from down the coast and asked if he could have a couple of kune kune for a wildlife park that wanted to save them. Charlie had donated two, though the guy then discovered that he had chosen two females by mistake and had to come all the way back to exchange one. This was a cause of great merriment to Charlie, as were the pigs in the back of our truck. They were clearly from the same litter. So much for Weasel's hermit story.

Charlie Marshall.

We happily exchanged stories, swapped one piglet and bought two more, but I was puzzled as to why some piglets had one or sometimes both tassels missing. With a broad grin Charlie pointed to his large tribe of grandchildren who had turned up, bare footed and runny nosed, to see the fun and play in the dust. 'They catch them by the tassels, and sometimes they come off,' he said, laughing. The pigs were remarkably quiet. Apparently the pure-bred ones never reverted to wild and just hung around like family pets. This was a great advantage in pā and villages, as there were seldom any fences, and yet the pigs would remain completely domesticated. We spent a delightful time with Charlie, who was free with helpful knowledge and suggestions,

CHAPTER FOUR KATCH ME A KUNE KUNE

and after saying goodbye many times, we backed carefully out of the yard to avoid running over any grandchildren, and headed off. It was now pouring, with rain bouncing off the bonnet as we felt our way down the roads, half mesmerised by the beat of the windscreen wipers. At least they were mechanical. I was still in fits of laughter about an old Holden we had pulled up alongside, stuffed with a Māori family and their dog. A piece of binding twine tied to each of the windscreen wipers led back through the half-opened rear windows to where a little boy sat pulling each one alternately, in time to the urging of encouragement from Dad in the front seat.

The rain was still drumming down and thoughts were dulling when we passed a sign saying Woodlands Deer Park. On the spur of the moment we made what turned out to be a fortuitous decision to call in and see if they could give us any information. After introducing ourselves to the owner, we were placed in front of a roaring fire and given a beautiful lunch prepared by his wife, while he rang around his contacts in the district to see if anyone could help. The bush telegraph worked its way up and down the various valleys until it led to a place called Kutarere, not far from Opotiki. Somewhere there lived Len and Daphne Helmbright, who had indicated that they might be able to help and so we headed off up winding gravel roads into the mist.

Bush roads usually lead only one way, which is up valleys, and this one wound its way through dense sodden forest that opened out into a clearing and a wonderful warm welcome by Daphne, who explained that Len was away getting reinforcements, but if in the meantime we wanted to pop up the road, we could talk to her neighbour, Mrs Mac Onekawa, and see some of her pigs. She turned out to be a lovely woman with two beautiful little kune kunes. They were the best specimens that we had seen yet, except that they had no tassels, but sadly and understandably, they were not for sale. According to Mrs Mac, who was reputed to be an authority on Māori lore, the first kune kune came over from Hawaiki on the original canoes. They had always been only Māori pigs, and were an important part of their lifestyle and culture. The fat from the animals was widely used to preserve their meat.

When Len, a big, active-looking man aged about 50, returned he had with him a short, stocky, elderly guy named Timi Kereopa, generally known as Kelly. He wore a heavy woollen tweed jacket and a crumpled hat pulled low over two shrewd black eyes. His English was not great but he always managed to make himself easily understood. Kelly agreed that there were few kune kune pigs left these days, but felt pretty confident that he could find us one or two. After working out a plan of attack over a billy of tea, we set off in the vehicles, with Len, Daphne and Kelly, towards a village Kelly had told us about. Periodically along the way we would pass a house or a group of houses, and Kelly would get out and talk long and loudly to the occupants. The houses were universally old, and maintenance was obviously not high on the list of priorities. In most cases they nestled into the bush as if they were slowly being reclaimed by the trees, and inevitably had a cluster of children in front, playing among dogs and chickens. The feeling of isolation was only occasionally broken. Sometimes it would be a lone man on horseback, quietly walking up the road with a few dogs tucked in behind and a rifle slung over his back, occasionally a vehicle. In all cases the conversations were conducted solely in Māori, and with many meaningful glances in our direction. It felt very strange to be in the country of my birth and yet have no idea what the indigenous inhabitants were saying. This was indeed Māori land and I was an intruder. As the sun went down, however, and the shadows darkened the valley floor, Kelly was convinced that the information he had gleaned was correct. Pigs would be found, but we needed to get further into the bush, and so we returned to Len's and waited until the morning.

At breakfast the next morning, to Kelly's delight, John agreed that he would pay him, should he find and acquire a purebred kune kune. As with the previous day we could have been in a foreign country as we headed away on a two-and-a-half-hour drive into the valley mists. Most men we saw had a rifle in their hand, or maybe over their shoulder, and were either walking in or out of the bush, maybe on horseback with sheepskins as saddles and, quixotically, often wearing bright yellow Ministry of Works wet weather gear. There was, too, a strong feeling of community. Even the road gangs tended to consist of the whole family, with Dad being responsible for the whereabouts of his shovel, and Mum filling the unpaid role of keeping the fire going, brewing tea for her man, cooking his lunch and foraging in the bush and streams for the condiments for dinner. Usually scattered along the edge of the road, and diving in and out of the undergrowth, would be the usual assortment of dust-covered children, who stood and studied us thoughtfully as we passed by.

It was early afternoon before we got the break that we wanted when Kelly returned with news of some kune kune. Unfortunately they were running freely in the riverbed, but if we were prepared to catch them, then we could take what we wanted. A couple of passing men pointed us towards the local rubbish dump at the foot of a steep drop into the bed of the river, where they had recently seen the pigs nosing among the car bodies and household refuse. With Kelly up on top to keep watch, John, Len and I searched the riverbed in vain for about half an hour, until we heard a bellow from Kelly,

CHAPTER FOUR **KATCH ME A KUNE KUNE**

Len Helmbright and Timi Kereopa, better known as Kelly.

who was waving energetically upriver, pointing with his stick. Following his directions, we came across a very grumpy black and white sow with about six half-grown porkers in the scrub. A quick consultation, and a planned scissor movement followed by a spectacular tackle by Len, led us to catching a black and white boar along with a small black sow. Exhausted but exhilarated John and I were triumphant at the result, but Len and Kelly were determined that what we really needed was the old sow. This was much more serious stuff, but we could hardly be seen to be ungrateful, so with some trepidation we rejoined the chase. Several times we thought that we had her bailed up, but each time she slipped away. John and I were hard on her heels with Kelly and Len some distance away upriver when we bailed her up among some tree roots under a bank, and stood back to catch our breath again and wait for some more backup.

69

Len was probably 100 or so metres away and out of view, when a battered Falcon ute pulled up on the track above, and three very tough-looking men got out and began shouting at us in Māori. Their meaning was clear and it didn't bode well. John and I, feeling most apprehensive, shouted back a very non-committal time-delaying comment. They threatened us again, this time in English, and started down the hill. Just as I was considering the merits of trying to explain to them that it was really all John's idea and I only came along for the ride, Len finally reappeared around the corner. John and I breathed tentative sighs of relief as the exchange in Māori echoed backwards and forwards across the riverbed. After what appeared considerable reluctance on their part, the men climbed back into their truck and drove off muttering, followed by our quiet blessing.

By now the old sow was fairly wound up, and had no intention of being caught. Upstream, downstream, uphill and downhill we all went to the tune of Kelly's conducting until we were absolutely exhausted and more than a little discouraged. Running backwards and forwards with his bandy-legged gait and furiously waving his stick, he was red in the face, breathless and perspiring heavily. Daphne was more worried abut him than any kune kune. He had recently had several strokes and was not supposed to do anything energetic. In his heavy woollen trousers, a waistcoat topped with an overcoat and the inevitable hat pulled down over his eyes, he resembled a soda bomb about to blow up.

Then around the corner, slouched in the saddle on a bag of bones wrapped in a bit of horse flesh, came a scruffy-looking Māori accompanied by a pack of dogs that a pound would think twice about. Reining up alongside old Kelly, he straightened up in the saddle with interest when he finally understood why the old boy was fizzing at the bung and almost incoherent with excitement. Pleased at the opportunity for a diversion, and also to show off his team of dogs, he put heels to the nag's sides and came stumbling up the riverbed, much to the growing alarm of the pig. It was only a few minutes before she was bailed up by the dogs in a thick patch of scrub with nowhere to go, had her back leg firmly grabbed by Len and was bundled triumphantly into the trailer. With a wide toothless smile, our saviour went on his way with his little pack of dogs, their tails and ears pricked high with excitement and pride.

We had one further contact to stop at before heading back, and as so often happens the last call is often the best one. Two beautiful little pigs, just as we imagined that they should be, except that they had no tassels. As had been typical of the Māori we had met on this journey, the people concerned would accept no payment, though we knew that Len and Daphne would one day address the balance with a side of lamb or some shellfish. The kindness and goodness that shone through these people was to have a profound effect on my life, and the act of giving created in turn a responsibility to ensure that the intent of the gift was honoured and passed on. At the summit of the road that led into the valley John formally paid the debt to a now much calmer Kelly, who by now had calmed down, much to Daphne's relief. Like a tortoise retreating into its shell, his wizened head and neck had shrunk down into his coat and he was fast asleep before we left the valley. An unexpected outcome of this extraordinary day was my decision to stop smoking. I had been puffing and panting behind Len, and I realised that if I wanted to maintain the fitness I needed, the cigarettes had to go.

The next morning, as the mist rose in the valleys, we were off again to visit another friend of Kelly's known as Paddy. We got a red boar off him, but what was of real interest was the way that Paddy was keeping his pigs. He had a number of steel drums lying on their sides, that he rolled around his property. Alongside the settling place of each drum he would drive a stake, and tie a pig to it by its leg. It was a bit like walking into a mustering camp run by Monty Python, except where there should have been dogs straining and barking at the end of the chain, there were pigs grunting and looking up at you with expressions of interest and expectation. The older pigs had noticeable marks around the fetlock of each leg, and so obviously the ties were changed periodically, or as maybe needed or, I hoped, noticed. I knew that in Britain tethering pigs with a belt around the shoulders was an old form of husbandry; maybe this was the Māori equivalent. I visualised rows of kune kune pigs tethered in orchards eating windfall apples while their babies wandered free, and I couldn't help but think that often we miss the obvious in its simplicity. We loaded our little boar and sadly farewelled Len, Daphne and the inimitable Kelly.

Our route took us north to Tolaga Bay, and then we retreated to the civilisation of Wairoa, where we thought we would try some stock agents. This led us to another Charlie, who was enthusiastic enough to abandon business for the day and take us home to show us his kune kune. Unfortunately they were no improvement on the assortment that we now carried in the back of the truck, and so although disappointed at not making a sale, he sat down and marked on a map some settlements that he thought we should visit.

At the first settlement, a wisp of smoke curling out of a whare chimney beckoned us, as we carefully made our way through a gate up an overgrown pathway, and onto a seriously rotten verandah, but with an open door

RESCUE ONE NEW ZEALANDER'S CRUSADE TO SAVE ENDANGERED ANIMALS

John pays his debt to Kelly.

welcoming us like a toothless smile. Our calls were answered from inside, and in the gloom we could make out the form of an elderly woman sitting cross-legged on the floor, weaving flax baskets. The room had no lighting and the smoke from the little fire she sat by drifted up in a haze, giving an ethereal appearance to the whole scene. Warm, serene and sincere, she was willing to be of any assistance. We stayed and talked of pigs, life and living, but then had to reluctantly leave her wreathed in smoke and smiles.

Through her we tracked down Sam Rurehe, who knew the kune kune well. His grandfather had told how his village had been involved in a battle up north in the mid-nineteenth century, joining forces with the tribe from Te Kuiti. They fought well, and in return for their help were given some plundered kune kune. Sam also explained how, during the Great Depression, they used to mix fat from the kune with golden syrup, to make a spreadable replacement for butter. In his opinion there were no kune left in the region now. An hour or two down the road, at a pub Sam reckoned might be worth a stop, we met a very buxom Māori woman named Ada McNabb and her elderly and rather deaf companion Auntie Kuini, commonly known as Auntie Queenie. The rather loud and boisterous conversations that took place over the next hour or so soon left us in little doubt that we were in the presence of a couple of influential and locally well connected women. It was a lovely evening and time well spent for we ended up with a contact called Ru Kotaha. The bar may have closed on us but Auntie Queenie certainly didn't consider the night finished, and insisted that we all drive around to Ru's place and knock him up.

It was to be a long night. Ru had to reluctantly arouse himself in order to show everyone his pigs by torch and truck light. Even in our fairly relaxed and rosy state we could see that they were magnificent pigs, kune kune as we had always imagined how they would be. It was like rediscovering old friends. The rosy glow diminished slightly when he said that really he didn't want to sell any, but then Ada crossed her arms over her magnificent breasts and Auntie Queenie leant on her stick and gave him such a withering look that he immediately recanted and offered us a young pair. They were soon caught and in the truck, and when I asked how much he wanted for them, one look from Auntie Queenie was enough for them to be gifted, with a wide and open smile. It had been a very special evening but we now had to leave the bush. As we did so, our journey lost an almost spiritual component.

We now had thirteen pigs on board. Some had been travelling tourists with us for some time now, and every time we introduced a new animal, the hierarchy and sleeping order needed to be re-established. Cleaning and feeding properly were becoming more and more of a problem, and so we decided to return to Staglands and drop the pigs off into holding facilities there. We had again been given some more contacts, back up the west coast above where Weasel lived, and we had got our first pigs. So it was with some degree of manipulative subtlety that we prepared our partners and families with the knowledge that yes, we had come back, but no, we needed to go on the same journey around the North Island again, in order to complete our mission. With the pigs offloaded and settled, and a domestic night doing dishes in order to build up some credits, we were repacked and away the next morning, again following the coast road north.

We were looking for Whare Hepi, who took some time and devious cunning to eventually track down. Whare had obviously been around a bit, and had little intention of talking about his past, and so the few answers we got to our questions weren't really forthcoming or reassuring. He may have felt cornered, but he said that he had no kune kunes himself and couldn't help us find any. We were pretty disappointed after travelling so far to find him. Maybe sensing this, he rather reluctantly told us about a person who could probably help us if we were prepared to take the risk. His name was

John Wilson. He had a reputation and we would need to be careful about how we approached him. Whare painted a vivid picture of an old recluse living in the bush, surrounded by his kune kunes for companionship, while trapping opossums for a living. He was passionately fond of his pigs, and living in a remote area among people who liked fatty pork and parties made him supersensitive about intruders. Anyone caught around his animals could certainly expect a shotgun blast. We got the feeling that there was some personal experience behind Whare's narrative.

Despite the rather hazy directions, we stumbled across John Wilson's place with surprisingly little difficulty, although without some prior knowledge, you would drive right past and never know it was there. No driveway, just wheel marks up a hill. No house, just two small huts close together and tucked away under the inviting bush, about three-quarters of a kilometre up the steep hill and off the back country road. We opened the gate into the paddock, and bounced our way up the grassy slope to the little encampment. It was an idyllic setting, tucked against a background of dark bush from which jutted huge rock formations that cascaded down the hill, laced with pools and waterfalls from a stream that cobwebbed them all together. We turned the vehicle off and a deep velvet silence settled around us, broken occasionally by the snore and grunt of a pig stretched luxuriantly out in the bracken, basking in the afternoon sun. Suddenly the realisation hit us: we had actually found the hermit, who lived up a four-wheel-drive track, about 80 kilometres out of Te Awamutu. It all fitted Weasel's rather convoluted explanation. After one and a half times around the North Island, we were back to where we should have started from.

We could see an old horse standing patiently still, reins loosely hanging down and saddle and working gear still in place. A couple of dogs ran around, cocking their legs on anything they felt was theirs to mark. A man presumably unpacking the results of a day's work must be the Mad Hermit himself. With a boldness that we didn't feel, we drove resolutely up the hill to the huts, fully expecting to be confronted with the twin muzzles of a shotgun. Tails wagging, the dogs ran around the trucks, pleased to be able to lift their legs on something new, and the horse cocked its ears forward with interest, but most surprising of all was the cheery wave and loud hello that came from their owner. A small wiry man in his mid-seventies, John moved and acted like someone half his age. His honesty and love for his simple lifestyle were quickly apparent, and he obviously had a wonderful and fulfilling relationship with his animals. His horse was his transport and mate, his dogs his mates, his ducks and geese produced enough to make him feel that he was productive, and his beloved kune kune gave him the reason for being there.

CHAPTER FOUR KATCH ME A KUNE KUNE

A kune kune sow greets us at John Wilson's.

They roamed freely everywhere, for there were no noticeable fences. All along the bush edge there were tell-tale movements, as residents returned home hoping for a bit of a scratch and supper, older animals shifted to make the most of the last warming rays of the sun and convoluted bundles of piglets tumbled over each other before getting lost in the bracken. There must have been well over thirty pigs visible and an undisclosed number still in the bush. Wild pigs would have turned the place into a badly ploughed paddock but here there appeared to be no sign of any damage or mess. The impression was one of complete love and harmony, and if I had been John Wilson and someone was trying to take one of my animals for a party dish, then I, too, would have had little problem in reaching for the shotgun.

Alone and unnoticed, John had worked to try and save and protect these pigs, after seeing many years before that they were in danger of disappearing. He had taken every opportunity to obtain and purchase stock, and must have frequently wondered about the rationale of continuing to maintain such a lonely and often futile crusade. I couldn't help but draw a parallel with Richard Henry, working all those years in Fiordland trying to save the kākāpō, only to see his work and dreams shattered. John was so excited at the possibility that other people might share his passion, that his welcome could not have been warmer or more forthcoming.

It may have been coincidence, but he said that we had arrived at exactly the right time: he was going to have to get rid of his favourite boar, because he had used him now over two generations, and needed another bloodline. He was a stunning creature, huge for a kune kune, probably weighing in at 150 kilos or more, and a light gold in colour. Because he had never had a bad hand on him, he was a gentle, good-natured animal, although old and big enough to view the world with some confidence. Loading him onto the truck was going to be a problem, as there were no yards, let alone loading ramps. Using food, we eventually enticed him into a small makeshift pen and backed the truck up to the side of it. A rope was slipped around his top jaw and then, with one person pulling and others on each back leg and around the middle, we lifted him, with much high-pitched screaming into the back, where he grumped and grumbled until he was given some food to settle down. To complete the breeding group, John then gave us a young unrelated black and brown marbled sow about nine months old, and a hand-reared three-month-old female.

We had now completed the full circle. There were no more real leads left to follow, and we were satisfied. As we turned the truck for home, we had a lot to occupy our thoughts and conversations. Did we now have an answer to the origins of the kune kune? Were they actually originally a pure breed, and if so how would a breed standard describe them? We had been gifted a responsibility. How would we handle it?

As far as we could estimate, there were probably about fifty or so breeding kune kune left in New Zealand, and so we were lucky to get sufficient animals to form two breeding groups. Of the eighteen animals we had collected, nine were considered to be purebred or so close to it that it did not matter. The others would be useful to grade up from, and bring in new blood in the future, while Staglands and Willowbank could work together and exchange stock as required.

What is now the Kune Kune Pig Breeders Association was born in 1988, originally under a slightly different name. Inevitably it started in a small way, but as the years passed it grew and grew, until it had several hundred members and a herd book with well over 1000 animals. As a society it grew to totally eclipse the National Pig Breeders Association, which was made up of all the other breeds of pigs combined, an ironic situation considering

CHAPTER FOUR **KATCH ME A KUNE KUNE**

> **Congratulations, Sir Michael!**
>
> For outstanding achievement in the field of conservation and saving the kune kune from extinction I dub thee Sir Michael Willis, and we must swap favourite recipes sometime.

Courtesy New Zealand Kunekune Association

those same commercial breeders didn't want to even acknowledge the kune kune's existence. With their cute little faces, snub noses and round bodies, they became a wildly popular designer pig. Kune kunes have been exported to Britain, and there's now a strong society there, as well as smaller ones in France, Belgium and, more recently, Austria. They have also been exported to the United States, where two societies fight each other for supremacy and registration systems.

Although the kune kune pig is no longer considered endangered, it still needs an eye kept on it, as nothing retains its popularity forever, and populations such as this can still crash. Over the intervening years the numbers have peaked and no one knows where the downward trend may end. These animals are lucky in that they combine good looks and personality with charisma, otherwise they would just be ignored like so many other breeds. Still no one knows where they came from, or how they arrived in New Zealand, but it appears increasingly likely that they arrived very early and that they certainly have an Asian background. No doubt one day some DNA tests will throw more light on the mystery of their origin. They are, however, a truly New Zealand breed, and should have a special place in our heritage, and yet we almost lost them before we knew they existed.

Left: Building a whare for the Māori village.

My experiences with Māori while collecting the kune kune pigs had quite an effect on me. Their culture was so much part of the country's identity, but certainly in the South Island, where I lived, it was relatively unknown. I felt an obligation to the people I had met, the gift of the pigs, and the hospitality that I had been given, to recognise that in some small way. I came up with the concept of building a pre-European Māori village, at least as a starting point. I wanted it to be a relatively authentic experience, and something that people could relate to. I didn't want to recreate a pā, with substantial fortifications and infrastructure, but a simple village or kainga.

After organising some students over the holidays, we went out and built one. We went scrub cutting and returned with hundreds of manuka poles from which we built palisading. We cut trailer-loads of raupo, which we dried and tied with flax into bundles for covering the little houses or whare that were half buried in the ground to retain warmth. We wove mats and made ropes of flax, and after months of work had created a little village and absorbed a lot of Māori culture while doing so. We had a grand opening ceremony conducted by the rangatira and orator Hohua Tutengaehe and attended by about 250 people. The village was officially named Te Pari o Whiro, or the place of the willows.

CHAPTER FOUR **KATCH ME A KUNE KUNE**

Above: Hohua Tutengaehe arrives to open the village.

Above right: Part of Willowbank's unique Māori cultural experience. Ben Brennan at left.

One of the key cultural figures who spoke for us that day was Hori Brennan, whose son Dave was a small boy in the haka party. Some years later he asked me if we wanted to establish a cultural performance group at Willowbank; he had been involved in doing such performances for a number of years. An hour later we shook hands on a deal, and the very next week started work on a performance area. At first we had a stage and nothing else, and the performers, barefoot and wearing fairly minimal costumes, froze in winter. Next a sail went over the stage, then some seating was erected, and finally, after two or three years, a fully covered area was finished, complete with changing rooms for the performers. We named the cultural experience Ko Tāne, and, run as a separate company from Willowbank, it has gradually developed to become the only cultural group of significance performing for tourists in the South Island. It is a valued and enjoyable relationship, and one that helps to fulfil our desire to be a facility representing New Zealand in culture as well as in wildlife.

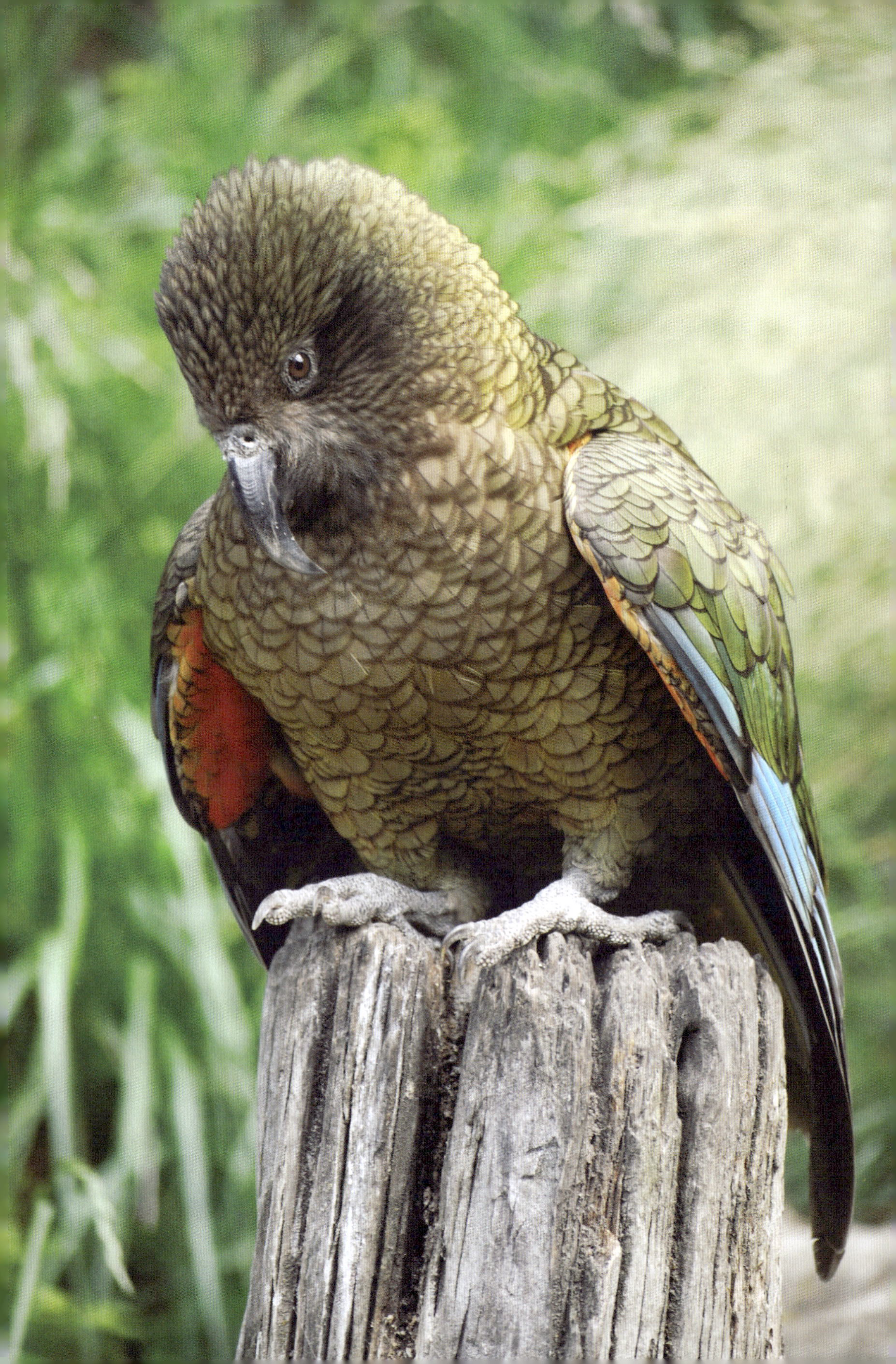

CHAPTER FIVE

WHEN IS A CAMEL NOT A CAMEL

The sun was just creeping down behind Mount Ngauruhoe, and its snow-capped cone stood proudly, etched in the evening sky. The very sound of the name Desert Road has a mystical air about it, as it leads the traveller across a bleak, harsh alpine plateau, dominated by the inspiring cones of the three famous volcanoes, Ruapehu, Ngauruhoe and Tongariro. Humans have never really dominated this region, and that sense of vulnerability eats its way into the very vehicle you are travelling in, and either stimulates or eradicates any suggestion of idle gossip. With me in the Land Rover was John Simister, and we were in pretty good spirits, for we had the prospect of a couple of entertaining and worthwhile days ahead. I wanted to collect a camel from Auckland Zoo and both of us wanted to attend a Clydesdale horse auction that was being held at Mystery Creek near Hamilton.

It had been a convivial night, so resting on the rail next morning was a welcome respite from pretending to be alert. Radiating inwards all around us were the huge rounded rumps of numerous monstrous draught horses, shifting patiently on their platter-like feet, and with what appeared to be monotonous regularity lifting their tails and breaking copious amounts of grassy wind that did nothing to dispel the fog in our own heads. With the prices high and beyond the reach of either of us, we lounged on the fence, taking no active part. It was right at the tail end of the sale when my attention was drawn to a nondescript filly that was being prepared to go into the ring. The bidding started and was slow. Late entry, not presented well, and I started to take a lot more interest.

Opposite: You will not fool me. I'm a kea, the cleverest bird in the world.

'Buy her,' I said to John. 'She's dirt cheap. If you don't bid on her I will.'

Shaking himself out of his reverie, John lifted his catalogue and took a bid. The price lifted slowly, John had disappeared into himself again, and she was obviously close to reaching a sale price.

'She's a gift, I tell you,' I said. 'Look, I'll go you halves then, but for goodness sake bid on her.'

As if in a dream he raised his catalogue again. A few more bids and she was ours. As far as we were concerned she was the buy of the sale. Our next stop was Auckland, and so we arranged for her to stay there overnight and we would pick her up the next morning.

That morning found us at Auckland Zoo outside the camel enclosure. I had arranged a young male for our female, and was thrilled to have this opportunity.

'He's a bit boisterous,' said the keeper. 'Needs a firm hand.'

The camel was almost 2 metres tall, but with the aid of several keepers and ropes we manhandled him into the horse float and closed the ramp up behind him. He immediately turned around and stood there facing backwards, with his head peering over the top of the door, and his large dark moist eyes round with a mixture of surprise and concern. It never pays to stand around when you have first loaded an animal, and so we bid our farewells and drove out of the zoo and into the heavy morning traffic.

After the comparative calm of the south, Auckland traffic is a nightmare, and in this case it was made worse by the camel, who stretched his long neck out over the top of the door, taking an evident interest in the chaos stretching out behind him. People in the overtaking lane would slam on their brakes and drop back to try and see what it was. Some would pass and then brake to make us pass them again so they could get behind and jostle for a position. It was like a demented funeral cortege, and we were grateful when he eventually must have got bored with the whole thing, pulled his head in and, like a mechanical toy, folded up his long ungainly legs and settled into the bed of straw. With the diversion gone, the traffic flow returned to normal, and we made good time to Hamilton.

Horses notoriously loathe and detest camels, and many and varied are the stories of camels putting to flight legions of horses. Somehow we had to convince the little Clydesdale that there was no truth in that rumour, and that a camel was really not at all a bad travelling companion. We backed up as close as we could to the stable where she was being held, and enlisted the help of a woman working there. She looked a little disbelieving when we said we needed a hand to load a horse because we had a camel on board, but

CHAPTER FIVE **WHEN IS A CAMEL NOT A CAMEL**

John works on persuading the little Clydesdale to enter the float again after arrival at Staglands.

after putting her head in the side door and being met by a soft velvet muzzle, overhanging droopy floppy lips, festooned with strings of glutinous saliva that fluttered as a series of moans emerged, carrying with them the gas from his stomach contents, she believed us.

We had a plan. We would push the camel over to one side of the float and get him to lie down by touching his feet. We then needed to hide him. Some old sacks we had found suited the purpose well and we covered him so he vaguely resembled a wool pack of dags, a character part we thought suited him perfectly. I then got a tube of toothpaste from my luggage, and smeared it around the nostrils of the little horse to mask any unsocial scents her unknown guest might have, and to give her that double ring of confidence that we all in fact needed. Preparations completed, we led the horse out, dropped the ramp and roped her straight in. As her tail passed the end bar we flung the ramp up and secured it tight. The sudden movement made the camel stand up, shaking his sacks off, and they looked at each other in mutual shock and amazement. Back in the Land Rover, we headed straight to Wellington, knowing that we would not get away with that trick again, and they actually settled into a reluctant acceptance of each other.

A couple of days at Staglands, and it was time to cross on the ferry to

RESCUE ONE NEW ZEALANDER'S CRUSADE TO SAVE ENDANGERED ANIMALS

the South Island. As usual in those days there was a charge not only for the vehicle but also for the animal on board, and so it became a matter of principle to outwit the authorities. The cunning plan this time was to put the camel in a crate on the back of an old long wheelbase Land Rover John had, and cover it with a tarpaulin. Applying the philosophy that if a squirt of toothpaste up a horse's nose makes a camel disappear, we decided that, with Carole's help, a few exposed areas of female flesh would have the same effect on the men at New Zealand Rail. John and I were to have a low profile.

We managed to get the camel up a ramp and into the crate and the tarpaulin secured. Unfortunately the sides of the crate weren't quite high enough for him to stand without making a bulge that moved around like a mole under the bedclothes, but there was little we could do but hope that he would lie down and behave himself. Carole went off and got changed, returning in a low-cut, almost see-through blouse that was perfect for our purposes. We thought the skirt with the slit up the side was going a bit far, however, as the doors of the Land Rover would often stick, meaning you had to exit by

Unloading the camel at Picton before heading home.

CHAPTER FIVE **WHEN IS A CAMEL NOT A CAMEL**

climbing out the window, so she opted instead for a pair of skin-tight jeans. Outside the ferry terminal John and I jumped out and walked onto the ferry, leaving Carole to her own devices. At the stern, we watched as the vehicles lined up at the first checkpoint.

'Dirty bugger,' John said, as we observed the official standing on tip toe with his head all but in the window of the Land Rover. 'Typical civil servant. Either act like eunuchs or sex fiends. Either way they can't keep their minds on the job for more than two minutes.'

This one proved him wrong because he lasted a good five minutes before he reluctantly waved Carole on. Smiling sweetly and waving, she drove onto the ferry. I met her as she came up from the vehicle deck looking like an advert for a strip club, and threw my arms around her, saying that I didn't think she would get away with it, and we would be discovered. 'I don't want to know,' said a voice behind us. Walking away was a close family friend, who to this day thinks I was being naughty. The next day, when John and Carole returned on the ferry, the officials had a different attitude and found the St Bernard Carole had purchased in Christchurch hidden in the back of the Land Rover and charged for it accordingly. On that occasion John was driving and Carol was draped in a heavy woollen sweater.

Bureaucracy and officialdom are never far from the surface when you're involved in the running of a zoo or a wildlife park. They can be the biggest hurdles to overcome, and ones that you have little chance of altering. It is sometimes appalling how whole populations can be put at risk because of the opinions of one or two people. A poodle as a pet, three years at university and many graduates are experts in the field of husbandry and population dynamics. Some attitudes are just hard to comprehend. A DOC scientist once tried to explain it to me. He said that there are two approaches, depending if it's plant or animal. If the plant people have a rare and endangered species, then they propagate it as much as possible, send it to as many nurseries as they can and encourage as many people as possible to look after it. The polar opposite applies to the animal people, who in effect shut such a species down, hold it tightly to their chests and rigidly restrict any outside involvement. It was a throwaway comment, but the truth of it was hard to avoid.

A typical example would be the delightful little flightless Auckland Island duck. A small number had been brought back to New Zealand, and we were lucky to be able to obtain a pair. The thrill of holding one of the world's rarest ducks became very tarnished, however, when the directive came from the species coordinator that no breeding was to take place. The species was to be left to die out on the Mainland. Eventually the last pair alive, which were then being held at the National Wildlife Centre by DOC, were euthanised, but because they were so rare and valuable their bodies were sent to Te Papa to be mounted. The same directive applied to the equally rare Campbell Island teal, with no justification that carried any merit. I made myself unpopular lobbying Ministers of Conservation and anyone else I could think of, but to no avail. Years later there has been almost a complete U-turn, with talk of going back to the Aucklands to capture some more ducks, to provide a secure secondary population elsewhere. Sometimes you just have to wonder at the shallowness of thought and narrow-mindedness that accompany such decisions.

Strangely enough, the zoo industry itself is one of the worst culprits. There was a good, cohesive and very successful organisation made up of individuals, groups and facilities that held captive species. But this was taken over and controlled by the larger zoos, which then set about dismembering it. Individuals and groups could no longer belong. Those controlling bodies have an elitist attitude, but at the same time complain that there aren't enough accommodation spaces to develop breeding programmes. Some large private avicultural and waterfowl facilities in New Zealand have collections far exceeding those of any of the large zoos, and yet all of this support is cut out. Big avicultural conferences with outstanding overseas speakers are held regularly, but seldom if ever attended by zoo or DOC personnel. The species coordinators are generally selected from the large zoos, and have almost complete control over what happens, and usually with little knowledge or experience to achieve an end result. Wildlife is suffering as much through disjointed human thinking as it is through other environmental factors.

Our kea population is another good example. Our Willowbank kea aviary is arguably one of the biggest and best in New Zealand. It has space for at least fifteen birds, which was the number put into it when it was completed many years ago. Across New Zealand, however, the coordinator for the species decreed that there was to be no breeding, eggs were to be destroyed and the numbers reduced in the captive population to under 100, with the idea of phasing out the population completely. Kea numbers in the wild were dropping, but few at that time believed it.

Over the years our kea numbers at Willowbank declined until we were left with a handful of old birds that behaved like a bunch of geriatrics. Finally, in disgust, I decided to take matters into my own hands and allow the birds to do what comes naturally. Few kea have ever bred in captivity but ours

Opposite: Kirsty with three of our kea.

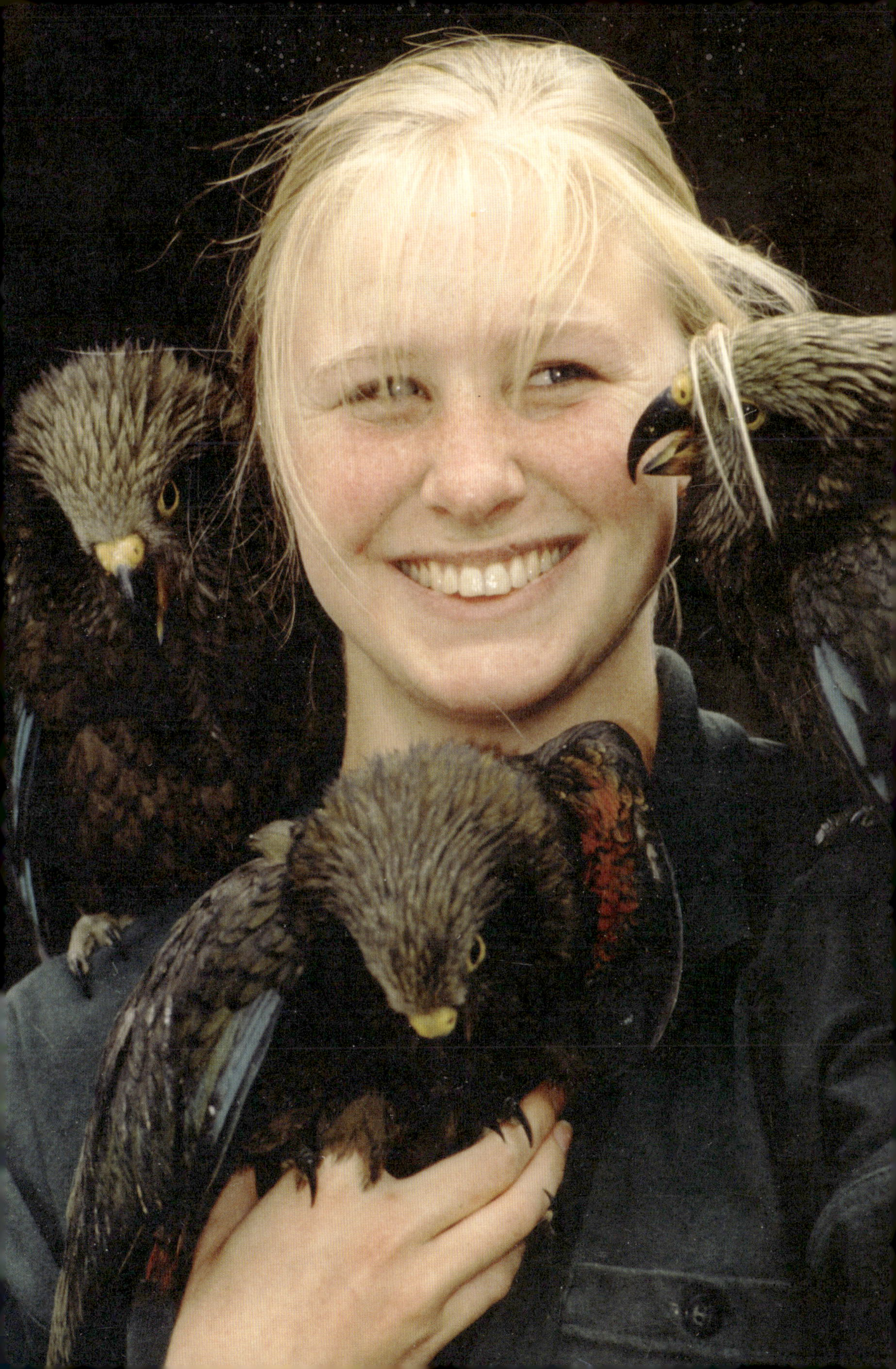

soon picked up the challenge. Two breeding seasons later, and we were back up to fifteen. The change in the dynamics of the population was enormous. The original birds had been dull and not very interactive. Now there were babies, juveniles and adults, all tumbling around together, and learning good and bad habits.

There was, of course, going to be retribution, and when we filled in our census forms with the new number, the coordinator threw her toys out of the cot and wanted our permits revoked immediately. Fortunately the area conservator made some pragmatic decisions and I escaped but with yet another black mark against my name in what was becoming a thick file. On the more positive side, the little colony of kea we created is now used extensively by DOC and researchers, to test for their attraction to poison baits and whether they can access a predator trap or various other intelligence tests. That's mainly because ours is the only captive group in New Zealand that displays the natural behaviour you would hope to expect from a flock comprising various age groups.

Kea being what they are, they occasionally work out a way of escaping. That is the nature of the bird and never a great cause of panic because they never seem to want to go away, and hang around being a nuisance until they are enticed back – which, it's to be hoped, is usually sooner rather than later, as they can cause a certain amount of playful damage. They have, for example, removed some of the plastic caps of the roofing nails of the main building, which tends to allow for unexpected leaks. Slightly more embarrassing was what happened with some neighbours who had a large and boisterous family, and an equally large Para swimming pool made of highly coloured and chewable rubber and plastic. It was the equivalent of a kea Disneyland. The backyard was flooded, the pool was empty and the insurance company had some difficulty in understanding how a mountain parrot could wreak such havoc in a city suburb.

Equally embarrassing was the visit of the wife of a senior politician, who was holding an important overseas post. Along with some friends, she walked into the kea enclosure, with her handbag, as she thought, tucked safely away in the pram she was pushing. She had totally underestimated the birds, who soon had the contents of her bag out and were sitting on a branch over the middle of the river, examining them with interest. The cheque book was the first thing to get bored with, and pages were ripped out and dropped with total disregard into the waters below. Certainly the lipstick and compact held their attention for a while, but in the end, everything suffered the same watery fate. It wasn't quite a diplomatic emergency but it had the makings of one.

CHAPTER FIVE WHEN IS A CAMEL NOT A CAMEL

Kākāpō, cousins to the kea, are amazing birds but they're locked away on Codfish Island, in a strange echo of the attitude of our British forebears sending their convicts to island isolation in the Antipodes. I've sat with kākāpō, and was completely besotted by these gentle and charming creatures, which ooze personality. One of our great natural icons and tourist advocates, they're hidden in an area that's hard and expensive to get to, difficult to manage and where only a special few can see them.

One breeding programme that has been opened up slightly is that for takahē. With fewer than 300 birds left in the world, they had been closely managed at a breeding facility at Burwood Bush in Southland. When DOC were looking for additional spaces in which to hold them, in spite of our unenviable record with officialdom, we were chosen to be the only other facility in the South Island. We built what we believe is the nicest and most natural takahē enclosure in New Zealand, and it was an exciting day when we received the birds and the then conservation minister opened it. We were given a pair that were thought to be past any suggestion of breeding, but three years later we bred the first chick to be born in a captive facility. And it came from the oldest male to have ever sired a chick, which was later moved on to become part of the breeding programme. Our head of natives, Nick Acroyd, has now given several presentations on takahē husbandry and breeding, and is one of the country's most experienced people in this field.

It's really important that a facility such as Willowbank serves a conservation function. One that appealed to us was the reintroduction of the buff or eastern weka. For reasons unknown, this bird died out in Canterbury in the early days of settlement. Fortunately twelve had been taken to the Chatham Islands, where they bred up to become a thriving population that was regularly captured and eaten by the locals – one of the few instances were it's permissible to kill and eat a native species on the rather dubious understanding that they're in fact 'introduced'. As they're naturally Canterbury birds, and thousands are killed and eaten, I thought that it would be easy to get the correct approvals. It became anything but. DOC wasn't jumping with excitement about the thought of a species being returned, and made any permit conditional on the approval of the Chatham Island Māori. After several consultations, reluctant iwi approval was given for a dozen birds to be captured and brought back.

So began the Great Weka Hunt. Eight of us flew to the Chathams and set up camp on the outskirts of the main township, Waitangi. It was a low-key but fun week, even though we had to work quite hard to get the numbers that we wanted. We got the birds back to Willowbank without too many

RESCUE ONE NEW ZEALANDER'S CRUSADE TO SAVE ENDANGERED ANIMALS

difficulties, and it wasn't long before we had them breeding. That was the easy part. The difficult part was getting approval to release them. DOC now regarded it as a 'translocation', which put it into another level of bureaucracy, while some newly qualified experts considered that the weka would have an adverse effect on the environment, because they're predators. So until all that nonsense is resolved, our weka are held on restricted breeding and the chance of having them back in Canterbury is in the hands of a conflicting few.

Projects such as these, however, were becoming increasingly important to the direction of Willowbank. To give meaning to what we were trying to achieve, we needed to try and tell a story. To tell a story you need to travel

Dave Matheson with an armful of weka.

CHAPTER FIVE **WHEN IS A CAMEL NOT A CAMEL**

on a single path, and so over the years we've established a one-way walking system that leads people on a structured journey. This starts with the arrival of the Europeans and the animals and plants that they brought with them and introduced, such as deer, wallabies and so on. It then talks about the exotic animals that were once kept in Christchurch, both privately and in zoos, which allows us to continue to keep some exotic animals including a group of otters as a reminder of the native New Zealand otter or waitoreke (see chapter six). It goes on to illustrate the farming in New Zealand and the introduction of livestock breeds and the need to conserve them. The final part of the journey travels through an area that focuses on native plant species with some emphasis on the part played by Māori. We hope that by the time people have walked through the experience, they understand the mistakes that were made in the past and the problems created, the importance of our largely forgotten heritage animals – the early European settlers introduced well over 70 mammal species alone, and that didn't include livestock brought in by farmers – and the battle to save the future.

In 1988, Helen McKenzie and Bobbie Ohara, two livestock enthusiasts from Carterton, called a meeting of people they thought may be interested in forming a society with the aim of conserving livestock genetics within New Zealand. They had seen similar work being done overseas, in particular that of the Rare Breeds Survival Trust in Britain, and recognised the need here for a similar watchdog organisation. Massey University gave it a lot of support, particularly through the involvement of Dr Mike Rudge, who went on to become chair, and also Professor Hugh Blair, who became its patron.

I attended that first meeting, which was the beginning of a long involvement with the society, including a stint as chair. For me it opened a whole new field of genetic conservation, which until then had been largely focused on species in the wild. To some it is about preserving heritage and the past, but to me it was also about retaining values for the future. In a frighteningly short time, agriculture as we know it may have to change, and these breeds now considered rare may be the building blocks of the future. Dr David Scobie describes such breeds as his sandpit to play in, full of bundles of genetics that he can dismantle and rebuild, or from which he can extract bits in order to establish desirable traits. We lose those bundles of genetics at our peril.

One day I received a newspaper cutting about a farmer in Ashburton who was retiring and selling up, but among his herd of animals were two Large Black pigs, thought to be the last in New Zealand. It was inconceivable to allow these animals to go to slaughter, and so I hopped in my truck and headed south. The farmer was thrilled that someone had taken an interest. They were both sows, an old pure-bred sow and her part-bred daughter. Pigs have always been a bit of a favourite of mine, and I was fascinated to see them. They were both exceptionally large animals, with huge floppy spaniel-like ears that hid most of their faces, and meant that if they wanted to see you, they had to hold their noses up high so that the ears fell away from their eyes. They were like a couple of schoolgirls who haven't made up their mind whether to have their hair shoulder length or in a pony-tail. Seen close up, the hair on their bodies was a bit sparse and the skin a slightly greyish colour, making them look for all the world like hippopotami, an impression reinforced by their massive bulk and big, fat, rounded bottoms. The farmer was happy to accept slaughter price, and within hours they were ensconced in a pen in the Willowbank farmyard.

In the early days the Large Black was quite common, and sought after as a hardy docile animal that thrived in outdoor conditions. Two, however, didn't make a breeding group, and our best option was to import some from Australia. It became a daunting and frustrating task, largely coordinated by Dave Matheson and requiring patience from all sides, before finally the fateful day arrived, the animals had passed all of their health checks and were on the plane to New Zealand. There were three of them all told: a boar to be named Aussie, and a couple of sows named Sheila and Matilda. After a lot of effort from a number of people, these established themselves as a breeding group, and Large Blacks are now represented throughout New Zealand, registered with the New Zealand Pig Association, and had their moment of glory when one won a championship at the Hastings Royal Show.

Some animals we heard about by chance. One day a friend, Rick Denton, happened to mention some sheep that were to be found up the Clarence River. They were, he said, extremely wild and secretive and lived mainly along the edges of the bush, browsing on leaf litter and what grass was available. Some rams had massive horns and were highly sought after by hunters, as well as DOC, who wanted them eradicated.

This, of course, piqued my interest and we arranged to go in one day and catch some. It was a long drive in up the river, but after parking the truck we set off with the dogs and soon ran into a small mob of sheep grazing on the edge of the bush. They were fully alert, though, and having seen us, dived for the cover of the forest itself, with the dogs right on their tails. My heart sank, as I heard the barking get further and further away down a steep

CHAPTER FIVE **WHEN IS A CAMEL NOT A CAMEL**

Lou Redwood with a Clarence sheep.

ravine. They had bolted like deer, and there was no way they were stopping. When we finally reached them, we found that, like wild animals, they had tucked themselves under a waterfall, and refused to budge. It was a long carry back up the hill, but at the end of the day we had in our possession a couple of ewes and a ram. Later we got another ewe and ram, making a nice little breeding group for the park, which we later moved on to other breeders. Today their future is uncertain, and they would have to be considered highly threatened.

Several months later AgResearch called into the park to borrow one of our Clarence rams for a project they were doing. They were collecting the genes of several old breeds of sheep, hoping to create an easy-care animal. One of the components for this pot pourri of genetic blends was already standing in the trailer, looking arrogantly down a long and aristocratic nose.

93

'What on earth is that?' I said in amazement.

'It's a Woodstock Merino,' was the response. 'There's a small group of them living wild up the Waimakariri Gorge.'

The animal's outstanding feature was the badger face pattern, which is thought to be a very ancient colour variant. It was an apt name, for the ram had distinctive badger stripes across the face which, along with a faint grey colour to his wool, made him a stand-out animal. The scientist stressed the importance of retaining the genetics of these types of animals, because they carried vital traits without which they would have little to work on.

The more Willowbank got involved with these breeds, the more important their conservation was becoming, and it's surprising how many unique breeds we now have. For instance, apart from the ones mentioned, we have Raglan Romneys, Mohaka sheep, Hokonui sheep, Stewart Island sheep, Diggers Hill sheep, Herbert sheep and Waipu goats, to name a few.

The amazing and exciting thing for me is that some of these animals aren't just sheep, cattle and pigs. I thought I'd seen most things in the high country until one evening I got a call from a friend, Dave Whiteman, who owned a station. That day his head shepherd had been out guiding a South African hunter. They were sitting on the side of a hill, glassing the valley opposite, when the visitor commented that there was a big cat down there.

'Nonsense,' said the shepherd. 'We don't have big cats in New Zealand.'

'Well, it's just down there, coming across that shingle scree,' said the South African.

Sure enough, there was a large cat strolling along a sheep track under some matagouri, before eventually going over a crest and out of sight. Later that day Dave went back and stood in the same spot with his dogs, so they could try and get a perspective of the size of the animal they saw. Measuring against his big huntaways, they judged it to be twice the size, at least 1.2 metres long, and with a long thick tail 80 to 90 centimetres long and carried low with the tip curled slightly up.

It wasn't the first time such an animal had been seen. The previous year five men on a neighbouring property had reported seeing a large black panther, as had a hunting guide with an American client. Many other people have reported sightings, which may sound impossible but can happen. Many years ago a woman living in the little settlement of Brooklands just outside Christchurch, woke up to see a tiger on her lawn. It quickly disappeared and nobody would believe her. I do, because I know a family-operated circus was in town, and took their tiger for a walk along the beach. She got away from them in the evening, and they went back the next morning and, more by luck than anything found her, and had her back in her cage, as innocent as the priest's wife.

If there were such a big cat in the high country, how would it get there? There are stories of a leopard escaping from a circus in Oamaru, but then it would also be quite possible for someone to import a cub and call it a half-grown moggie. It may sound far-fetched but ... I've heard of Russian pigs coming into New Zealand off a boat, but slightly more bizarre was a phone call I had from a gentleman I knew who had imported twelve rhea eggs into New Zealand. Rhea are a South American bird a bit like a stunted ostrich, and are recognised worldwide as being highly protected and endangered. He just bought them off the Internet, and they arrived in a brown paper box labelled eggs. When they all turned out to be infertile, he reordered and brought in eight more. Again they came through customs but this time somebody notified the authorities, who descended on him in force. When I was speaking to him he was surrounded by police, customs and MPI agents. As the eggs had been declared, nothing further appeared to happen. Later I had a ridiculous meeting at the park with enforcement people from MPI, DOC and customs, who said that they never considered air transport to be a method of bringing in eggs.

An acquaintance working for DOC in Wellington rang me one day. I knew him through hunting days, and he was a very experienced bushman and hunter. He had just had the head of an animal brought into his office, and had no idea what it was. A hunter had shot the animal in the bush of the Tararua Ranges. It was described as being of creamy colour, and about the size of a donkey. He sent me down some photos to see if I could throw any light on it, but I couldn't help. It did look as if it could have come from a Blue or Argali sheep, which would have huge value if established and bred in New Zealand. He took it around to MPI, who examined it with little interest. They had never issued a permit for anything that looked like that, so it was no concern of theirs. Still no one knows what that animal was, or how it got there.

There was another animal in New Zealand that fascinated me. Otters are a favourite with most people and yet can be incredibly secretive. You can live on an otter-bearing river all of your life and never see one. It was hard to imagine that such an animal could exist in such a small country as ours, or could it?

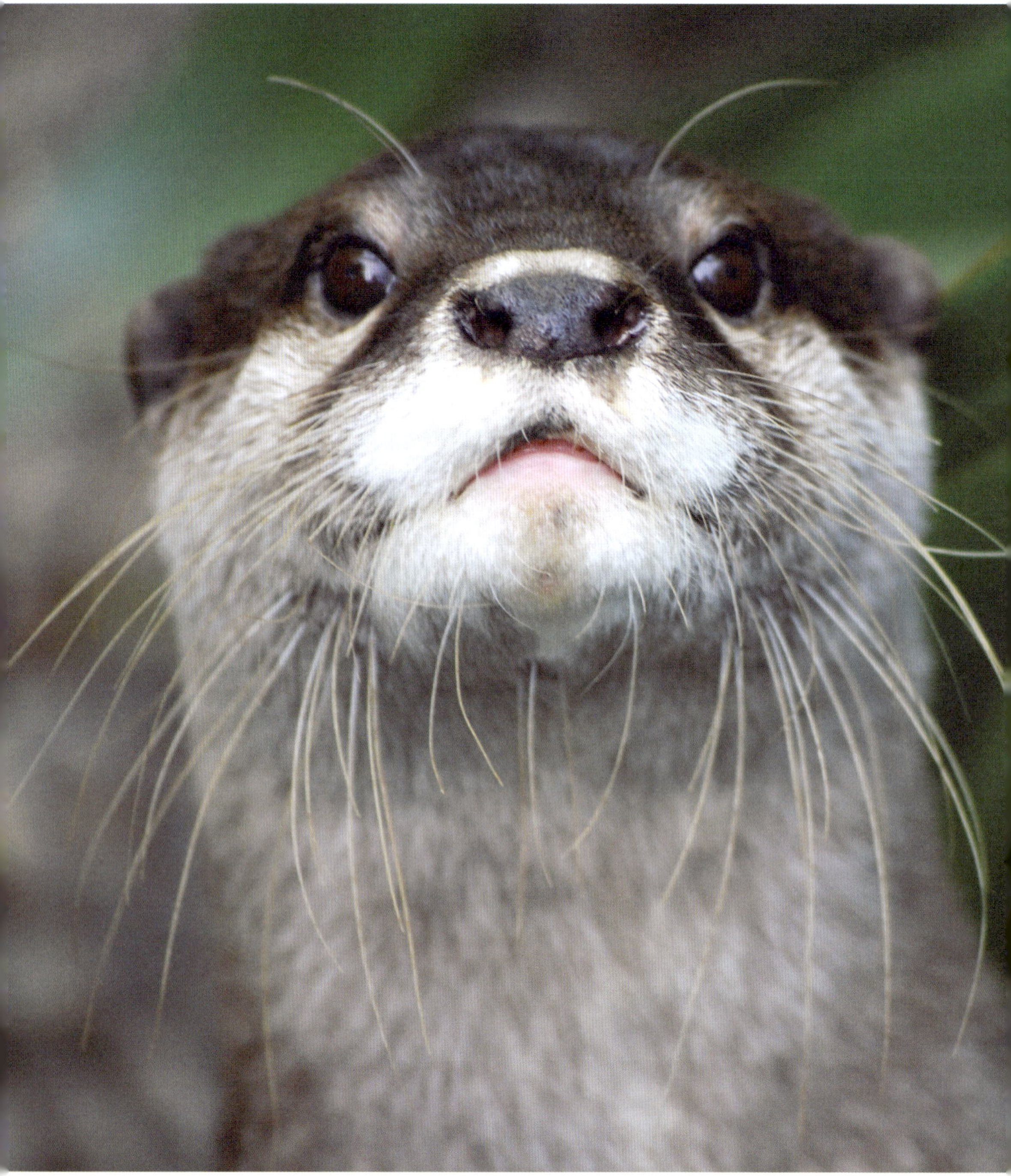

CHAPTER SIX

ODE TO AN OTTER

In the 1980s there was another small zoo at New Brighton near the sea in Christchurch. It had started life as an aquarium some decades before, and after several owners had been bought by a bit of a character called Bill Grey. He had accumulated a hotch-potch collection of cast-offs from larger zoos and circuses wanting to rid themselves of surplus and often maladjusted animals. Because of this it didn't have a very good reputation, some of which was unjustified as Bill loved those animals, and cared for them deeply. For many of them, their time there was the best of their deprived lives. Among the collection Bill had a pair of otters. They were commonly kept in other zoos, but seldom ever bred, and to the larger zoos' consternation, Bill was very successful in breeding them. When he asked one day if we wanted a pair, we jumped at the chance to get such a delightful species.

First we had to build an enclosure, and that was a major project. Bill's enclosures were practical but not really very good, especially for allowing the animals to display their natural behaviour. They were rectangular with a high concrete wall, a square pond large enough for a goldfish at one end, and a concrete dog kennel-like structure at the other. I wanted more than that. Certainly I wanted a pond that looked natural and, importantly, had an underwater viewing window. How to achieve this on a shoestring budget was a problem, but the only way to solve such a problem is to start resolving it, and see what comes out the other end.

The window was remarkably easy to resolve by purchasing a large armoured glass door that I found in a demolition yard and no one wanted.

Set horizontally, it would certainly be a good start and I could even leave the handle on it, so that sticky little children's hands could hang onto it, rather than smudge the glass. One Saturday I was digging the foundations with a shovel when the neighbour from up the road, Peter Stevens, turned up. Peter owned a large timber and construction company, and had been a great supporter since moving into the district. When I explained what I was hoping to do, without hesitation he offered to supply the concrete for the foundations and pond and so on. That was a fantastic start, and once the base was down, I sourced some cheap concrete blocks and was able to build the retaining walls where the public stood to see the otters, as well as fitting that essential window. We used fill to create the shape of the pond, which was then concreted in with a waterfall outlet. A den made for the otters using concrete blocks had sleeping quarters and an outside holding area. To make the whole enclosure secure, I located some unwanted steam pipe, and one of the mechanics from the local garage came down and spent a couple of days welding it all up and basically creating a cage over the whole thing. Painted black, it looked fine, and once it was netted and the pond filled, we had not a bad otter enclosure. The final stages were the landscaping. Trailerloads of boulders were brought in and manhandled into place, so the pond looked like part of a riverbed, and planting around the outside softened everything into a natural environment.

Eventually we were ready, and the big day arrived when I could go over and collect our pair of otters. It is always a good feeling putting an animal into a new enclosure, and this was made even better by otters' natural curiosity, which is second only to that of monkeys. They explored every nook and cranny. Long whiskers quivering with excitement, they spent hours exploring every part of the enclosure. Even with the little gaps that they couldn't get into, they would thrust their hands in up to the shoulder and feel all round to see what exciting things might be found inside. It became very obvious that these animals were going to be supreme escape artists. Once they discovered the pond, they were in their element, and it was fun to watch their bodies shooting past the glass window, glistening silver with beads of air trapped in their fur. They had an absolute ball, and I had just as much pleasure watching them.

Their names were Ricky and Rana, and they soon became firm favourites. They were always as pleased to see us as we were to see them, and would come squeaking with excitement as we approached, standing up on their hind legs to get a better view or climbing high up the wire. They were high-revving little creatures and because of that needed feeding three times a day, an

CHAPTER SIX **ODE TO AN OTTER**

event that was met with much excitement as the food was inspected and taken away to be washed thoroughly and generally played with before eating, on the off chance it may still be alive. Cleaning their enclosure became a battle of wits. For them it was as much fun as playing rugby on a Saturday. First they had the broom to jump on and attack. Once they got past that, there were those fascinating things called human feet encased in black shiny gumboots. They could be another otter that had encroached on their territory, or they could be an eel that was good to eat. Either way those things needed to be killed. Otters have long needle-like teeth, perfect for gripping and grabbing slippery objects. They would launch themselves into the backs of your gumboots and, locking in their teeth, would twist and turn in an effort to permanently maim whatever was inside, so they could then check its potential for gang warfare or play.

Much has been written about otters, most famously by Gavin Maxwell in his 1960 book, *Ring of Bright Water*, based on his experiences with wild otters as pets on the Scottish coast. It popularised otters, and gave the impression of rather cuddly aquatic creatures wanting to blissfully share their lives with you. I thought he had developed a lovely relationship, until I found out that his assistant had lost two fingers to an otter. It was about then that an orange caution light started to glow. As a handler, the first thing you find out about otters is how difficult they are to handle. Their skin doesn't seem to stick to their bodies. You can hang on around the middle, but the whole animal then slides backwards and forwards inside its skin, and you can never be quite sure where its head is going to turn up next. It becomes a ball of twisting and turning muscle, and the best way to control an otter is to wrap it up firmly in a sack or towel, and expose the parts you want to inspect a little bit at a time.

My fears about them being escape artists were well founded: sometimes they took an opportunity and made the most of it. Later we learnt not to panic too much if one did find its way out, because they were just as good at putting

The otters are always pleased to see us.

themselves back home again. It was still, though, a nerve-wracking time as you did some gentle exploration in order to establish the whereabouts of the miscreants. The worst thing you can do in such a situation is pursue an animal, because once it's chased away from its familiar territory, it will often just keep going, as Auckland Zoo found out in 2006. One of their otters, Jin, went halfway across the city and kept the news media and public entranced before being caught about a month later on the other side of the Waitemata Harbour. The same thing happened at Marineland in Napier when one of its otters was finally caught on the edge of the city, and the whereabouts of one from a West Coast zoo are still unknown.

Ricky and Rana settled in well and after a year or so they were old enough to breed: I could see that indeed she was pregnant, with a much bigger belly. Otters are very secretive and all evidence pointed to the fact that they will not tolerate nest disturbance. Accordingly, everything was kept to a minimum and they were left alone as much as possible. Every morning I would give Rana a titbit, and make her climb up the wire a little to get it. That way I could check her belly and also her teats. One morning she didn't appear and all we could do was wait and hope that everything was okay. Ricky was in and out of the sleeping area and obviously a little agitated as if he didn't quite know what to do. The next morning Rana came out when I called and climbed up the wire for her titbit. I could see her belly had gone down and her nipples were slightly enlarged, but best of all I could see wet rings in the fur around her nipples where it looked like something had been suckling. We had babies.

Three or four weeks went by and all appeared well, and then I noticed that her teats had gone down and she didn't appear to be milking. A day or two later and there were no wet rings, and she had obviously lost her milk. Something had to be done and so I opened up the box and found two little otter pups, hollow bellied and a bit weak but still alive. Clutching them to my chest, I carried them up to the house, put them in a box to warm up and sat and pondered my next move. The obvious answer was to hand feed them, and I found a kitten teat and started warming up some milk. Otters are very similar to dogs, and so, I thought to myself, the milk from canines should be suitable. I then glanced into the back room where my son Mark's little Cavalier King Charles dog had just recently given birth to three puppies. Maybe I could get some milk from her? And then I had another more outlandish thought. Was there any chance that she would feed them? They had fur, their eyes were firmly closed, and although they didn't look like her pups, they were about the same size. The most off-putting thing was their fishy odour, so rubbing

CHAPTER SIX **ODE TO AN OTTER**

Jeremy Maguire feeding Jala, Jandra and Nadi.

them as clean as possible and rolling them in with her pups until they smelt like one, I settled down to wait.

Nellie was lovely, possibly not the brainiest dog in the world, but a much-loved pet. She looked at me with those big black orbital eyes that Cavalier spaniels have, and seemed slightly confused at the rather increased squirming mass that seemed to have appeared around her stomach. One of her pups latched onto a teat and she lay back contentedly, which allowed me the opportunity to pick up the little otter cubs and fasten them onto a nipple each. There was no hesitation, and within a minute or two they were sucking noisily and their stomachs were filling. From that moment on Nellie became their mother, and the two little otters were brought up as house pets. As pups they would all play together, going for walks in the garden, and it was a funny oddball relationship until the time when we decided that they needed to be weaned away from their friends and go back to being otters again.

Otters in the house aren't a very good thing. Later we had another who had become quite ill and needed nursing. As she got better she had the run of the house and was like a dynamo to live with. Her little paws were like hands, exploring everything. She would be into all the cupboards, rummaging around. She particularly liked the pot cupboard and would bang the pots around and throw them out in some sort of private amusement. The worst thing, however, was the odour that followed her everywhere, owing to the otter diet being mainly fish. In a confined space it became something you couldn't avoid – definitely anti-social, and a really off-putting experience at a dinner party.

Running a zoo and inviting people for dinner are not always compatible. Nowadays we have a wildlife hospital on site, but in the early days we often received sick and injured birds, and the wash house or the bathroom were usually the only place for them to go.

One day a little boy, who turned out to be called Davy, accompanied by his mother, arrived with a huge carton and told me that he had captured 'this big albatross thing'. Intrigued, I got the little fellow to put the box on the ground and then knelt beside it, cautiously opened the lid and looked in. There was the clack of a beak that sounded like a sprung opossum trap going off and, rubbing my nose, I hastily shut the box again.

'He seems awfully vicious,' said the mother. 'Took a great hunk out of my husband's finger, and he said if we don't get rid of it, then he'll back the car over the carton, bird and all.'

Davy was clearly pleased to relinquish his rescuing responsibility, and so I endeavoured to look as if they had given me just what I had always wanted and expressed my gratitude. Once I had the box in the wash house, I shut all the windows and doors, pulled on a pair of gloves and investigated. In fact, rather than an albatross, which can have a wingspan of some 3 metres, I was facing an adult black-backed gull, whose outstretched wings would make a mere metre or so. Like some strange hybrid between a black and white angel and a penguin, it took up a position on the freezer, shook its feathers vigorously and stared at me coldly with its yellow fish-like eye.

Since there had been some storms recently, I assumed the bird was suffering from exhaustion and malnutrition. When I held up a fish from the fridge, Albert Ross, as he became known, lunged forward and grabbed it. Looking rather surprised, he tipped his head back and swallowed the food eagerly, clacking and shaking his beak thoroughly afterwards. After several

CHAPTER SIX ODE TO AN OTTER

more pieces of fish, he looked quite smug and contented and soon settled down into a deep sleep. As the day went on, we fed him more fish each time he seemed to be waking up, and he remained on a shelf in the wash house, as still as a monument on a tombstone.

That night we were having important people for dinner. Before anyone arrived I fed Albert Ross a last huge meal of fish fillets and wished him good night. One of the women guests was terrified of birds: it had taken a good hour and a half, and most of a decanter of sherry, to convince her to stop looking anxiously behind chairs and curtains, and she would go nowhere near an open window. But the meal, at a candlelit table, went well and we felt we were making a good impression. We had reached the pavlova and cream, to be followed by coffee and liqueur, when I heard the crash of things falling off the shelf next door and the flap of wings. I was as puzzled as anyone but the mystery was soon solved. Albert Ross, perhaps caught in a nightmare about being pursued along a beach by an overenthusiastic dog, had launched himself off the shelf, flown through the kitchen and was heading for the glow of light around the corner. He had somehow managed to negotiate the doorway, and with only the candles on the table to guide him, came flapping down the living room like some great auk out of the adventures of Sinbad. Just before he reached the table he started to back-flap in preparation for a landing, a manoeuvre that successfully distributed the contents of the icing sugar bowl over everybody. Then, with his enormous webbed feet held out stiffly like a pair of water skis, he hit the pavlova. This had much the same effect as jumping into a cow pat while wearing oversized gumboots. He skidded down the table, a bow wave of pavlova and wine glasses ahead of him and a trail of debris behind.

Most of us were too stunned to say a word, but the poor woman who hated birds screamed in terror and was out the door and into the car before anyone had a chance to move. Albert Ross himself wasn't that impressed, either, and continued to create havoc until I managed to roll him into a curtain. We eventually got him under close confinement, but it was clear that, despite our profuse apologies, the dinner party was at an end.

We went on to become so successful at breeding otters that our animals went to zoos throughout New Zealand and Australia, and we were actually asked to stop breeding because our bloodlines were overrepresented. But did New Zealand have its own otter? For years I had heard rumours and received titbits of information, but nothing of substance. That changed one day when I noticed a man walking up towards the house, making hard work of carrying three large and obviously heavy cartons. When I went down to relieve him from some of the weight he introduced himself as Jim Roxburgh, and said, rather apologetically, 'My uncle was named George Pollock. He spent the later years of his life studying the existence of otters in New Zealand. He died recently and expressed the wish that you were to have all of his papers and notes. I hope you don't mind, but I've brought them all around.'

Mind? I was ecstatic. I knew the name George Pollock well, for I had read bits and pieces written by him regarding the otter, and had always hoped to run into him sometime. That was now not, I hoped, going to happen for a while, and so I couldn't wait for the nephew to depart so that I could start opening boxes. George was a retired solicitor, who had spent most of his later life painstakingly researching and collating the scraps of information regarding this creature. It was a project that almost became a crusade, and took him along some tortuous routes. For me the boxes were full of history and intrigue, a window into the private life and hopes of a dedicated man, and a fairy-tale chapter into parts of New Zealand's history that is largely unknown. And so I buried myself in the accumulation of one man's unshakable belief, born out of optimism and research, but running against the tide of most established knowledge.

Who or what, then, is the New Zealand otter? Periodically over the years I had always kept running into snippets of information on this creature. The mystical waitoreke was in fact nothing new. The name is the one given to the creature by Southland Māori, who described the animal to early observers such as Herries Beattie, who assumed by the description that the animal was an otter. Cook's men started the European side of the story in 1777, if rather inconclusively, when they described an animal they saw in Fiordland. The tale, however, gained momentum, and many early explorers claimed to have seen sign, or the animals themselves. Respected men such as Julius von Haast and Ferdinand von Hochstetter noted in their journals the existence of such a creature, before the introduction of animals such as opossums and ferrets.

Other early colonists reported seeing the creature, and among the mountain of correspondence were some more recent sightings, many from people I either knew or had heard of – landowners, veterinarians, prominent schoolteachers, museum directors and a host of others who had eked out their leisure or existence in remote parts of the South Island. In 1920 two men repeatedly saw an animal in Middle Island near Dusky Bay on the South Coast. It had a strong smell and a thick tapering tail. About the same time the

CHAPTER SIX ODE TO AN OTTER

owner of the Te Anau Hotel was told by track hands at Milford of a dog-sized animal that lived at Lake Ada. In 1968 a man who had studied otters in Britain watched an animal through binoculars, as it cautiously came upstream and onto a riverbank. It was about 900 millimetres long and had dark spiky fur. It was joined by three cubs. In 1971 a shooter in the Hollyford valley heard splashing and saw an otter repeatedly climbing up from the water, and glissading down a well-worn slide. In another account, the owner of the Hollyford lodge saw otters engaged in similar play in the lower Hollyford Valley. On a bright summer's day in 1972 a man got close enough to an otter on a riverbank to distinguish its webbed feet, small ears and reddish coat. When the 900-millimetre-long animal dived into the river he found it had been eating a freshly caught eel. In 1975, at a meeting, the Fiordland National Park Board considered to be reliable evidence given by a local fisherman, who had seen two otter-like creatures playing in the Wild Natives River that flows into Bligh Sound.

And so it went on: letter after letter, document after document, note after note. Myriads of sightings and many well documented with names, dates and details. Could all of these people over such a length of time be so wrong? Were they all deluded? Were they all pranksters and con men? The answer would have to be no. Several had risked ridicule and their own personal reputations to report sightings they knew were controversial. After a week of digesting, analysing and trying to rationalise such an amazing wealth of information, I leant back in my chair and decided that I wasn't brave enough to call the whole thing a myth. It only took one of them to be right. No jury would ever throw all that evidence out the window. No judge would dismiss such a trial. The case just had to stay open, particularly when it also had such strong roots in Māori lore. So how could such a creature have arrived?

One answer lay in the notes. George Pollock didn't confine his interest to otters. He was also very interested in history, and his legal mind sifted out and filed a mass of miscellaneous facts that he drew upon to paint a possible scenario. For me one of the most conclusive pieces of evidence was that over much of New Zealand there *was* no evidence. Almost without exception, the sightings were confined to two main regions, inland Canterbury and Southland/Fiordland. If the sightings were as a result of misidentification, then you could reasonably expect people from throughout New Zealand to mistake ferrets, seals, eels and other forms of wildlife for otters. Not so. Virtually all of the evidence came from these areas. Was there a common link? Yes, said George Pollock.

His hypothesis was that Indians, possibly Tamils, were shipwrecked on the New Zealand coast well before the arrival of Europeans. He based this on links that go back to independent and isolated bits of history that on their own don't have the least bit of relevance. One was the Tamil bell found in Northland in 1836 by the missionary William Colenso, and then there is the Korotangi Stone or Crying Dove, a carving found imbedded in the roots of a huge manuka tree that was blown over in a storm in the late 1870s. The carving, certainly not Māori, is generally thought to be of Indian origin and also some centuries old. It is thought that Tamil voyagers may have reached northern Australia by the fourteenth century and maybe even made it across the Tasman. Tradition has it, too, that some of the Māori found around Lake Ellesmere, Te Waihora, in Canterbury had different skin and hair colour. Cook noticed that some of the Māori he met in Fiordland had thin bandy legs, and reported that his Māori interpreters couldn't converse with them. There's an ancient tradition among Tamils and others of using trained otters, on a harness, to catch fish. Just suppose, Pollock argued, that a Tamil vessel was wrecked on the West Coast and that some survivors, and their otters, came ashore? That would explain why Southland Māori are the only ones with a waitoreke tradition.

Among George Pollock's notes were recent references to sightings that had been made down in the swamps around Lake Waihola, just south of Dunedin. The television programme *Wild South* had made a documentary about waitoreke, and it had received a certain amount of credibility. So I decided to go and have a look for myself. Horrie Sinclair, the contact, lived in Outram. He was a short, heavily built late middle-aged man, who seemed to perpetually wear a hat either indoors or out. If Horrie had a strong point it was talking, and as soon as I told him why I had come to visit, I was whisked inside his house as swiftly as a praying mantis catches a fly.

The house was small, very old, and although Horrie kept referring to things kept in his filing system that contained all of his information, it must have been in the bedroom or the bathroom, for there certainly wasn't space for it in the living room. In the centre, presumably, was a table, because there was a gap between the pile of essentials sitting on top, and the bundles of newspapers and other not so essentials underneath. In one corner was a TV set surrounded by empty bottles, while facing it about 2 metres away was an armchair, Horrie's chair. Graciously he waved for me to sit in it, while he manoeuvred some piles to clear a space for himself alongside the TV. Perched there dressed in trousers and singlet, with a stomach that refused to be contained, he regaled me for two hours with tales about his swamp and its otters.

CHAPTER SIX **ODE TO AN OTTER**

Above right and right: Working with the extraordinary Horrie Sinclair.

Fascinated by the house, I kept glancing around. I had never been in such an incredible assortment of what to most people is rubbish, but to him was one day going to prove to be worth keeping. It was the sort of place that you read about, where people die and are eventually dug out several months later from under a pile of yellowing newspapers. An unusual contrast were two beautifully kept automatic Browning shotguns, leaning casually on each side of the door. As one visiting American sports writer put it, 'Horrie has his priorities all right. His house may be a mess but his shotguns and mai mai are immaculate.' He was very proud to be, as he put it, an honorary ranger for the 'Whole of New Zealand', as well as the 'Whole of the Offshore Islands'.

107

He had some delightful expressions. Before seeing the otters for the first time he was a 'vast septic' about their existence, but now having seen them, he would never forget them, thanks to his 'photogenic memory'. At the end of a couple of hours my mind was reeling, but he offered to show me around the swamp the next day. As we stepped out from the clutter within the house he stopped short, for he could see my little dog Fey was in the front of the Land Rover. 'I wouldn't have a dog in my vehicle,' he said in a reprimanding tone. 'Messes them up.'

Horrie had bought his 315 hectares of land for a pittance in 1960, and let it revert to swamp. The result was what is now known as the Sinclair Wetlands (Te Nohoaka o Tukiauau), a wonderful area bordering on and becoming part of the lake, and home to an amazing assortment of wildlife. Horrie, who ended up with an MBE for his services to conservation, had worked in pest destruction for most of his life. If anyone should be able to tell an otter from something else, it would be Horrie. He told me of standing on the shores of the lake and watching them play, a story corroborated by his foreman, who had turned up to join us, and who in addition had seen paw prints up the Hunter River at the head of Lake Hawea. As far as these men were concerned it wasn't 'Was there an otter?' There was no question about it at all.

I went back to Lake Waihola with a group of people, and we did a quick search but without uncovering anything of interest. We have continued the search into Fiordland but the country is so vast that it would be opportunistic to actually come across one. The otter sightings were consistent up until about the mid-1970s, and since then have tapered right off, although in 2018 two Southland men appeared on a national current affairs programme to say that they had both seen otters in the past. Again this is significant: it shows that they were unlikely to be wrong or cases of misidentification, but, rather, point to a population that has possibly declined to extinction. I find it a bit sad to be extinct without anyone knowing that you were even there in the first place, but just maybe that's the cost of living in New Zealand among vast septics.

The breeding ban for otters in captivity throughout the Australasian region largely continues to be enforced – to the degree that they are close to being functionally extinct. Our animals are sixteen to seventeen years old and, at this stage, unable to be replaced. Through the direct actions of humans, they will probably join the waitoreke as part of history.

CHAPTER SIX **ODE TO AN OTTER**

Could these be the prints of moose?

Fiordland was not only a reputed home of otters, but also once held a small population of moose, liberated at the top of Dusky Sound in 1910. Some were even shot, but for many years there were no sightings, and of the few who knew of their existence, even the staunchest supporters were having doubts about the animals' continued survival. While I was living and working in the area, a local hunter shot one. I knew the man, but unfortunately he should not have been hunting in that area, and with past convictions for poaching, went to ground and denied all knowledge.

That was enough, though, for me to launch an expedition into the area, for now I had moose as well as otters to consider and it was a great excuse to visit a fabulous area. Sadly, no sign was found. However later on another trip into Wet Jacket Arm, I found hoof prints that were extremely large, and appeared to show the imprints of the dew claws, a typical moose characteristic. Could those prints be those of the last one?

And so the jury is still out regarding moose in Fiordland, but my son had to bear an unfortunate result of my hunt. When his school friends heard about it, there was much ribald laughter and he was stuck with the nickname 'Moose'.

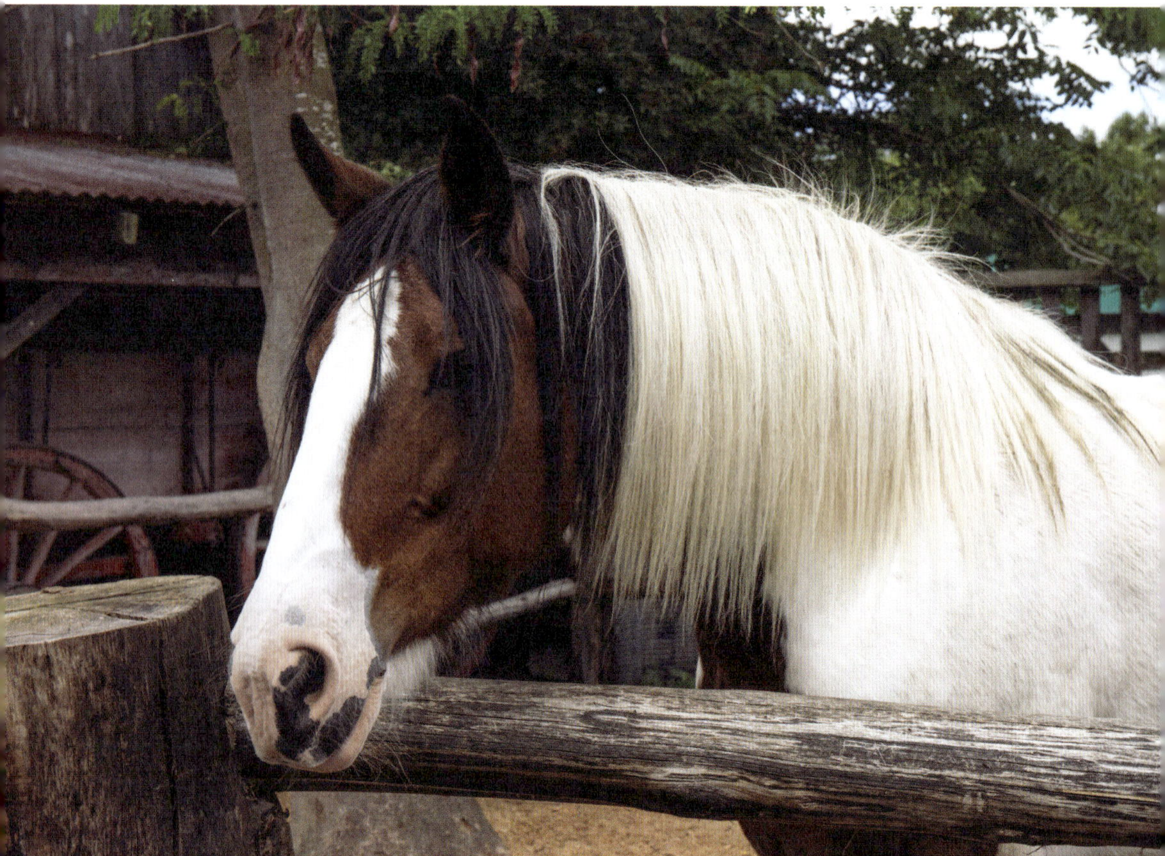

CHAPTER SEVEN

A COUNTRY FIT FOR HORSES

'Do you know what I've often dreamt of doing?' I asked John Simister when we were driving to Mystery Creek for the Clydesdale sale.

'Having a baby?' he suggested helpfully.

'No, not that. I've always wanted to ride horses from Cape Reinga and down to Bluff.'

That made him sit up in his seat, and I could tell by the way the ends of his eyebrows started to curl, that he was very interested.

'Yes,' I continued, 'I think that it would have to be the ultimate that New Zealand could provide in the way of a horse trekking experience. Going straight down the centre of both islands on a riding horse, and with a packhorse carrying all your supplies so you were completely self-sufficient.'

We discussed the pros and cons of the concept for a while, and somewhat to my surprise I found that John was taking more than a passing interest in the idea. The kilometres ticked by until just before Taupo, when he turned to me and said, 'I know it's your idea and all that, but if you want company, then I'm happy to go too.'

Expecting the matter to lie there, I assured him that if I did it there was no one else I would rather do it with, but he was like a terrier with a rat and wouldn't let it rest.

'Good,' he said, 'then when do you think we should leave?'

This was taking things far too fast. I certainly hadn't got around to considering any dates yet, and hadn't really anticipated attempting it for some time to come. 'It'll take a year or two to get all the gear together and a

Opposite: Sam, my current riding horse.

route sorted out, so perhaps we could start planning for a couple of years' time.'

'Far too far away. We'll either be incapable of doing it by then, have thought of something different, or come up with some other bloody excuse.'

'Well, I suppose we could possibly consider next year.'

'What's wrong with this year? It's May now. As long as we're both back by Christmas, we have about four months to plan it.'

Inwardly I groaned, and desperately tried to think of some face-saving way that would keep my comparatively organised year intact, but couldn't come up with any idea that would really hold water. How the hell was I going to explain to everyone back home that I wanted to go away and ride horses for three months? But the excitement of the idea was too much to hold any negative thoughts for too long, and the kilometres flew as we discussed all the different angles of such a venture, and its implications.

A lot of preparation went into organising and planning, acquiring equipment and, most of all, finding the horses. I had two Welsh Cob types, Bev and Bella, whom I had used extensively in the back country and were very experienced mounts. John's choices were two light Clydesdale-type horses, named Bob and Debbie. Eventually the big day arrived, and a rather nervous little group assembled early one afternoon beside the lighthouse at Cape Reinga. Feeling rather like someone who has been taken to the top of a twenty-storey building and told to jump, I tried to overcome my apprehension by admiring the scenery, which was superb. To the right lay the Pacific, glistening blue and calm. To the left lay the more unpredictable Tasman, while between them, the flax- and scrub-covered headland of Cape Reinga jutted out like a knobby little finger separating them and signifying the starting-off place of not only idiots like ourselves, but also the spirits of Māori, who by tradition departed from here on their journey to the afterlife. Our projected journey may not have been quite as spiritual, and we hadn't yet taken leave of our bodies, even if we had of our senses, but the place certainly had a mystique and aura that were all its own.

The horses were cramped and stiff from travelling and coated in dust, so first of all they had to be cleaned down. Because the Land Rover was going to stay with us for the next couple of days, we did not waste too much time packing properly, but just got the gear basically sorted, and the horses ready to go. Last goodbyes, and we swung our legs over and into the saddles and set off back down the road, for the first stage south. The horses, pleased to be off the floats and walking, strode out with vigour. Our first night was to be at Te Paki Stream, about four hours away, which was all the time we would

CHAPTER SEVEN **A COUNTRY FIT FOR HORSES**

Gathered at the Cape Reinga lighthouse before the trek begins.

have that day, and was also the start of Ninety Mile Beach. Northland is quite narrow, and surprisingly short of streams and water for the horses. As far as we could make out, only three streams crossed the whole length of the beach, and this was the start of the realisation that, no matter what we might think, we were bound to work within the requirements of our animals. Part of our decision-making process had been to decide that we would stay with the horses throughout the trip. Where they camped, we camped.

We arrived at Te Paki just as dusk faded into night. It was a beautiful campsite, on the edge of the stream with luxuriant grass, flax and scrub on one side, while on the other was a sheer white wall of sand that broke out

RESCUE ONE NEW ZEALANDER'S CRUSADE TO SAVE ENDANGERED ANIMALS

into kilometre after kilometre of rolling dunes. Lying in our tents that night, we could hear the avalanches of sand falling off the cliff into the stream, and it was obvious that this part of the country was young and in a constant state of flux. The very soil layer is thin, easily torn, like the skin of an elderly person, and so hard to heal. Ninety Mile Beach was the perfect spot to settle the horses and get into a daily routine. It was a fascinating area and very deceptive with its wind shifting sands and massive dunes and changing tides. The soft sand was too hard to ride on, so we tended to ride on the edge of the water, and have it constantly flowing in and out under our horses.

    Distances were deceptive, especially in the simmering heat. At one point we saw two small objects way off in the distance and decided they must be people. As time went on, and they became bigger, we decided they might be motor bikes. On they came and we could see they weren't motor bikes at all and must be cars. As it turned out, they were two large buses, which raced past at speed. They almost caused a problem as Bev, whom I was riding at the time, half reared in fright and turned around, crashing into Bella, who was

I prepare Bella for another day of riding.

plodding along behind. I thought nothing of it until later when I saw blood running down Bella's leg and found a large cut just above the cornet, where Bev's shoe had struck her. The salt water kept the wound clean, but it was a timely reminder of how easily the whole journey could end.

Even the ground couldn't be trusted, as we found out when we turned off the beach one lunchtime to go up a small creek in search of some grass for the horses and to have lunch. I had an uneasy feeling up the back of my neck when I looked at a patch of sand ahead, for we had been told about the quicksands that had, on occasion, buried whole trucks. It was duller, flatter with almost an oily look, and none of the debris on top that you usually associate with beaches. There was no visual demarcation line, however, though all too soon the hooves of my horses started to sink and the surrounding sand trembled like jelly. I yelled back to John and spun the horses, urging them out, which they did with much floundering and sucking of their feet. Had we hit that at a trot it would have been a different story.

The Land Rover, which was still accompanying us in stages, came across a natty little sports car stuck in the sand with breakers all around it. A pretty young woman was sitting high on the back of the seat, and a panic-stricken young man was waving them down. They got a rope to the car, but couldn't get close enough to double it, and three times it broke. On the last and final time a breaker crashed into the boot and the car pulled free and could be towed up out of danger.

We had an interesting few days of exhilaration and moments of boredom. It's amazing how lonely it can be riding a horse, even in good company. We would inevitably travel in single file, which left us metres apart. On a calm, still day the odd exchange might be possible, but with any sort of wind blowing attempts at communication reverted to sign language. To a large degree, we planned the next day's riding in the tent the night before; any further discussion necessitated reining in the horses. So we would travel for hour after hour with very little communication at all, but as we rode we would both note things mentally, and when the opportunity to talk did arise, conversations that started some hours ago would be continued as if there had been no breaks.

With our support vehicle now well gone, we were making our way down through Northland. It was largely Māori country, and the relaxed and friendly hospitality we encountered made this part of the trip much easier than it might otherwise have been. We were getting into a better routine now, too. We were up at five or six in the morning and normally away by 7.30 after breaking camp, packing all our gear and catching and saddling the horses. We would ride for about an hour, then let the horses graze or walk with them for ten minutes. We would then ride for another hour, and stop and let the horses graze for up to an hour. That pattern would be repeated until lunchtime, when we would strip the gear from the horses and allow them to graze and rest for an hour. This was repeated in the afternoon so that roughly the horses did eight hours of travelling with rest periods in between, which made a normal eleven- to twelve-hour day for us. We rode six days, and had one rest day. We had heard of many people who had started such a trek and failed, largely because their horses lost too much condition. We were therefore very regimented in sticking to a routine to protect the animals as much as possible.

We bummed a lift on the barge across to Rawene, rode down through Opononi and on into the majestic kauri of the Waipoua Forest, where we gained some peace until coming back out and into the final leg to Auckland. This was to be one of the worst sections for us, as we couldn't get away from the roads and had to ride through traffic that, to put it mildly, posed a considerable hazard. With the packs on, our horses were almost 2 metres wide, and the continual stream of cars and trucks roared past in what seemed

John and I couldn't always chat like this. Often many hours went by when we rode out of earshot of each other.

a suicidal manner. It was like playing Russian roulette. The cuttings were the worst: there were no verges, just a sheer cliff-like bank that you hugged as close as you could. Alternatively you had to ride on the edge of the road. We became very litter conscious, for the wind generated by the traffic picked up bits of paper and rubbish and swirled them around. I could understand why they call them disposable nappies. Chuck them out the window of the car along with the beer bottles that shattered on the cutting face and created a minefield of broken glass, waiting to slash a horse's foot open. Tarpaulins flapped, containers rattled and the more enthusiastic drivers gave a blast on the klaxon as they rumbled past. I was sitting lighter in the saddle than a hen on eggs, putting my faith in my horses and blindly following the white line south. Miraculously we survived the open road until, like floating logs drawn into rapids, we were engulfed into the maelstrom of the main street of Wellsford.

The horses' nerves were at breaking point and the red lights were the last straw. Bob threw a shoe in the middle of the main street, and as it clattered onto the road behind us, a woman dashed out, picked it up and was off with it. It was too valuable to lose and, throwing me his reins, John took off after her. Four horses were impossible to control in the middle of a busy street and we were just about to back into a chemist's shop when, to my relief, he returned with the shoe and we were off again. We considered ourselves lucky to later enter the comparative peace and calm of Puhoi.

South of there we had a problem: New Zealand's largest city, Auckland. How were we to get over the harbour bridge and through that part of the CBD? The council solved the problem by saying that we were definitely not allowed to, and so the horses were loaded onto a cattle truck and offloaded again just before the Bombay Hills. From there we slowly made our way south, heading for the pine forests of Tokoroa and Lake Whakamaru. Ahead of us was the Central Plateau and the inhospitable Desert Road. The horses were travelling well but Bob was struggling.

We had had many comments about poor Bob on the way down: 'He'll never make it'. 'All show and no go, that horse.' I don't think Bob even had much faith in himself. He made a forlorn picture, standing with his feet apart like tripods for support, while his bottom lip hung low and his eyes barely opened. I've never known a horse to go so far and do so little, without being actually dead. When Bob slept, he slept. Lying full out on his side, he stretched his hooves out in blissful relaxation and then, letting his whole gaunt framework go slack, he snuffled and burbled himself into sleep. At first I used to think the snoring that floated over the camp in the early hours of the morning came from John's tent. I realised my mistake one evening when I went out to investigate and found Bob lying on his side in the moonlight looking like a desiccated elephant, nostrils flaring and trumpeting, limbs jerking spasmodically, as in his dreams he cleared the last fence at Aintree while his ears flicked in the grass to the roar of the crowd as he came into the home straight.

To tether him at night always meant a broken sleep. Invariably he would get his foot caught around the rope, and then a few moments of silence would pass while he pondered on how to overcome this predicament. Instead of turning around like the other horses, he would begin to slowly and rhythmically stamp. Whether it took five minutes or five hours mattered little to him. Gradually and methodically his great hoof would rise and fall, shaking the earth and shattering all sleep until the blissful moment when the loop of rope slipped down and peace would reign again, for a while anyway.

To leave him loose was equally nerve-wracking. He was a very kindly and sociable animal, but the other horses, all female, found him a complete and utter bore, and rejected him, sending him back to the only available male company, John and me. Like an unloved and deprived child, he would hang around the camp, and as the dark and loneliness of the night crept in, he would shuffle closer and closer to the tents for protection and comfort. In the darkness you lay awake, cringing and waiting for the inevitable to happen when he got himself all wrapped up in the guy lines of the tent. Time and time again I ended up rolling across the floor, arms up for protection as the walls and roof flapped wildly, and I was convinced that he was going to fall over and flatten the whole structure. He never did but I had little faith in his ability to get himself out of trouble.

Just before the Desert Plateau John arranged for a food drop to be left there hidden for Bob, and one night Carole turned up with some oats for Bob, and treats for us. The weather had been pretty bad, bucketing down with rain, and the last few days had been a struggle. Everything got wet and life was pretty unpleasant, so we were pleased when, by the time we had skirted the western shore of Lake Taupo and passed through Turangi, the clouds lifted and we could start to dry out. As we climbed up and onto the plateau the temperature dropped and the wind chill made it bitterly cold. The mornings were frosty and food was scarce for the horses. The food drop wasn't there: someone had found it and taken it. The horses got hollow and we searched for anything edible to keep them going.

Some people we met on the journey had said that we would never make Auckland. Several had said that we would never be able to cross the plateau,

CHAPTER SEVEN **A COUNTRY FIT FOR HORSES**

so it was with considerable relief that, some days later, we eventually reached the other side, and began a descent. Soon we were back into grass and food again and gave everyone a much-earned rest. We had some leisurely days wandering down the Turakina River before making our way down the coast and on to Waikanae. The traffic was starting to build up again, but we were well used to it by then. It just didn't make for pleasant riding. Our routines were now pretty well established. As the landscape became more built up, our biggest problem was always trying to find somewhere to sleep. We would cover 45 to 50 kilometres a day, but if we hit a largish town late in the afternoon, we might not make the other side by evening, so normally around five o'clock we would start looking for a suitable spot to hold four horses and two tents. We slept under bridges, in cemeteries, behind churches, domains and riverbeds. We found places in the most unlikely spots, much to the puzzlement of several people. But we all managed to stick together, and from Waikanae rode over the hill and down the Akatarawa Valley to Staglands and a hot shower.

During our two days there we overhauled the gear, reshod the horses and generally made last-minute preparations. It was a good chance to catch up with all the news from home. We had baby otters, a new baby monkey and photos of the Clydesdale filly we had just acquired. My worries were groundless: Willowbank seemed to be thriving without me. It must have been hard for John and Carole to come home after being away for so long, and then to pack up and leave again. Although I enjoyed the interlude, I was impatient to be back in the South Island. The excitement was tempered by the fact that we still had one day of bad riding to get through: down the valley, through Upper and Lower Hutt, and then down the river to Petone, which was as close to Wellington as we were allowed. The horses were loaded onto the floats, taken aboard the ferry and soon we were in the South Island.

To begin with, the journey from Picton was rather boring – a bit of traffic but nothing like the North Island, and long, straight roads. We made our way up the Wairau Valley, and as we got higher the vegetation changed until we were back into tussock flats heavy with manuka scrub and deeply eroded by steep rocky creeks. The dense manuka made for warm welcome shelter as it was cold and windy and the horses also found shelter in its clearings. Eventually we arrived at Rainbow Station and turned in to go south, virtually running parallel to the Southern Alps all the way to Tekapo. The track led through a spectacular rocky gorge, via the appropriately named Hells Gate.

RESCUE ONE NEW ZEALANDER'S CRUSADE TO SAVE ENDANGERED ANIMALS

Negotiating our way through Petone as we near the end of the North Island leg of the journey.

We stopped for a rest and while dozing in the scrub heard a rumble and rattle of rocks and boulders, followed by a very heavy thud. Bob, in his typical dozy way, had wandered up to the edge of an overhang, which had given way and he had fallen about 3 metres, landing on his back in an avalanche of boulders. His feet were jammed up under the bank, and his head stuck under a tree, but he was still alive. He was grunting and groaning but couldn't get up, so we unhitched his gear and set to work removing the tree. Getting his head free allowed us to drag the front legs out, and then, hanging onto his tail, we pulled him downhill and managed to get him to his feet, where he swayed drunkenly. We got him back into the riverbed below, where he stood propped up on all four legs, happy to remain on the flat. When he had recovered sufficiently we repacked and carried on slowly, shooting a hare for tea as we went.

The valley opened up as we went but retained its rugged beauty until we crossed a low saddle and into the famous grasslands of the Molesworth

Station, massive country that stretched as far as the eye could see, especially as we continued to climb higher until crossing over Island Pass and into Lake Tennyson. Crossing the pass was bitterly cold, and because of the altitude, there was limited feed again for the horses, so it was a relief to get back down into bush and grassy flats. Our route then took us through a series of swamps, over Malings Pass and down into the upper reaches of the Upper Waiau. This is a magnificent valley, part of the well-known St James Station and home to some herds of semi-wild horses. We passed the deserted station outbuildings, and continued down the valley, crossing the river several times. The water was high, up to our boots, and sometimes I could feel the horses swimming beneath me, but we always managed to clamber out the other side unscathed. Leaving the Waiau, we rode through the picturesque Magdalene Valley and the Boyle Huts. From here we crossed the main highway of Lewis Pass, and headed up the Hope River Valley, over the pass and down to the top end of beautiful Lake Sumner. Another low saddle took us to Lake Mason, more swamps to traverse, and then we began a long steep climb, heading for Mount White Station in the Waimakariri Valley.

The slope ascended almost in a series of knobs disappearing into the sky. It was cold and drizzling at times. The cloud kept coming down around us and it was difficult to keep ourselves orientated as we were blanketed in clammy whiteness. Every now and then a gap would allow a brief view of the country below, and we listened to the roar of Deep Creek Basin somewhere down on our left, knowing that we didn't want to go there. We were now in rocky alpine scree, well past the point of no return, and kea made a welcome diversion as they came down to inspect these invaders. Once we had gained the main ridge we picked our way along carefully, referring constantly to our map and avoiding several blind shoulders that led down into bluffs. We found the spur that we thought we needed, sidled around to it and headed off down to Andersons Creek, happy to have survived our first real alpine test.

Rivers were always going to be a severe test. The Waiau had been bad enough, but now in front of us we had the three biggest in Canterbury. The first was the Waimakariri, but we found a very good wide ford and accomplished that crossing with relative ease. A few more days of riding brought us up to the banks of the Rakaia, and we followed the north bank up until we reached the Wilberforce, which we approached with considerable caution. The Wilberforce is a river to be reckoned with and has claimed a spectacular number of lives over the years. It was running fast but fordable, and although the horses were swimming, we crossed successfully and rode on to the Rakaia. Here the river was well braided and by taking our time we could select crossing places

RESCUE ONE NEW ZEALANDER'S CRUSADE TO SAVE ENDANGERED ANIMALS

without too much difficulty, and we were soon clambering up the banks and into the yards at Glenrock Station, home of Charlie and Judy Ensor. Since the next leg of our journey would involve a very arduous alpine crossing, we made the most of their grass and hospitality, and all had a couple of good days' rest before heading off up the Rakaia Gorge on the next leg, which took us through to Lake Heron and on to Arrowsmith Station.

On the way we were tucked in some scrub when we saw Charlie fly over in his plane. He had offered to drop off some feed at Mesopotamia, then the Royal Hut and finally Mount Gerald at the head of Lake Tekapo. It was doubtful that he saw us, even though he spent time circling overhead. From there we followed the Potts River down to where it joined the Rangitata. This, the third mighty Canterbury river, also had a reputation for quicksands, which were known to have swallowed up several horses. Sure enough, before we were halfway across Bev's hind legs broke through the crust of a patch, fortunately just on the edge and she had little trouble breaking free. Bella,

River crossings in the South Island high country were one of the biggest challenges.

however, with the heavier load, was struggling, and without the additional pull from Bev could well have been in trouble. It was eerie and strange to see the gravel and shingle stirring up all around us like a stew.

Next morning we set off up Forest Creek as early as we could, knowing it was going to be a long day. The climbing was steep, but the footholds were good, and we slowly worked our way up and around a patch of bush before coming out directly below the Bullock Bow Saddle. If we thought the climbing had been steep before, then we were in for an awful shock now. There was no way you could ride up – the horses had to be led – and it wasn't long before Bob's muscles were shaking with exhaustion and nervousness. The climb seemed to be straight up, and went on, and on, and on. Just when you thought you had reached the top, another ridge would break out above you. We were now climbing in shingle scree. Alpine plants were scarce, but a colourful array of lichens crawled all over the rocks, covering them in a myriad of colours, while big fat grasshoppers jumped around among the black and blue alpine butterflies. As we neared the tops we ran into large patches of snow, not huge but soft and deep enough for the horses to be shoulder deep at times. By the time they finally broke over the last ridge, they were bathed in sweat and snorting with indignation.

The country now dropped away from us into a huge alpine basin, with its own little hills and tarns. On the far side was our destination, the Royal Hut. We wasted little time in getting off the saddle, sliding down the scree and after an hour or so, reached the hut. Hugely relieved, we stripped all the gear off the tired horses and then looked for the sack of oats that Charlie had air-dropped for us, but we could find no trace of it. Nor did we see his plane door: we discovered later that it had blown off as the oats were thrown out, and was never seen again. That was an expensive trip for Charlie and I felt bad about it.

The horses weren't happy either, as there was really no food for them. John had a few oats left, which he gave to his two, but mine had to make do with what little they could find to chew on. The sky became overcast that night and it started to rain. If the weather packed in and we couldn't go over the tops tomorrow, then our situation didn't look good. Although next morning the hut was closed in with fog, we were pretty confident that it would lift and so packed up. The horses were hungry. Bob and Debbie were almost coming in through the door of the hut for dinner. Bev, on the other hand, had to be tied up or she would have disappeared and gone back to where she knew there was grass. John was away first with Bob, leaving me to tidy up and follow shortly with my two and Debbie. Today we were making for Stag Saddle and beyond. I moved fast, got high and found myself on a bench that seemed to go in the right direction. Below in a creekbed I could see the tiny figures of John and Bob, slowly making their way up. Everything was going well, although the country was getting a bit steep, until the tussock tapered out and we were on a very precipitous shingle slide that went from top to bottom. With every step the horses' hooves slid down in a little avalanche of gravel, and they were getting pretty edgy about the whole thing. Even I couldn't keep my balance and had to keep fending myself off the slope with my free hand in order to stay upright. Because the horses were forced to scramble a lot, I had to be pretty quick on my feet in order to keep in front and prevent being trampled.

I was leading Bev, with Bella tied on behind, when there was a bad moment: during her plunging, Bella got a leg over the lead rope tied to Bev's tail. Both horses were being pulled in all directions and I cut the rope with my knife to release them. Halfway across the slide Debbie decided that it was all too much, packed a sad and refused to move. There was little I could do but move on and hope that she would follow, but she just stood there, a lonely figure glued to a shingle slide, too scared to move, and receding into the distance as we battled out in front. Below in the creekbed John was slowly coming up with Bob, also having some difficulty but making progress. We eventually made it out into a high alpine basin, where there was water and firm ground to relax on. John went out and rescued a very reluctant Debbie, and we all rested to recover our wind and nerves. The horses' fetlocks and legs were cut and bleeding from the rocks, while their bodies were running with sweat that dripped off their bellies.

We still had a couple of hundred metres to climb out and up onto a ridge, but the going wasn't too bad, and once we breasted the ridge we could see our goal, Stag Saddle, out to the left. There was no vegetation, just a jumble of barren rock, and we made our way carefully across a lunarscape of large broken boulders, leg-breaking country and quite dangerous. Bob chose here to wedge his great hoof in a crevice between a couple of rocks and, in extricating it, plucked off and bent the shoe, which then had to be reshaped and replaced on the spot. A bit more climbing, a scramble around a couple of bluffs, a final flounder through a snow drift capping the ridge and we were at the top of Stag Saddle. It felt like being on the top of the world, and we were light-headed with accomplishment and exertion. Way below to the left were the pastel-blue waters of Lake Tekapo, straight across we could look Aoraki Mount Cook in the nose, while stretching out behind us, filmy in the haze, rolled the Canterbury Plains. Much as we would have liked to have sat and

CHAPTER SEVEN **A COUNTRY FIT FOR HORSES**

Replacing Bob's shoe in less than ideal circumstances.

drunk in the view, we wasted little time before starting our descent, as the wind was icy, blasting straight off the glaciers.

The first 300 metres or so was just bare rock and boulders again but after that we could move out onto a leading spur that led us down towards the valley floor. There was still nothing for the horses to eat, however, and it was now over thirty-six hours since they had had any real nourishment. Even as we got lower the horses were slipping, their feet going like toboggans in the snowgrass that formed a hard, smooth, shiny surface when trodden on. Far, far below us we could see the toy-like buildings and tree lines of Mount Gerald Station, and we headed down towards the green paddocks as fast as we could. The horses would get their grass, and the hard feed that Charlie had flown over for them. It was a real pleasure to see them roll, eat and generally relax after what had been quite an ordeal for all of us.

The next day, though, we were back in the saddle and travelling down the north side of the lake to Tekapo. We were low on supplies and expecting to be able to restock there. As we left the station boundary the fence crossed the road and lying against it was an old dog kennel, a remnant of the past. I still have difficulty with the concept of what were known as boundary dogs. Often old dogs no longer capable of a full day's work, their reward was to be chained to a kennel and lead a cold, hungry, lonely existence. Their only relief from boredom was to howl in the night air and hope to hear the answering wail from the next poor sod somewhere out over the hills. You often see road signs indicating 'Dog Kennel Corner' or similar. Fortunately the practice is now well outdated, but the ghosts of those old dogs remain, still refusing to believe that their master isn't coming back one day to take them home.

We arrived in Tekapo township in the evening and rode along the lakeshore past the famous monument to the collie dog. We had permission to use the saleyards across the road, which were deep in grass so that we could turn the horses loose into an area divided into several small holding paddocks. Early next morning John went off to check on the horses while I was hanging out a lot of sodden gear to get it dry. He seemed to be away for an awfully long time, and when he did appear he was walking up the road like a schoolboy on his way to the dentist. 'Debbie's hurt herself,' he muttered. 'I'll have to get a vet in.' Unable to believe it, I went and had a look for myself. There on the inside of her thigh was a huge gash, almost big enough to put my hand in. I found the steel waratah that she had walked over in the night. It was bent over and still had blood and skin attached to the burred edges on top. A pleasant and competent vet arrived later in the morning. The verdict? Any excessive exercise would pull the stitches out, and only aggravate the injury further. We couldn't believe this had happened. We were safer away in the mountains. The local pub seemed to be a very reasonable and natural place to become our headquarters, while we considered our options. We couldn't afford the time to wait around for the wound to heal, but nor did we want to leave Debbie behind. John could retire, but that wasn't a prospect either of us wished to consider. After tossing around various ideas, we came up with a compromise that we thought might work. If we could get Debbie sent on ahead somehow, then we could meet up with her and reassess the situation then. In the meantime my horses would have to carry the extra gear.

The news media, which had been following our journey when they could, took up the challenge and sent a plea out over the radio. Later that evening, as we sat sipping morosely in a corner, a strongly built weatherbeaten man, hiding behind a big black beard, detached himself from a group at the bar and came over. He pulled up a chair and introduced himself as John Simpson, the local builder, who had heard the news on Radio Caroline. He was jovial and yet quietly spoken. I liked him right from the start, and even more so when he offered to transport Debbie south. I contacted a friend, Bob McRae, who had a station at Glendhu Bay just out of Wanaka, and was more than happy to look after Debbie until we arrived. At last we had a plan and a way of moving on.

As our smaller cavalcade left Tekapo, we were pleased to be leaving but had mixed thoughts about what lay ahead. Despite the rain and bitter cold, it was nice to get back to camping again. The harsh wind sweeping up from the south only seemed to highlight the warm sense of security within the frail walls of the tent. Cooking a meal again over the burner felt almost like coming home. Past Lake Pukaki, and the tussock grasslands rolled out ahead. The horses were walking out really well and we started pushing harder and harder, increasing the distance we covered each day. Over the Lindis Pass we went and a few days later rode around the shores of Lake Wanaka and on to where Debbie was paddocked.

The news, however, was all bad. She had pulled some stitches and the local vet strongly recommended that she not be ridden for some time. We reluctantly decided to leave her there and continue on as we were. It was a big wrench turning our backs on her, as she had done so much and come so far, but we consoled ourselves with the thought that, if we made Bluff, then we would make sure that she was there too. Our journey now took us through the beautiful Motatapu, following old gold miners' trails, over the Motatapu Saddle and past deserted, ruined buildings. Those men must have been tough to survive up here: you could see the remains of the workings and stone houses carved out of rock faces. The trail led to Arrowtown and then on to the bustling hub of Queenstown. Across the lake were the iconic stations of Walter Peak and Mount Nicholas, which led us up the valley of the Von, over the Mavora Saddle and down the Mararoa to Burwood Station. It was all familiar territory to me, and it was with considerable regret that we came out onto the main highway and turned down for the final leg to Invercargill and our final destination, Bluff.

It was a strange rendezvous as we all gathered again around the signpost that marked the bottom of New Zealand. Best of all, we had Debbie, whom Carole had picked up on the way down. John's big black labrador Hades was also there, greeting his master with undisguised enthusiasm, as was my little border collie, Fey. It was with mixed feelings that we loaded the horses, headed back up north and returned to our normal lives. For three tough, disciplined months we had never known what the next day would bring and we had lived and slept with our horses in some odd and occasionally ridiculous places. At the end of it all I could easily have continued, rolling up my swag and seeking more horizons.

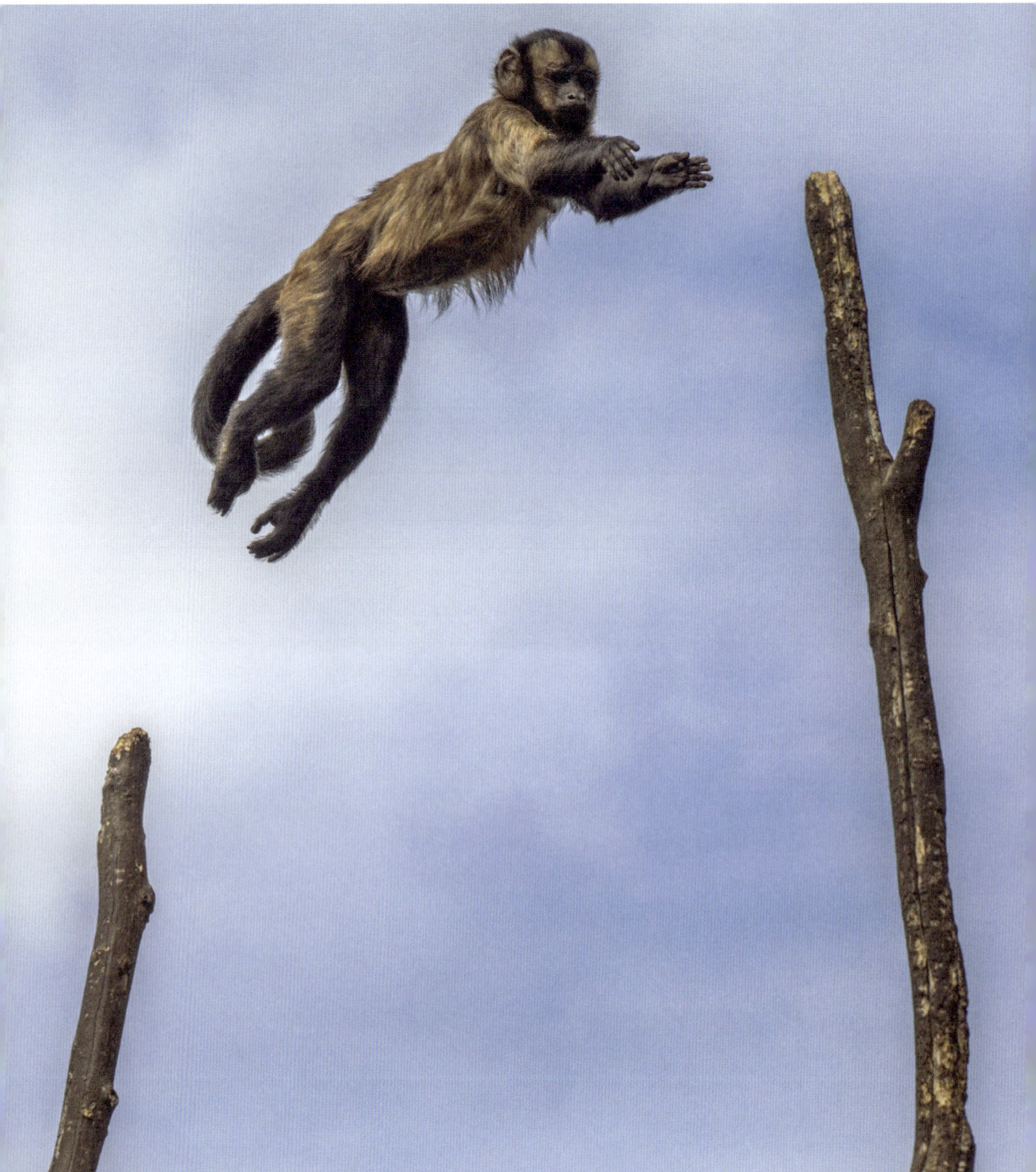

CHAPTER EIGHT

A CHANGE OF LIFE

Having the otters made an appreciable difference to the park. They were fun, exciting and people related well to them. Also they had that New Zealand association with the waitoreke, which felt comfortable and allowed them to fit in. For some reason, though, I felt that we still didn't seem to have the aura and status of a 'big zoo'. What we needed was a larger icon species and it came up in Dunedin, just north of Waihola.

For several years the Phillips family had been trying to establish a zoo in Dunedin. They started with a small collection at Taieri Mouth, just south of the city, and then after a few years took the plunge and moved to a more accessible spot on the outskirts of the city itself. As with Bill Grey's establishment, the majority of the animals were misfits that no one else wanted, and Trevor Phillips was pleased to be able to offer them a home. However, in spite of giving the project all the energy and resources they had, they became another casualty of a fickle public, bureaucracy and an unsupportive zoo industry. The inevitable phone call came, and I drove down to Dunedin. They had lost almost everything. Closure was now the only realistic option. But how do you find homes for exotic animals that nobody really wants, and those who do want them aren't allowed to keep them?

It wasn't fun going along the cages and looking into the faces of monkeys you couldn't take, and for whom you could see no future. I had seen nothing that that fitted our future plans – until I walked past a concrete block shed with a heavy chain link front. There, looking up at me, was the intelligent face of a chimpanzee. Some chimpanzees have quite pink faces, but his was black like a gorilla, with strong but delicate features. His eyes were gentle and he pursed his lips towards me as if wanting to kiss me through the netting. He hooted softly and held his fingers out through the netting. 'Don't trust him,' said Trevor. 'His name's Charlie and he's already removed two of my fingers.' Gently I stroked the back of Charlie's hand and he settled down, grunting softly to himself, while his other hand scratched idly through the straw. Behind and at the back of the pen was a pile of straw and a shape that moved slightly under a humped sack that fully covered it. 'That's the female, Coco,' said Trevor. 'She's a bit timid.' And then peeping around and looking inquisitively at us from under the corner of the sack was a little pink face with two black soulful eyes, and surrounded by funky, spiky fur. 'Yeah, that's a baby. We call her Samantha.'

Thoughts rushed through my head. Did we want a family of chimpanzees? What would happen to them if we didn't take them? What would happen to us if we did? It was a thoughtful trip back home, and after a few days of thinking it all through I rang them up and said yes. That decision was to start a mind-altering experience. The look deep down in Charlie's eyes had unsettled me. That animal needed a home, and surely having charge of such a creature and his companions would have to be one of the pinnacles of owning a zoo.

With only a few weeks before the Dunedin zoo closed, there was a fair bit of pressure to get things ready for the chimpanzees. We had recently built some new enclosures for the monkeys, and so decided we could use their original one. It was very strong and with some minor modifications would be suitable. The day came when all was complete and I headed off down to Dunedin in my trusty Land Rover with a large steel crate on the back that had been used in the past to transport some large cats. The little chimp family had been locked in a small holding area that had a trapdoor leading outside, and by placing the crate against that we managed to get them in without any real difficulty. Then, picking the crate up with a tractor, we loaded it back onto the open back of the Land Rover. That was easy, I thought, and headed north towards home. My journey took me back up through the main street of Dunedin, which was busy and full of people but I had plenty of time. I stopped at a set of red lights and was idly watching people go by when suddenly all hell let loose. The inside of the crate was being hammered as if by sledgehammers and being thrown around and making the whole vehicle roll vigorously from one side to the other. This was accompanied by a terrible guttural screaming that was being amplified by the steel of the crate. Traffic came to a standstill, people on the pavement stood staring open mouthed and

CHAPTER EIGHT **A CHANGE OF LIFE**

Charlie the chimpanzee surveys his realm.

the lights turned green. I took off as fast as I could, hoping the movement would settle down whatever mayhem was taking place in the crate, which still rocking furiously on the back, making the whole vehicle weave from side to side. It was my first introduction to the volatility that goes hand in hand with keeping chimpanzees.

I have never understand how I made it out of town without having half a dozen police cars chasing me. Recently I had been in Wellington, and after

131

visiting the zoo was heading through the city with a crate of animals plus a very vocal Corrella cockatoo, who had a deafening scream and a large and varied vocabulary. He was getting sick and tired of all this travel, and halfway through town started to vent his annoyance and frustration. It was only a few minutes before there was a wailing of sirens and flashing lights, and I was unceremoniously pulled over in the middle of an intersection. The police had been informed that there was someone in an obvious life and death situation in the back of the truck. It was a tense moment until I could pull back the covers and they could see the avian Charlie still bouncing up and down on his perch, excited about all this new activity and diversion that he had created. Odd that they were both called Charlie, I thought, as I pulled into the Willowbank gate and drove the chimps up to their new home. They were happy to be out, and we could all settle down now and get to know each other.

Samantha was easy. She was just a delightful little baby chimpanzee who had been born in the Dunedin zoo. Coco, the mother, was in her late thirties, which is middle aged for a chimpanzee. She always had an aura of sadness around her, and you got the impression that she had lived a joyless life. She was very standoffish, and would always keep a good distance from anything that might cause her any stress or grief. If pushed too much she would scream, hold her arms out in front of her and wave them in the air, presumably in an attempt to drive away whatever was annoying her. She had been born in an Australian-based circus and had spent all of her life travelling with it. The owners were happy to sell her off to Trevor Phillips when they had the opportunity, thinking she had reached the end of her shelf life as a performing animal.

Charlie had had a much more chequered career. After being wild caught as a baby, and his mother no doubt shot, he was sold to an animal dealer in Belgium, who kept him for a few months. He was then sold to a showman, who used him as part of his performance. He brought Charlie up as being one of his own family, and the chimp could dress himself and eat at the table. When the showman died in a car accident, Charlie was reputed to have been found lying down and cuddling the body. The widow had no use for a chimp and he was sold on to a circus. Charlie performed in the ring for a number of years until inevitably he reached puberty, when he became potentially very dangerous. This is a familiar story for performing chimps, who have a working life of about thirteen to fourteen years, and then become impossible to handle and a liability. In the States large facilities have been set up at great cost to house many of these maladjusted animals, former pets or relics of laboratory testing, space experimentation and tea parties. All are kept isolated, too dangerous to handle, and their hominid status makes euthanasia very difficult. Charlie had thrown his bike at the ringmaster and generally behaved like any adolescent teenage boy on steroids. The ringmaster, a big tough man, not to be reckoned with, solved the problem by welding Charlie into a steel crate that was just big enough to sit on a trailer. It had an area of grating on the floor so that it could be hosed and cleaned out, and one side was heavy mesh so Charlie could be paraded for people to see. He spent some years incarcerated in that crate, until the opportunity came to sell him to the new zoo in Dunedin for a quick profit, and to pass the responsibility over.

I found it amazing that Charlie kept his sanity during all this, and that, in spite of never being able to behave like a chimp, when he met Coco he became a loving husband. He was also a very good father, which some males are not. For two animals that had come from a cruel and alien background, they were as loving and normally adjusted a pair of parents as you could have wished for. That's not to say they didn't have their arguments. Every now and again Charlie would lose his temper and create mayhem. After he had finished his demolition derby, Coco would often tell him off. By screaming and grimacing and waving her arms wildly, she usually had the last say.

To grasp Charlie's tantrums you have to understand chimps' natural behaviour in the wild. Regularly, something will set the males off, and they'll behave like a bunch of maniacs in a full moon. In a typical example, they might gather at the foot of a hill, and one by one trudge up the ridge to the top. Once there they will start to scream and bounce up and down with their shoulder hair standing erect. Then they will take off and charge madly down the hill, demolishing anything breakable and leaving a swath of destruction behind them. They will arrive at the bottom, panting and exhausted, and then turn around and trudge up the ridge again to repeat the whole performance. No one quite knows why they do it. It's just a major release of pent-up energy and steam, and once over it they settle down to normal behaviour again.

You could see a tantrum coming and it was frightening to watch. Charlie would start strutting around the enclosure, hooting softly, with his shoulder hair standing erect like a muff. Coco would grab little Samantha and, holding her closely to her chest, would huddle in a corner with her back to Charlie. (In such a relatively small space it was all Coco could do.) Charlie's hoots would build up and so would the hair around his upper body until he appeared twice the size and became a devilish mountain of muscle bouncing up and down on the spot. The hoots would build up to a climax of screams, and he would rush around the enclosure, throwing anything moveable away until finally he leapt up onto the sides and, gripping the steel mesh, would shake the hell out of the whole place. You could only watch helplessly and hope that the sides held together. Moments later it was all over, Coco would abuse him and he would sit there quietly withdrawn into himself. The strength of a chimpanzee is phenomenal. Charlie wasn't a huge animal as chimps go, but when he was in that mood he could easily pick up half a telegraph post and throw it seemingly without any effort.

On the other side, Charlie was such a cool dude. We would play games running backwards and forwards along the front of his enclosure, each trying to pretend to evade the other until we collapsed, worn out and laughing to each other. In special quiet times we would sit together and he would just gaze into my eyes, hooting softly, his mouth rounded like a tube blowing kisses. He would shuffle as close as he could to the netting, hold his fingers out, and I would stroke the backs of them and we would sit there and communicate as best we could. My personal relationship with Charlie was very special. Without being told, he knew where everyone fitted into the staff hierarchy. New people on the block were given the run around until they had proved themselves. I was top chimp for Charlie, and if I was anywhere near the enclosure, then he was always watching out for me. He also kept an eye on the staff and what they did. Some of the other staff also played running games with Charlie. Guy Atkinson was playing such a game when, unknown to him, his radio fell off his belt.

Radios were vital for us as the park continued to develop — for safety reasons, and just to co-ordinate what was happening. We started with a few cheap walkie-talkies, and then went on to some good hand-held radio sets. Initially they were on a common band, which meant that anyone within range could hear what was being said. The more they were used, the more the problems developed and some messages were inviting some strange responses from outside. Anything with a sexual connotation was fair game for some ribald comments from half the tradesmen working in the district. Eventually we went onto our own unique waveband.

Nobody saw how Charlie ended up with the radio, but it's well known that chimps have developed the ability to use tools. He must have found a stick or something similar and dragged the radio close enough for him to pull it through the netting. Meanwhile at the front desk, all the staff monitoring the base set could hear were popping noises, crackling and banging. When Guy realised he had lost his radio, he tracked it back to Charlie, who was walking around the enclosure holding the radio to his ear, and then out in front of his mouth. Nothing, however, was working for Charlie the way it seemed to work with the staff, so he gave the buttons a few flicks — they flew into the

CHAPTER EIGHT **A CHANGE OF LIFE**

Charlie and I have a chat. It's easy to see how a moment's inattention could lead to problems.

air satisfactorily – and then removed the aerial. The rest became history but Charlie was so nearly there. Chimpanzees and humans are reputed to share about 98 per cent of their DNA, depending on how you measure it, so his behaviour shouldn't have come as a surprise.

Our relationship hit a bit of a low one lovely, peaceful morning when I was crouched down in front of Charlie's enclosure, with a palm full of sunflower seeds, which he loved. For normal safety reasons my arm was lying parallel to the mesh and he had shuffled up quietly and was engrossed in picking them out of my hand. Then one of the staff came up to ask me a question. Without thinking, I took my eyes off Charlie for a few seconds, and during that time his fingers shot through the netting, grasped my hand and pulled it close. My thumb went through the mesh and he bit a large part of it off. It all happened so fast that I really couldn't believe it – until I took another look and, sure enough, a good chunk of the thumb had gone.

Wrapping my hand in a tea towel, I went off to hospital again. I was feeling pretty sorry for myself until I ended up sitting in a waiting room with a young guy as white as a sheet, clutching a jar holding two fingers. Mind you, I guess that he had those reattached. When the surgeon eventually arrived he asked me what happened and where the rest of it was and could I go back and get it. Fat chance of that, so we dealt with what was left. I've been bitten heaps of times, but in many ways this was different. Human bites are the worst sort for infections, and those from a chimpanzee are considered to be roughly in the same category, so it was a course of intravenous antibiotics before I was allowed to walk out the door.

Getting hurt is part and parcel of animal work, and it's often the unexpected ones that cause the most problems. More people get injured on farms by sheep, mainly pet rams, than by any other animal. I haven't actually been hurt too much by sheep, but have certainly had my hands ripped to pieces by a pet Captain Cooker boar. I had my top lip stitched back up after an altercation with an emu, who also ripped my shirt off and punched me all over. A leopard put a claw through one shoulder, and a few years later a mountain lion did the same. Cuts and bruises were just par for the course, but the closest I came to something really serious, was an altercation I had with a little Highland cow. She was fairly stroppy, but, having bred her, I knew her pretty well. She had a calf a few days old, and I could see that it wasn't well and needed some attention. With a big stick in my hand, I proceeded to try and work them both towards some yards. Without warning she turned around and charged, sending me flying backwards onto my back. She stood over me, trying to hook me with her horns while I was trying desperately to hang onto them. She was pounding my chest and the horns had punched holes inside my thighs and I was in deep trouble. Then, with a hook, she threw me over the fence so that I lay winded on the other side. Thank heaven I'm out of there, I thought, but then there was a twanging of wire and she was ripping the fence apart to get at me again. She meant business, this cow. Once again she got me down on the ground and was grinding me with her head. I had run out of options until, as luck would have it, the calf tried to follow its mother and got tangled in the fence and started bellowing. The cow left me to run back to the calf and I managed to get over another fence and away.

It was a slow and sore walk back to the house, where I had a shower and got myself strapped up. The calf still needed treatment, and so I thought I would have another go. This time, someone drove the truck into the paddock

CHAPTER EIGHT **A CHANGE OF LIFE**

The cow who tried to kill me.

and we tried to use that to move the cow, with me hobbling alongside. I was on the opposite side to the cow, but she saw me through the windscreen. Her head shot up and then she was off, coming around the side to attack me again. I was getting a bit stiff by this time and was trying to lever myself into the back with my stick when she hooked her head under my bum and threw me in, along with another pile of bruises. By then I had had enough. A week or so later I got her into a secure paddock surrounded by a 2-metre fence, but every time I walked down the drive, she would pace beside me, snorting. She was the boss and she knew it, until I resolved the problem permanently by sending her off to the yards to be sold, with a big notice saying 'DO NOT TRUST THIS COW'.

I now had a similar problem with Charlie. He was top chimp with a strut and a swagger to match as he contemplated my bandages thoughtfully. One day, hiding a plasterer's trowel under my arm, I went to the enclosure and, crouching down, dribbled some sunflower seeds along the edge of the concrete where my hand was. He fingers came out to grab some and I smacked them hard with the edge of the trowel. He jumped back in shock and ran

137

around the enclosure, shaking his hand and holding it under his armpit. We were square now. The strut had gone, I was boss chimp again and we remained the best of friends, if not blood brothers.

The public reaction to the chimpanzees was interesting. Some were fascinated and stood in awe of them. Some were rightly petrified. A surprisingly large proportion had no comprehension of their potential to be dangerous, and considered them almost a plaything. Parents would lean over the rails holding their babies out, close enough to be within reach. Adults, especially fathers with children, would often pretend to act like a chimp and jump up and down, scratching themselves with maniacal laughter. It was bizarre watching them, and the chimps themselves must have wondered what humans really got up to. They hated being laughed at, and after a day of abuse they would be morose and depressed. So much so that they would pick at themselves and cause skin disorders. We had a healer come in regularly to try and sort their mental state out again, especially after a busy period.

Samantha grew up to become a fine young lady, if one who took life rather seriously like her mother. Coco then produced a fine handsome boy that we called Milo. He had Charlie's good looks and was the perfect specimen. When Milo was about four years old, he was found comatose in his pen one morning. He had been fine the night before, and now was close to death. The other chimps were separated, the vets arrived and the staff gathered. Milo was having trouble breathing and I rushed off to get a bottle of oxygen, but came back to find the vet kicking the tyres of his truck and Milo dead. The shock was absolute, and we were all numbed. We left Milo in his bed and let the other animals in. They came in sombrely and all sat around quietly, touching him, putting their lips on him and stroking him gently. It was two days before we felt that we could remove Milo, and they watched from the roof of the enclosure as I dug the hole that was to be his grave. It was a life-altering experience, and one that was repeated about two years later when Coco succumbed to a lung infection. Her lungs had been damaged early in her life, and dealing with them was a constant battle that became harder to win as she got older. It was a fairly small group when we were left with just Charlie and Samantha.

Surely, I thought, after the chimpanzees first arrived, we were getting close to being a really proper zoo. But I still wondered what we needed next to make the place even better. There must be a special wild animal out there somewhere that we could add, that would put the place on the map. I had always wanted a zoo, and now I was close to achieving it. It had driven me for years, and been the focus of most of my life. But when I started to think of what other animal I wanted, it came as a shock to realise that I couldn't think of one, and I began to seriously doubt the value of keeping the animals that we already had. The conservation value of most was nil. We were largely keeping them for public entertainment, and why should an animal like Charlie put up with the abuse of being in captivity? Was he even an animal? How do you measure that? After months of soul searching my mind was made up. We couldn't perpetuate something that just wasn't right. New Zealand had too much wildlife that needed to be preserved and advocated for, and few people were doing this. We needed to change. We needed to be more honest in our conservation messages, and maybe the rest would follow. We would become a New Zealand park, not merely a collection of animals and birds. It was a turning point both in my life and that of Willowbank.

Having made that decision, we still had Charlie and Samantha to consider. There was no long-term future for them, and appropriate homes would have to be found. That wasn't easy. Only a handful of zoos around the world have facilities suitable for chimps, and they had all the animals that they needed. We kept the word out and years went by. We were contacted by a circus working around the Pacific, but in spite of the money offered that was not an acceptable option. More time went by and we were starting to doubt that it would ever happen when, in the 1990s, we had an approach from a new zoo being established in Australia. They wished to hold chimpanzees, and were building facilities for them. Located south of Sydney, 10 minutes from Batemans Bay, it was called Mogo Zoo. I flew over to take a look. It was going to be impressive. The huge open enclosure and massive indoor facilities for the chimps were far better than anything we had been able to offer, and I was thrilled to give Charlie and Samantha to Mogo. It was a bit like being accepted into the country's top school. About two years later and the enclosure was finished and we made preparations to fly them over.

This was both a major logistical exercise, and a hugely costly one. Emirates agreed to fly the chimps over at no cost, crates were built and plans made for the big shift. Not without difficulty on the appointed day we managed to get both animals into their respective crates and flew with them to Sydney, arriving in the middle of the night. After a three-hour trip with a couple of trucks, we arrived at Mogo, where a large team was waiting to unload Charlie and Samantha and get them inside the holding area. We stayed for three or four days to be with the animals and settle them in, then left them, content that they had an excellent future. They were to be joined by two other chimps, a large male called Louie, and a female, Holly. Both had also been circus chimps, and had had a fairly chequered past.

The intention was to eventually integrate them all as one group, and until that time they had good facilities to keep them apart and accustom them to one another. It was to be a managed integration. Over the months we had progress reports and everything was going well, with specialist staff from Sydney's Taronga Zoo coming down to help with the process and the chimps integrating successfully into a mixed group.

Unloading Charlie and Samantha at Australia's Mogo Zoo.

And then came the phone call that you dread. They had tried a total integration, and Louie had jumped on Charlie's back and bitten through his neck, killing him instantly. No blame could be apportioned, but it reinforced my belief in the new approach we were taking. Later Samantha was transferred to Rockhampton Zoo and in 2019 had a lovely baby of her own. We all grieved for Charlie, deeply affected each in our own private ways. My daughter Kirsty was hugely upset. It had been a steep learning experience and, in spite of all the good times, it was a pathway I didn't want to go down again.

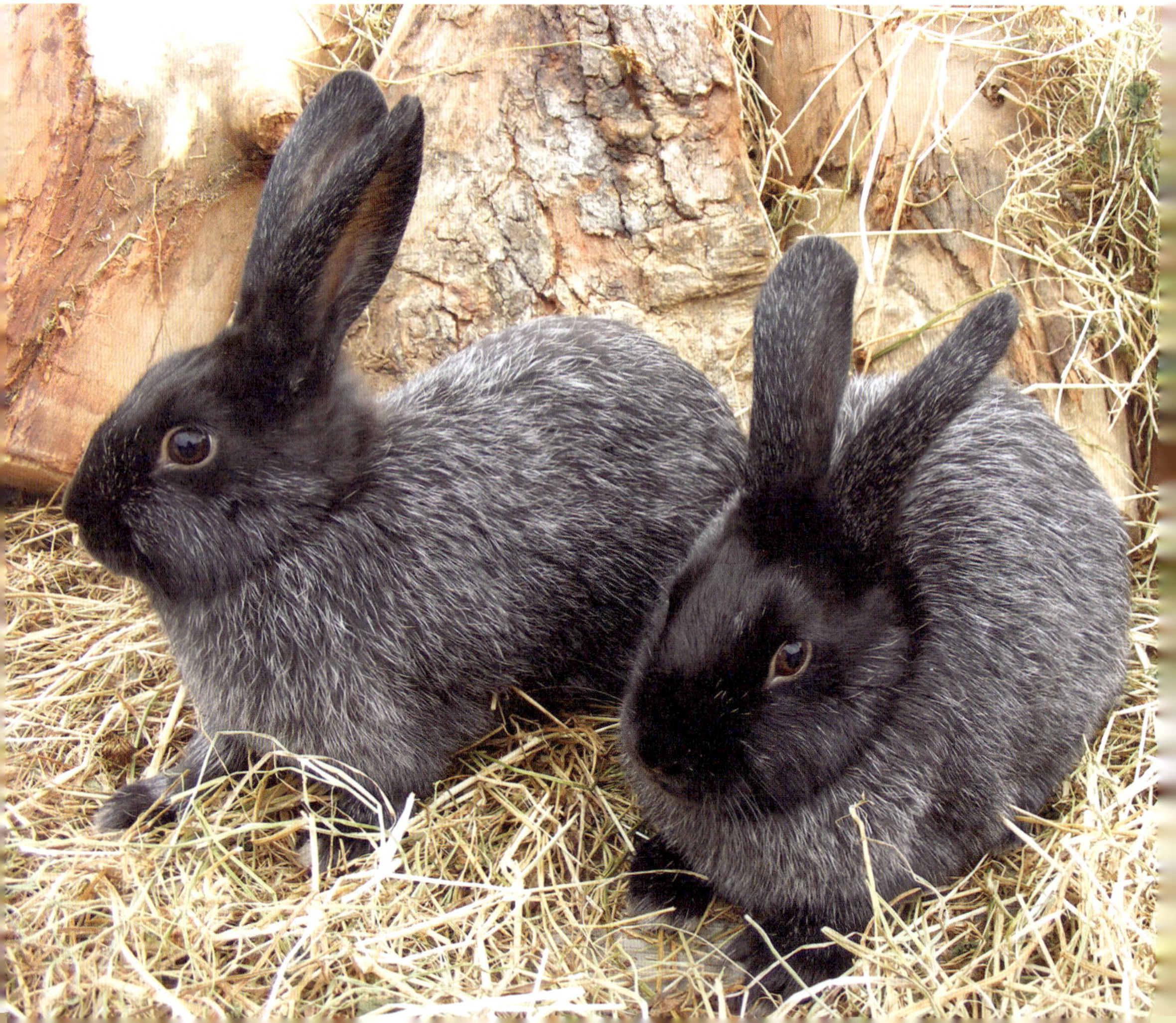

CHAPTER NINE

THE END OF THE RABBIT

'Hey Dave, do you want to go to Enderby Island?' I asked into the phone one evening.

'End of which island?' was the rather terse response.

'Not end of the island. Enderby Island. It's an island off Auckland Island.'

'What would I want to go up there for?'

'It's not up there, it's down below. Halfway to Antarctica,' I retorted, 'and we're going there to catch bloody rabbits, that is if you stop being a difficult sod and listen.'

'Why would we want to catch rabbits? I've got heaps of the little buggers in my back paddock.'

'Because these ones are actually a rare breed of rabbit. Probably the only ones left in the world, and they're going to be exterminated,' I said with all the patience I could muster. 'So we're going to go down, catch some and try and save the breed.'

This was the start of several rather difficult conversations, regarding a dramatic rescue attempt in one of the world's most inhospitable regions. Dave Matheson was a veterinarian I had known for a number of years. His wife Judy was a nurse, and they both had an infectious enthusiasm for life and living. As well as a successful practice they had a home farm. They loved their animals, they loved the outdoors and we met regularly on endurance rides in the mountains. These are long-distance horse races up to 160 kilometres, rides that Judy took as a challenge and at which Dave officiated as a vet. We often met socially, or to go on trips to various out of the way places.

Opposite: Two silver grey Enderby Island rabbits.
Photo: Sitereh Schouten

The bunny story started way back in 1865 when the then Acclimatisation Society of Victoria in Australia put twelve rabbits on a ship bound for the Auckland Islands, with the intention of releasing them to provide a food source for shipwrecked mariners. Quite by chance these animals were highly distinctive, being silver grey in colour and reputed to belong to the French breed, Champagne d'Argent. With few predators on the islands, the rabbit population expanded, with the main limiting factor to its growth the vicious winters. Lacking any other stock to mingle with, they had bred true and unchanged for over one and a half centuries, before humans again began to take an interest in them. In the past, the advantages of the winds of what is known as the Roaring Forties, along with the sea currents, made a route through these waters pretty attractive, in spite of the perils of the wild weather and the constant risk of shipwreck. With the advent of steam, however, and the opening of the Panama Canal, everybody breathed a sigh of relief and headed directly across the world, leaving the rabbits settled into a life of anonymity, discarded now as an offshore larder and forgotten about until the rise in conservation awareness brought them once more into the spotlight.

Under New Zealand government policy, any introduced animal starts with a heavily weighted bias against them, and these rabbits were no exception. Studies were done, and the verdict given that they were having an adverse impact on the vegetation, and to top it off their burrows had turned into miniature tank traps in which young sea lions were apparently becoming smothered. The jury never left the room. The rabbits had to go. The fly in the ointment, however, was other studies which had shown that these rabbits were, in fact, a rare breed, potentially an unusual and valuable genetic resource, as well as being of historical and heritage interest. A sufficient number of individuals and organisations knew this to make it extremely embarrassing should the rabbits be eradicated without a lot of consideration, as had happened with other species in the past. A lot of lessons had been learnt after Arapawa Island, and DOC was not keen for a repeat of that.

Early one evening I got a discreet phone call, saying that my name had been brought up as someone who just might succeed in such a venture, and asking if I was interested in organising and leading an expedition down to the island in an attempt to catch and bring back sufficient animals for a breeding group. Unlike Dave, I knew exactly where Enderby Island was, and had read many fascinating and intriguing accounts of the shipwrecks and abandoned settlements and farming ventures of the Southern Ocean. Without the faintest idea of how I was going to do it, it was a 'yes' from me, and a blind commitment. I would deal with the problems as they arose.

CHAPTER NINE **THE END OF THE RABBIT**

A lonely fingerpost on Enderby Island pointing to the nearest castaway shelter – a poignant reminder of long-lost settlement. The dark shapes in the water are whales playing.

Saying yes was the simple part. Once I had got over that and started to think about how we would actually achieve what was expected, a bit of reality started to sink in. A big plus was that Dave had agreed to leave his veterinary practice unattended for a while, and accompany me on the trip. Aside from his veterinary qualifications, he's great company and can be totally relied upon to still be carrying a pack at the end of the day with a smile on his face and mischief in his eyes. Together we discussed information as it was garnered, and most wasn't very good. Rabbits, it appeared, have a high stress level, and die like flies when put under stress. After assessing all of the information, we came up with various solutions, one being our secret weapon, a cocktail of drugs that we hoped would keep the rabbits bouncing happily and relaxed on fluffy green clouds until we got back home. That is, of course, providing we caught some.

Port Chalmers in Dunedin was to be our point of departure, and so on the appointed day Dave and I arrived and met up with two other DOC personnel, who were also going to the island to do some baiting trials in order to poison the very rabbits we were hoping to save. There was no conflict, however: we

145

all respected one another and offered mutual support where we could. So after a quick introduction and briefing, we all went through a gear check in order to make sure of no mice, seeds or any other undesirable stowaways, and then headed down to the docks and HMS *Manawanui*, a small specialised naval diving vessel. With space at a premium – they had only three spare bunks – I got the short straw, the decompression chamber perched on the aft deck of the ship, like a steel coffin. It was a bit like sleeping in a horizontal space rocket with portholes and a heavy round steel door that ominously sealed shut. It was just wide enough to crawl into with a stretcher to lie on, but I didn't mind it at all. Partially out in the open on the stern, my posse offered both privacy and spectacular views of the sometimes mountainous seas that rolled up behind the ship, threatening to engulf her until, at the last minute, she would lift up and the sea would hiss and roar past on each side.

Dawn a few days later, on 15 September 1992, brought views that are indelibly etched into my mind. Low rata bush on the island came down to a rocky coastline spreading in a semi-circle around us. To the left the bay was marked by huge basaltic granite columns that rose out of the sea, while the eastern part of the bay was sandy with rolling light-coloured dunes that created an incongruous desert-like setting for what almost appeared to be a carefully choreographed Walt Disney show. Rows of black and white penguins plodded from the shore and up into the bush, like serious mismothered waiters who had lost both their sense of humour and their menus. All along the sandy beach, groups of sea lions roared and bellowed, and humped and hollered in jostling groups that appeared to be both confused and ill-mannered, but obviously had a structure they could understand. On the grassy sward back from the glistening sand could be seen grazing the little grey dots that were the rabbits we had come to catch, while giant albatrosses, skuas, petrels and a host of other birdlife wheeled and soared over our heads, and skimmed the waters around us. As if all that wasn't enough, all around the bay, rolling and lolling in the water, were the massive black hulks of huge Right whales. They were having what can only be described as a whale of a good time, as they conducted their slow and ponderous courtship dances, for this bay was a recognised collection and mating point, and we had arrived right in the middle of their nuptials.

We had little time to admire the view, however, and swung straight into action. All the gear had to be ferried ashore by Zodiac and the black-suited frogmen, who were in their element. As we headed for land some of the whales would follow us, and we watched with some apprehension as the great creatures slid underneath or came alongside. One surfaced just out of

Opposite: Sea lions on the beach at Enderby Island, with green grass behind and tangled rata beyond that again.

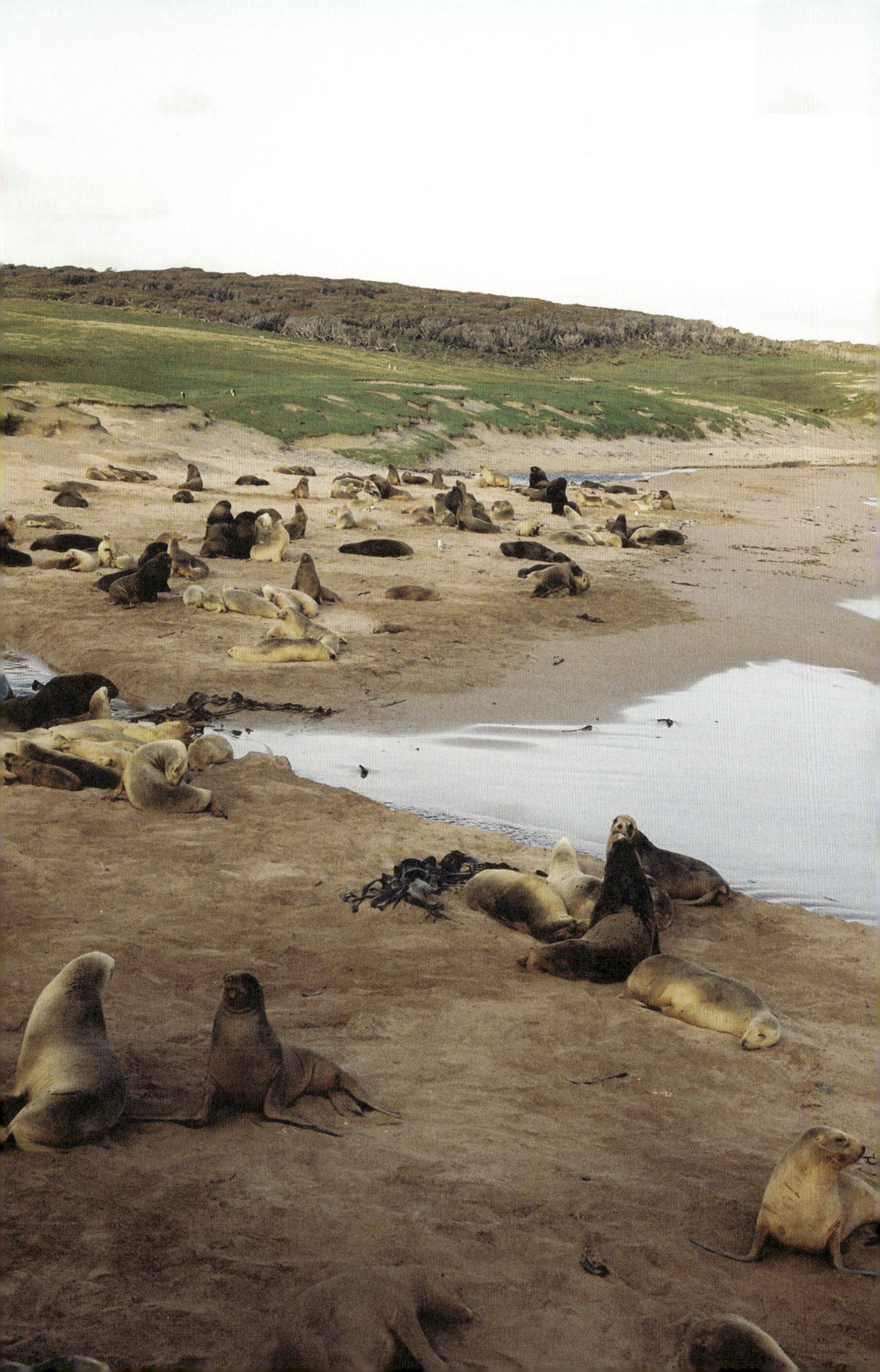

Frogmen in their black suits bring our supplies ashore by Zodiac.

arm's reach, and swam lazily by the vessel, looking at us intently with its saucer-shaped eye. It was a moving experience. Then the huge beast sounded and moved away effortlessly, leaving no feeling of fear or aggression, but rather disappointment at our lack of ability to communicate or play. Once ashore we set up a base around a couple of old huts that had been used by researchers in the past, and a boatshed that dated back to the days of early settlement.

Our immediate plan was to begin feeding some of the rabbits that were handy to the hut and get them as quiet as possible. They were to be our insurance rabbits. We had brought plenty of carrots because they held no environmental risk, all rabbits seem to like them and they travel well.

Accordingly we diced some, sliced some, and spread them around in the close vicinity of the camp, and were gratified to see that within a relatively short space of time, they were being eaten. This was probably not surprising as food was one of the main determining factors in the survival of these rabbits. Vegetation growth was very slow, and the winters severe, so anything vaguely consumable was considered edible. We spent the next few hours setting up traps and nets. We had trap cages against rabbit holes along with a number of the funnel nets with drawstrings favoured by poachers worldwide. In scrapes we set soft-jawed leg hold traps, which we monitored hourly. The grassy sward extended from the shoreline 100 or so metres to the belt of rata forest that encircled the island, leading into the high centre of scrub and tussock. A large number of rabbits had set up home in this hobgoblin forest of twisted rata and came out onto the grass to graze. We set up holding pens within the edge of the bush, with wings that came out in a long wedge, into which we hoped we could feed and drive them.

The *Manawanui* weighed anchor and headed off to Campbell Island to drop supplies and exchange some personnel from the meteorological station based there. Once she had gone a profound sense of isolation seemed to settle over us like a mantle. It was an odd feeling, knowing you were the only people in thousands of square kilometres of world, with no one to help should anything go wrong. At one stage I was bending over my traps when I heard a noise that sounded vaguely like a lawnmower or motor boat. I was on the cliffs above the sea and looked out as the noise grew in volume and died away before growing again. Then there was an enormous explosion that echoed around the bay and the noise started again, joined by another. It was the whales rolling and enacting their foreplay just metres from the beach. Far out in the deeper water a whale leapt into the air and came crashing down, beating the water with his flukes. A few seconds later and the explosion rolled across the ocean to us. Standing out from the others was a white female with a calf of the same colour. The female obviously had serious intentions of getting better acquainted with a large black male who was circling her in anticipation, while the little calf, in all innocence and ignorance, nuzzled them, bumped them, came between or just rolled over them, excited and buoyed with the play. One look at the enchanted expression on Dave's face as he gazed in wonder at the wildlife around him, and I knew that we both had the same problem.

A couple of days later and the mood was changing. Although we had covered a good proportion of the island by now, we still didn't have a rabbit in the bag. It wasn't an unexpected problem but time was against us and we

RESCUE ONE NEW ZEALANDER'S CRUSADE TO SAVE ENDANGERED ANIMALS

were getting a little bit depressed. I must admit to a certain pressure as we cooked dinner in the dusk, and watched darkness fall on another day. We had set a variety of traps and caught nothing so far. We had tried to dig the rabbits out, think them out, work them out, but the game was firmly in their court and something different was needed. That night there was no moon, the sky was as black as ink and the temperature was dropping fast. Time to think outside the square. Pulling on warm clothes and full wet weather gear, we armed ourselves with spotlights, nets and sacks and headed off. We had gone only 200 metres before we ran into our first rabbit. Unsure how it would react, Dave held it in the beam of the spotlight while I circled around and came quietly up behind. A quick swoop with the net and we had our first bunny. Suddenly the spell was broken and we now had something to work on. From then on we were out every night. Our government-issued permit allowed us to capture up to 50 rabbits, so that was our target.

Above left: In 1880 the crew of the New Zealand vessel SS *Stella*, led by Captain McKersie, built this A-frame timber castaway depot to replace an earlier hut that had been destroyed by fire.

Above: Dave Matheson with two Enderby rabbits in a net.

Opposite: The rabbits in their cages, ready for the return to Bluff.

CHAPTER NINE **THE END OF THE RABBIT**

The rabbits, however, were quick learners. The first few were relatively easy to catch, but they soon realised that the light meant trouble, and each night became that much more difficult, trying to out-think them as they became harder and harder to fool. Only one person could have a light; the other had to be in complete darkness as they encircled the prey and crept up. If, as often happened, the rabbit took off, then the chase was on and we were running blind, crashing through and over scrub, twisted rata forest, sea lions and broken terrain in pursuit of our quarry. We had to keep the pressure on. Even a snowstorm sweeping in from the south did nothing to deter our efforts.

The days were now passing all too quickly, but slowly our numbers were growing. As we caught more, so we had to make up more holding cages, and spend more and more time looking after our captives. Every morning they had to be fed and cleaned, and some sort of natural food sourced so that the diet change was not too sudden. This was harder than it sounds. Anything even slightly edible had already gone, and we were reduced to cutting grass with scissors when no one was looking, as removing any vegetation was very much frowned upon. We found to our surprise that there was some variety in the colours of the rabbits. The very young ones started out black, and changed into their blue colour around twelve weeks. Even the blue varied, with some being steel blue, and others having a brownish tinge. There was one rabbit that I really wanted, however. He lived up in the bush by the castaway hut, and he was a very light beige, almost white. We had watched him every day and established his routes, and the evening before we were due to leave we shifted the wing nets and holding pens and rebuilt them over his runs. He ran straight in, and Old Whitey, as we called him, was in the bag. We had our rabbits. We caught fifty, but one injured himself later, which still made a satisfying forty-nine.

That night when we achieved our total, the *Manawanui* arrived back from Campbell Island, and the rattling of the anchor chain signalled the start of the end of the trip. Our taxi home was waiting. At first light we broke camp and took everything down to the beach. The wind had come up, which meant that the Zodiacs had to stay well off from the shoreline rocks. Fortunately this presented few problems for the navy divers, and the wet-suited sailors ferried everything out through the rollers. In many cases it meant a complete soaking, but none of us had any choice if we were to go home. My heart sank, however, as I watched the divers, holding the cages well above their heads, being engulfed in breakers, to resurface from the foam a few minutes later. Having no wetsuits, Dave and I just got wet, and it was with some difficulty that I dragged myself over the pontoons and into the bottom of the boat, laden

Opposite: A frogman in his wetsuit takes back our precious cargo.

CHAPTER NINE **THE END OF THE RABBIT**

down by my heavy, wet clothes. As we came alongside in the lee of the ship, the seas were still too rough to tie up. Synchronised passing and catching was now required, and with the last cage I jumped for the rail as we hit the crest of a swell, and eager hands dragged me on board.

There was no time to get changed. A tarpaulin was laid out in the workshop, and the first of the cages brought in. Every cage had to be stripped down, the bedding changed, the rabbits checked, fresh food and water given, and then on to the next one. Dave came on board with the last load and joined me working side by side. It was an hour or two before we could straighten up, blue with cold, but after hot showers, clean clothes and a cooked meal we really began to feel that we were back in civilisation again, and even my stretcher in the dive chamber began to look attractive.

Dave and I got to know the workshop of the *Manawanui* intimately over the next few days. The rabbits had to be fed, cleaned and watered twice a day. The cages were all stacked in a heap, which we had to dismantle completely to get at the bottom ones, and then work our way back up. Because the workshop was tiny and cramped, space was at an absolute premium and we could manage only by stacking everything and wedging in everything, including ourselves, against the pitch and roll of the ship. Most of the day was occupied with tending to the animals, and so far their inclination to die was gratifyingly absent.

The Otago Harbour is pretty at any time, but it never looked prettier than the afternoon we cruised up the length of it and docked right below the city of Dunedin. Home, but not quite home. In spite of the fact that the rabbits had basically undergone 150 years of quarantining, they were still required to go to the quarantine station on Matiu Somes Island in Wellington Harbour for more testing. Furthermore, they had to stay in isolation on the ship, and footbaths were put down outside the workshop and against the gangways that led on and off the ship, and anyone going inside had to change their clothes. Dave, who needed to get back to Christchurch and a clinic of long-suffering dogs and cats, slipped away early the next morning, leaving me to continue on alone.

The weather was fine and sunny, and we had a couple of days to wait in Port Chalmers, so I decided to take the opportunity for a really good clean-out. I opened the bulkhead door to the aft deck and some of the crew gave me a hand to manhandle the crates out onto the steel plates, where they lay in the sun while I had a thorough scrub inside. The sun and the warmth put everyone in high spirits and once all was shipshape again, I asked the crew to pass everything back in. As they came in, I mentally made a count and we

CHAPTER NINE   THE END OF THE RABBIT

were one rabbit short. Back outside everything went and was then returned, counted both ways. No doubt about it, we were one bunny short of a pack. The feeling that went through me was indescribable. An escaped animal in a quarantine situation was either a MAF dream or a nightmare, depending on how they took it, and the resulting publicity didn't bear thinking about.

The problem was I hadn't counted the rabbits out, so didn't know if the missing animal was still in the workshop, or had escaped when the crew stacked the cages on deck. I stripped out every centimetre of the workshop, and still no rabbit. The others all went out and in again. There was no avoiding the situation. By this time the commander had heard there was an 'incident', and had come down to assess what the problem was.

'Yep we have a bit of a problem,' I said, trying to make light of it. 'We seem to have lost a rabbit.'

'So that's *your* problem. Nothing to do with me and the ship. If you *have* lost a rabbit, what will they do?'

That was a very good question. Some officials would be pragmatic about it, and we could work our way through it. Some of the more serious career governmental types, however, could make things quite difficult.

'Worst case scenario,' I said, 'is that the army would be brought in to hunt it down if it's made it ashore. If they think it's still on board, they may well quarantine the whole ship.'

The look on his face left me with little doubt about his opinion of either of those options and the person who was causing him these hassles.

'I have military exercises in the Pacific. Find that bloody rabbit or solve the problem.'

Now I had had several talks with the commander during the voyage and enjoyed his company and respected his position. He was very much a career seaman who had overcome a number of early obstacles in his life. As a result he had some very fixed views on how to control things, and one of them was that if something or someone was causing a problem, then you should remove it. You don't have time in life to have it cluttered with things that you don't want. I had a very strong feeling that I was cluttering up his life, that he didn't want me and that he was probably regretting that plank walking was no longer an option.

To compound all my problems, DOC then rang, generally tidying up paperwork and entry details.

'How many rabbits did you bring back?'

'Forty-eight on board,' I said quickly, little thinking of the consequences.

'Strange, I thought the ship's radio on the way back said forty-nine.'

'One must have died. We only have forty-eight.'

I got off the phone with a sinking feeling that while it wasn't a complete lie, equally it wasn't the full truth. I hadn't really solved the problem yet and I was in danger of digging a bloody great hole for myself. Where was that rabbit? I went back to the aft deck where the crew had offloaded the cages. They had searched the deck and found nothing. There was a shipping container there that they were lifting off. I waited for the lift to start and stopped it a couple of metres above the deck. Nothing underneath. I started to doubt that we had ever had forty-nine rabbits. Maybe we had made a mistake right at the beginning. Trouble was, Dave as the veterinarian had signed the entry permit for forty-nine rabbits. I got a pen and altered the document to forty-eight.

When I walked in the commander was sitting in the messroom with his head in his hands.

'I've found the problem,' I said. 'We made a mistake right at the beginning. We only ever had forty-eight rabbits.'

He looked at me, stony faced. 'If that's what you say then it must be right,' he said and walked off, shaking his head.

I congratulated myself that I had sorted that problem out until later in the day when I returned to the after deck. It was quiet now; the crew had all gone. I may have convinced some people there were forty-eight rabbits, but I still hadn't convinced myself. I went around the deck slowly and ended up right aft where there was a life raft and chain locker. Metres of heavy coiled chain went back under a low bulkhead. When I got down on my hands and knees and peered in everything looked normal, but what was that lump at the back? After getting a torch, I shone it in and saw, to my relief and disgust, one very greasy rabbit. Looking at him in the eye, I had to decide if he was going to exist or not, but after all the effort that went into getting him, he had to. So, hauling my trophy back, I locked him into his cage and went off to find the commander again.

'You can relax now and go back up into the Pacific to play war games again. I've found another rabbit. We're back up to forty-nine.' Before he could go on about my ancestry, incompetence, procedures and discipline, all of which I deserved, I scuttled away and re-altered the entry form back to the original figure.

Just when I thought I had everything sorted out, a MAF official came on board with a clipboard and a large plastic bag, which he waved at me.

'Come to pick up the corpse,' he said. 'Have to do an autopsy on it, of course.'

CHAPTER NINE **THE END OF THE RABBIT**

More quick thinking.

'Sorry, but it didn't actually die. Thought it was going to but amazingly enough it recovered fully. Don't know what was wrong with it. It's that one over there.'

Before he could question a rather difficult situation, a bevy of television crews and reporters arrived, all wanting to capture this historic event, and the MAF became the centre of attention while I gratefully made yet another undignified disappearance.

Following the shore leave we weighed anchor and headed directly up the east coast of the South Island, headed for Wellington. The lines were hot with DOC, MAF and a host of publicity machines gearing up for the arrival of these bunnies. The quarantine station on Matiu Somes Island was coming out of mothballs and getting prepared to accommodate them. Everything depended on the date and time of the ship's arrival, and once I had obtained that from the commander, I passed the ETA on to everyone concerned. I was now back to my old routine of feeding, cleaning and trying to keep everything stable as we punched our way into a vicious sea off the Kaikoura coastline. Half a day out and I got a call to go to the bridge. The commander was there, pacing agitatedly backwards and forwards.

'I told you we were going to arrive Thursday at Somes, right?'

I nodded.

'You've told everyone that, and they're all expecting us, right?'

Again the safest thing to do seemed to be to nod, which I did.

'Well, you're wrong. It's Wednesday that we get in. Okay, so you lost a rabbit and I've lost a day. I don't know how it happened. Get on to comms and sort it. Tell them I've cancelled some defence manoeuvres or something and that's why we're going to be a day early.'

I must admit I felt a hell of a lot better, and my relationship with the commander was restored. Because there was no docking space on the island for a vessel the size of the *Manawanui*, MAF was sending out a smaller vessel to rendezvous with us, and it was to be a ship-to-ship transfer for the rabbits. That was the rabbits sorted, but I still had to get to Wellington somehow. Since there was no way off Matiu Somes, it looked as if I was stuck with nowhere to go, and no way of getting there. 'No worries,' said the commander, pointing on the chart to a small stony bay on the very edge of the city. 'We'll anchor off, and the boys will run you ashore in a Zodiac.' This is going to be a great climax, I thought. The chances of some public-spirited citizen not seeing a Zodiac with black-suited frogmen landing a man in civilian clothes with a suitcase who then walked into the city, were small, and I would spend

157

the night in some watch tower trying to explain to disbelieving officials that I wasn't a spy. It was going to be a long night. As it happened, however, MAF wanted me on the island to do the transfer and settle the rabbits in. They then ran me across the harbour to a small jetty near Petone, where John Simister was waiting to pick me up, and within an hour or so I was back on land with a welcome gin in what was left of my hands. The last couple of weeks had seen them torn and scratched so many times that they and my forearms were a bloody network of injuries, and it was to be a long time before they were socially acceptable again.

The phrase 'breeding like rabbits' now has a totally new meaning for me. If I thought that the Enderby rabbit was now safe and well, then I was sadly mistaken: the problems were far from over.

The quarantine period for the rabbits finished and I drove up to Wellington and picked them up from the boat that brought them across from Matiu Somes Island. Four different breeding groups were identified, and these were given out to breeders who had expressed an interest in their conservation. We sat back waiting for the numbers to explode.

It didn't happen. As the months passed and the results came in, they showed very little breeding activity, and more than a few heads were being scratched. What the problem was, nobody knew. The months turned into a year, which turned into another and so on. Still the results were dismal and the answers missing. I took a couple of pairs home to my breeding farm, and released them into some enclosures. Much to my surprise they started to breed, and within a short space in time I had had several litters. It was hard to identify why, but as they were being run in a semi-natural environment and were lean, fit rabbits, possibly the others were being looked after just a bit too well. After four or five years of breeding, the number of females had still not risen above 100. It was a setback that no one had predicted. Rabbits are supposed to be easy to breed, and this was showing every indication of being embarrassing for all concerned. Animals were exported to the United States where a small group of breeders became established, but they, too, have had mixed and limited results.

One evening when I was at Staglands John referred me to a book that he was reading about rural life in Britain. It talked about the royal rabbits of Carperby, in Yorkshire, which were unique in that they were born black and changed to an attractive silver grey colour as they matured. No one knew of their origin, but local legend had it that they were introduced by Sir Walter Raleigh, after one of his marauding sea voyages. They were called royal rabbits, not only because of the Raleigh connection, but also because the pelts were highly prized, and the royal families used their fur to trim their ceremonial clothes. Tsar Nicholas of Russia was presented with a fine cloak lined entirely with the skins of these rabbits.

Over the years that records had been kept, several of the rabbits had been exported. Could these be the origin of our bunnies? A house had been built alongside the warren for a gamekeeper to live in and look after the rabbits. According to the book, it's called Warren House to this day. It had been a long night, so we got on the phone and eventually, rather to our surprise, were connected to Warren House. They were equally surprised, but once we made our way through the more difficult explanations, it was a delightful call. The remains of the warren were still there, but unfortunately they could give us no more information than we already had.

No one knows the exact origin of the Enderby rabbits. No one knows why they are born black and go grey as they mature, unlike any other rabbit breed except perhaps those royal bunnies of Carperby, which are extinct now in the rest of the world, but may be just hanging on in the Antipodes. A fairy tale maybe, but then maybe not. As I watch the little grey rabbits hopping around their enclosure at Willowbank, I sometimes half shut my eyes and can hear the crash of the surf, the calls of the birds and shipwrecked sailors, and visualise that endless cacophony of wildlife carrying on as it has for centuries. These animals are our heritage and our responsibility, and should not be allowed to just disappear and be swallowed up into the past.

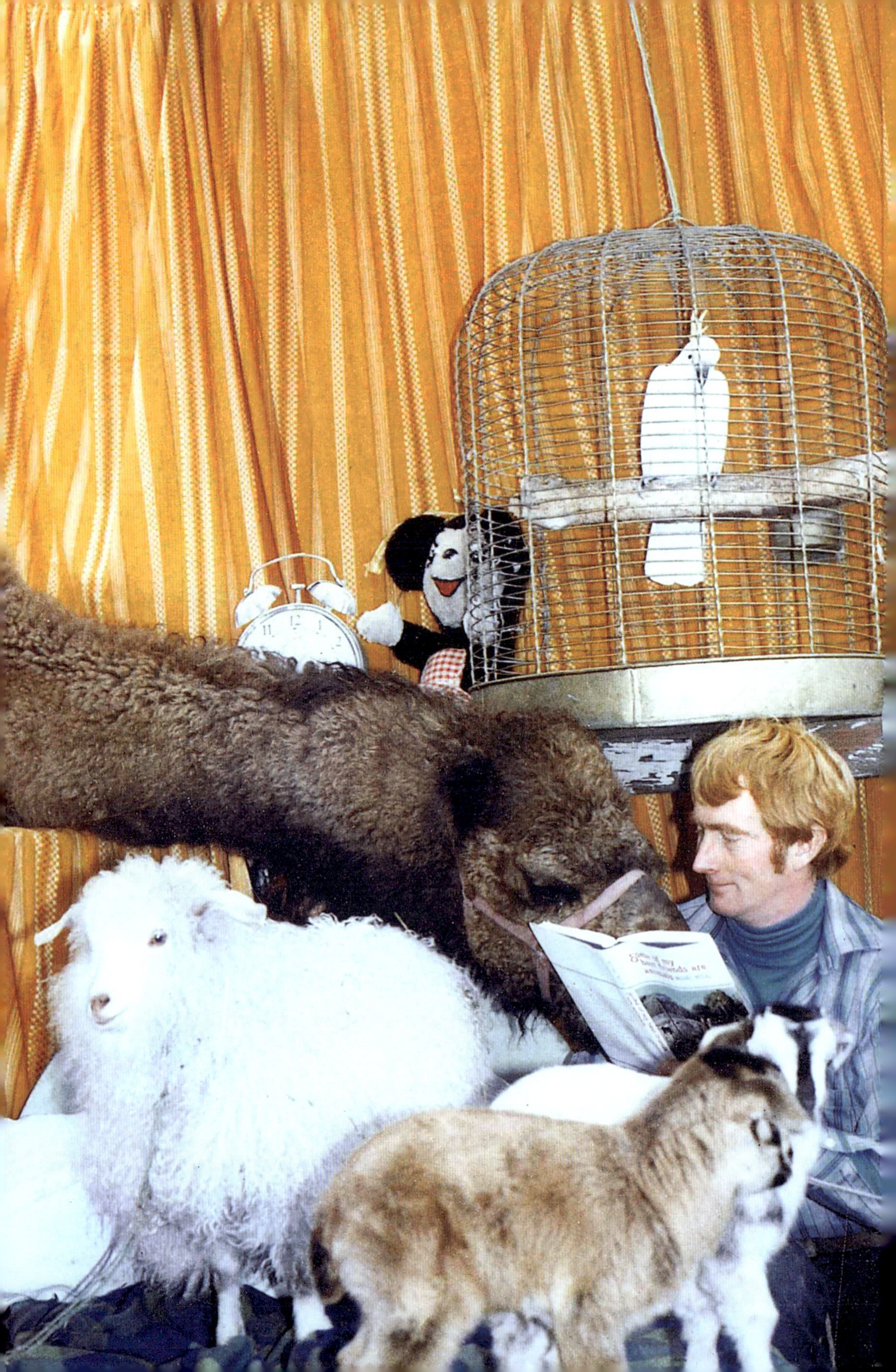
Some of my
best friends are
animals

CHAPTER TEN

CHASING RAINBOWS

Opposite: Along the way I wrote a book. *Some of My Best Friends are Animals* was published in 1983. Kasbah the camel and some mates helped with the publicity.

Following two pages: Tractors have been used for a variety of tasks at Willowbank over the years.
Press

The years passed, and Willowbank slowly developed in line with our growing income. It was a Catch 22 situation: we needed to make larger improvements than we could afford, but weren't in a position to take out a loan. No one animal was going to improve our situation, and so we needed to do something different and big with the park.

I made an exception to not extending our financial commitment when our neighbour offered to sell me some 3.2 hectares of his land. It was an opportunity that I couldn't turn down, further supporting my father's opinion that I lacked any commercial judgement. So now we had just over 8 hectares, but were also almost broke. We decided to shift the park entrance down to this new block of land, which allowed us, for the first time, to create a carpark. I was offered an 8- by 2.5-metre shed off a poultry farm that had closed down, and was full of old chicken brooders. I borrowed a truck, got some car jacks and wooden pallets, and lifted it high enough to sit on the pallets and back the truck underneath. Hoping that there was no one around to pull me over and ask awkward questions, I began a nervous sweaty-palmed trip down the motorway and into the new carpark, where the process was reversed until the shed sat triumphantly on its piles. The brooders inside I sold for enough to cover all of the costs with a few left over for the park. Next we were given a garage that we dismantled and I built it on as a lean-to extension. With a verandah off the front it looked quite quaint, if rather rustic.

One day while picking up some slab offcuts at the local timber mill, I noticed a large tower-like structure lying against a high hedge. The owner

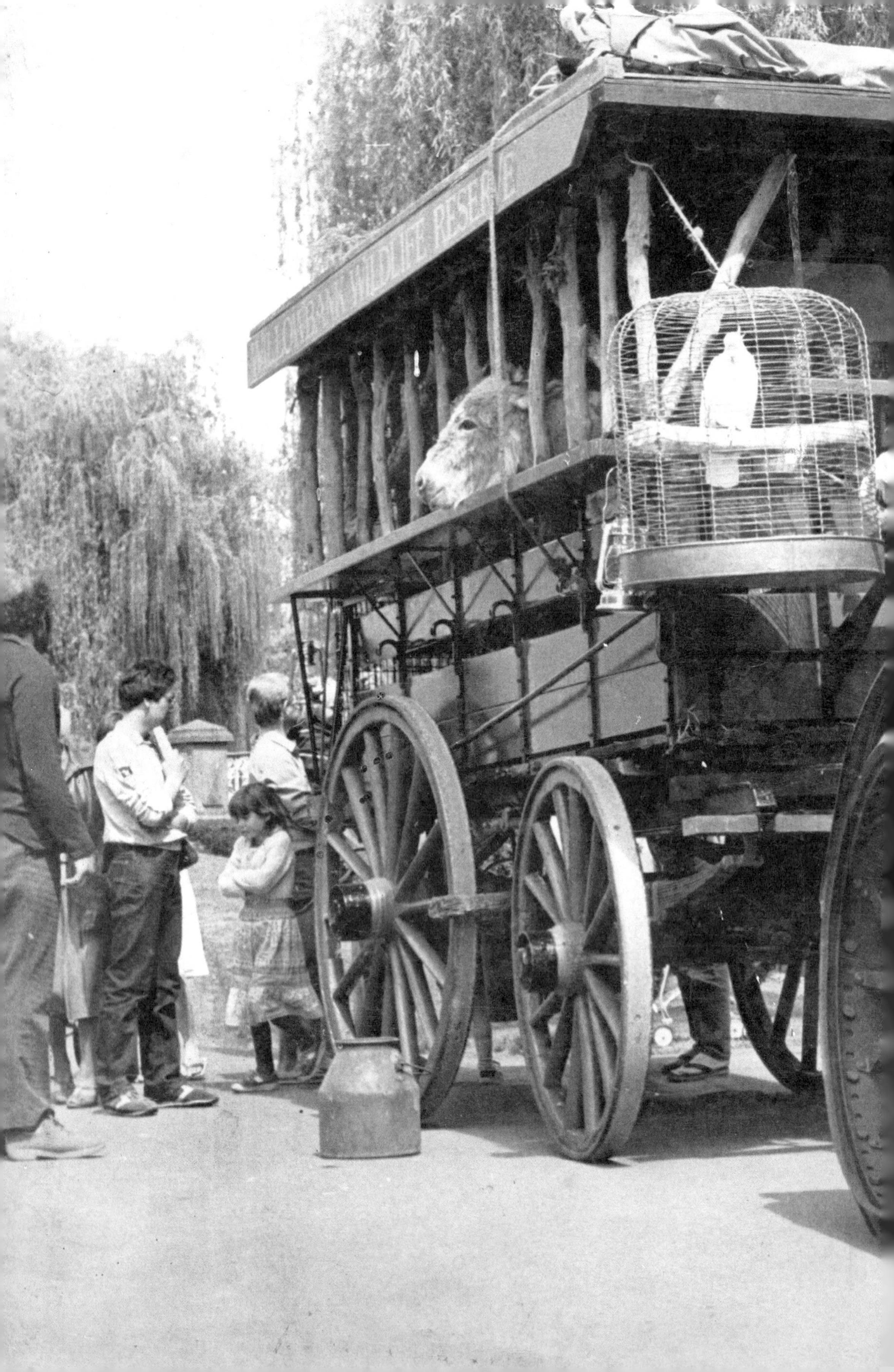
WILDLIFE RESERVE

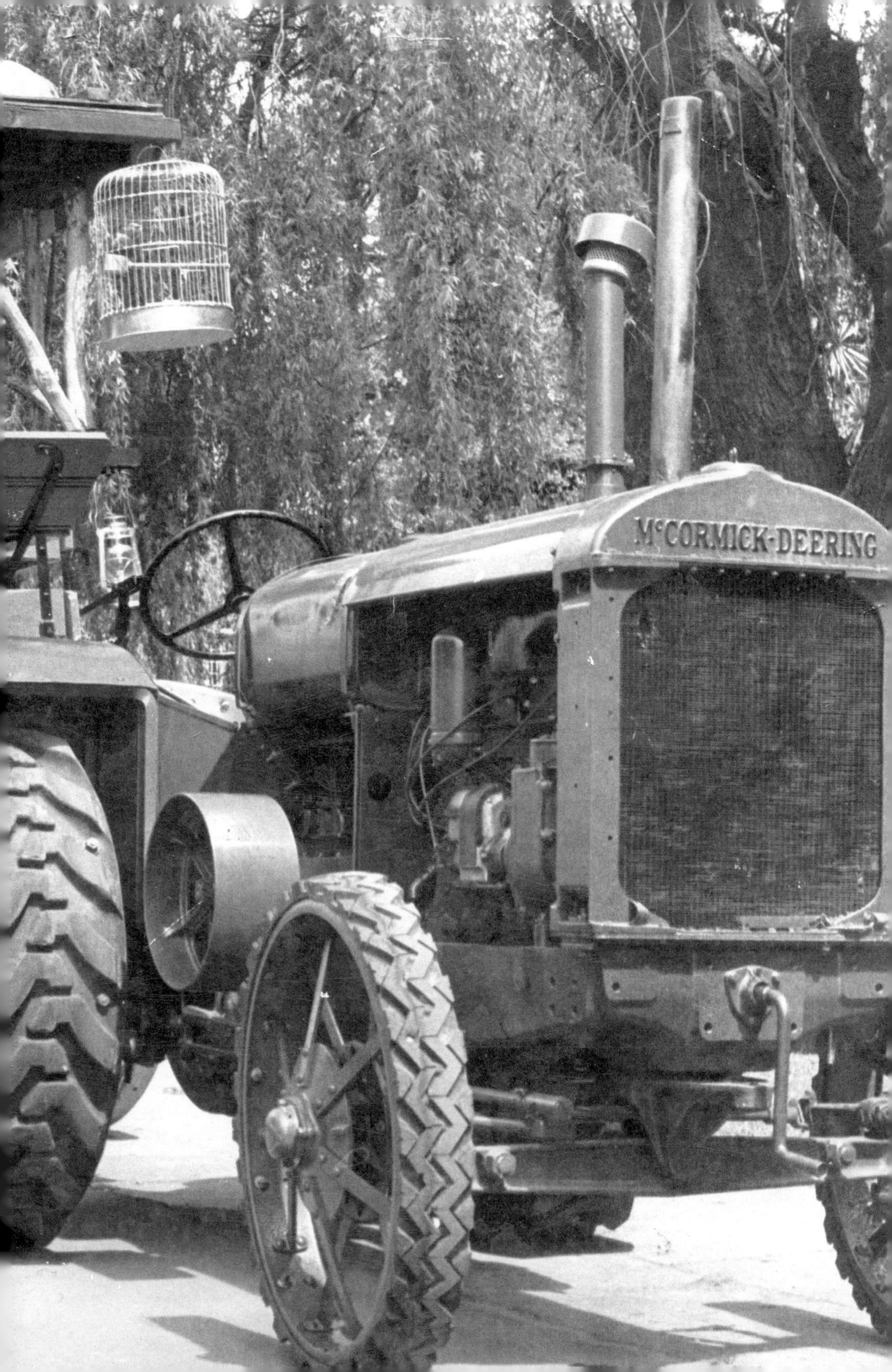
McCORMICK-DEERING

told me it used to be an old railway water tank tower, and had been there for years. Some serious negotiations took place, which led to me purchasing the tower, delivered, for $100 plus two turtles for his daughter. A few days later it arrived around five in the morning, transported with forklifts front and rear. Stood up next to the new entrance sheds, it made an imposing structure, and on top, instead of a water tank, I built a dovecote with a slate roof. The whole structure, made of solid kauri, is still one of the most photographed objects at Willowbank.

Now that we had shifted the entrance to its new site, the building we had used in the past for entry also needed to be relocated. The plan was to tow it up the road by using fence posts as rollers, and on the appointed Saturday we had everything ready. With the aid of Don and the Beagle Boys, we jacked the building up and slid round fenceposts underneath. I had an old Fordson Super Major tractor, and with wire ropes around the building slid it first sideways onto the road and then started our slow 200-metre crawl. As the building rolled forward we would pick up the posts from behind and put them in front and so on as we rumbled our way up. We took up almost the full width of the road but vehicles could get past by going onto the grass verge. As we progressed, however, the building got a sideways shift to it, almost blocking the road and creating a reasonable sort of traffic hazard. Fortunately at that stage it wasn't a busy thoroughfare. The 200 metres went very slowly, and we just got to the entrance of the carpark by the end of the day. There, though, we stuck. Once we were off the seal and onto shingle, we lost traction and the tractor was just digging holes in the gravel with its wheels. It was an awkward situation that lasted until the next morning when I managed to cajole a couple of guys with forklifts to come around and pick the building up, finally clearing the road. Once it was placed on the piles that had been prepared alongside the new entranceway, we had a conglomeration of buildings that we could then join together to create a new ticketing, retail and refreshment complex. You could never plan an arrangement like that. It was a dynamic thing that just happened, would never be replicated, but was functional. In a way, too, its character reflected that of the park itself – solid, quirky, created with love and enthusiasm and at a price we could afford.

At one point in the 1980s we had a visit from some people we knew who largely owned and managed a major tour company. 'Were we interested in selling?'

Answer: 'Definitely not.'

'Would you be interested then in a joint venture?'

'Keep talking.'

CHAPTER TEN CHASING RAINBOWS

New Zealand was in a good commercial space at this time. Business was booming and tourism looked to become a major player. This company had decided in principle to buy up what tourist facilities that they could throughout New Zealand and had already made some significant purchases. The more we talked about it, the more the idea had some appeal. They were heavily into transporting tourists, and they would bring the people and had the promotional and administration to assist with the growth. It was a case of lose some to gain some, but we thought that it might just be the lift that we needed to get into the big time. So we agreed to sell 50 per cent of the park, and that began the start of a whole new development.

After all the work we had done, our new entry buildings were no longer suitable for the numbers being projected, and we asked three architects to draw up plans for a replacement. One looked like Sir George Grey's Mansion House on Kawau Island, one looked like a castle that should have dragons in the moat, and the last was from a local architect, Stewart Ross, who based his design on old farm buildings. He won hands down, and the contract to build it was let to Peter Stevens, our neighbour up the road who had helped with many things in the past.

Along with the entrance building we also needed to upgrade the park itself. There wasn't enough money for the whole lot, and so we focused on what we called the New Zealand area, and its wildlife. I got in big diggers and turned the place upside down, creating hills, ponds and landscaping by placing truckloads of the biggest boulders we could get down from the mountains. We built a massive free flight walk through the kea cage. We made our own wire rope by twisting up No. 8 wire on a tractor. We drove nails through skis so we could walk all over the roof of the structure on the netting, working from above to fasten it down. This job usually fell to my son Mark, who at that stage was one of the lightest and more biddable participants. We created a bush aviary over the Māori village and fenced off and planted a large area of native bush for kiwi viewing.

It was to be a one-way walk that went through a series of experiences ranging from a fish-laden pond, to an alpine re-creation, through the bush and on to the kiwi viewing area and out. I had an idea for this, which was based around the restaurant we were creating and the tours. I wanted to create Wildlife By Night, which was aimed at showing the animals in their natural surroundings. I had been to Singapore Zoo and seen the way they did night tours there. Nothing like this however had been done before in New Zealand, and it became an exciting project creating lighting effects and ways of generating displays that people could easily view and participate in. We

Following two pages: Willowbank at night became a magical place, as this photo of the impressive front entrance shows. The reception area and shop are to the right, the cafe further back in the building, to the left. The Māori figure advertises the park's popular Ko Tāne experience.

welc
WARNING!
Kotāne
the Maori experience
• kiwi tours
• restaurant
• wildlife

Willowbank
CLUB
Willowbank
JOIN NOW!
• Best Value
• Unlimited Entry
• Exclusive Events & Discounts

The heights we went to when building the aviary. My son Mark is on the skis.

won a tourism award for that development, and after a grand opening we were full of confidence. It was, however, short-lived. We were on the crest of a wave, and there was a big trough underneath us.

In October 1987 the sharemarket crashed. Tourism died along with many of the companies that relied on it. We had been a little bit naive in the beginning, but all we could see was the way forward. Our partners were now in deep financial trouble, had been bought out by another international corporate and wanted out. Interest rates were rising and hitting over 20 per cent. The water in the sink was going down the gurgler fast, and it would not be long before we were left high and dry.

CHAPTER TEN CHASING RAINBOWS

By now we were the only ones dealing with the bank manager, and the meetings were becoming more frequent and uncomfortable. During one he was morosely studying some figures I had given him to read when Kathy brightly offered, 'And of course we're separating as well.' The bank manager leant back in his chair and studied his fingernails for a moment. 'You may think that I have horns,' he said holding a finger on each side of his head as if to illustrate the point, 'but someday you'll thank me for this. So many people in your position just need someone to make some decisions for them. So I'm referring you to the top floor of the main branch.' I didn't quite know what that meant, but it didn't sound too good.

A couple of weeks later we presented ourselves on the top floor, where we were met by not one but two bank managers. We must be becoming important, I thought. They were an odd combination: one looked like a cheerful little Irishman with a ready smile, while the other could easily have been an All Black prop. They started off with the usual jolly conversation about how they were going to do us a favour, and we would thank them in a few years' time. I interrupted them. 'If you think you're going to close the park down, then it's not going to be that easy. If I have to shoot all the animals, I will, then I'll load them into a horse float and drop the whole lot on the steps of this bank with the TV crews waiting.'

There was a long silence. They looked at each other, then, shrugging their shoulders, turned back to me and said, 'Well, what do you want to do?' That was actually the start of a long and fruitful relationship. I soon worked out that the moment I didn't have a plan or showed any sign of weakness, then they would jump in, but they were reluctant to do so if there was anything in place that may help the situation. So at every meeting I would have some scheme that I had dredged up to create some money. Some ideas were good and they worked. Some ideas were crazy and the bank men would shake their heads in disbelief. But overall many worked and money still kept coming in. On top of that, they were really helpful with advice, and after a few months we pretty much had two free business advisers who helped to make an appreciable difference to the outcome. Interest rates slowly dropped and after a year or so we had weathered the worst, and a couple more years later were back on a regular banking footing. It had been a steep learning curve and left me with even less desire to ever owe money again and have the future of the park and its inhabitants exposed to the whims of others.

Our partners still had their 50 per cent shareholding and were desperate to sell. This wasn't going to be easy, for anyone who bought in had to deal with me, and I was now a bit cautious about having another partner, so it wasn't an attractive situation for any potential investor. Our partners had been taking no active interest in the operation for some time, including the running of the restaurant, for which they were supposed to be responsible. It was a big headache, very specialised and high stress, with a large turnover of often melodramatic staff. After the last chef threw his pots out the door I contacted the partners and asked what they wanted to do. 'Nothing,' was the response. 'It's all yours.' By this time Kathy had put her own family money into the retail and souvenirs, and so I decided to take the gamble and run the restaurant in my own account. It was the start of a new appreciation of an utterly different and completely alien world.

I started from scratch. I peeled the spuds and washed and cut the carrots. I weighed the meat and did the costings. I started to grasp the skill that went into being a good chef, and the difference between being a cook, a chef and a top chef. I couldn't afford top chefs at that stage, and I soon learnt that some were a fairly fickle if fascinating breed in their own right. At one end of the scale they could be incredibly temperamental. As someone advised me, if you have to admonish a chef for any reason, then get him out of the kitchen and away from the knives. This was actually pretty close to being right.

One of the first chefs we employed came with excellent qualifications, private school education and from a well-respected family. We had great hopes for his future, but then came a few incidents that started to cause us some concern. It culminated one wet miserable winter Sunday when no one really wanted to be out visiting a wildlife park. We did, however, have a booking for a small group for lunch, and at the appointed time they duly arrived. I watched in some disbelief as the chef, wearing full dinner suit and tails, and with a bugle slung over his shoulder, met them at the front door with a low bow and greeted them effusively. Although a bit taken aback, they said that they would be quite happy to have a warm seat by the fire and look at the menu. No, the chef was having none of that. He marched them through the building and out the back door and into the rain and told them to wander around the park as he wasn't ready for them yet. Thrusting umbrellas in their hands, he instructed them to listen for the tune from his bugle, 'Come to the Cook House Door, Boys', and then they could come back in for lunch. About an hour later he bugled them back in and sat them shivering at the table, wondering what was going to happen next. He was the wine waiter, the waiter and the chef, and could never quite sort out what role he should be doing next. I got a better understanding of what the problem was when I saw him sitting in his car between courses, sucking on what was left of a bottle of sherry. The people arrived about midday, and left about four. When

CHAPTER TEN **CHASING RAINBOWS**

they left he produced his bugle with a flourish, and played 'Reveille', as he escorted them to their car.

It had been a funny afternoon, and I would hate to think what the customers thought, but from a commercial view it wasn't really a very good performance. Back in the restaurant as he was tidying up I mentioned that his behaviour needed some attention, whereupon he picked up a casserole dish and hurled it across the restaurant at me to shatter all over the fireplace. Bursting into tears, he then disappeared back into the kitchen, and I never saw him again.

Another chef who stands out was a big powerful guy who used to cook on the Interislander ferries. He had worked at Willowbank for a few months, and although he wasn't particularly good, we were grateful to have him since it was the Christmas period and we were very busy with group bookings. One evening I was relaxing at home when the phone went and it was Christine the maitre d'. 'We have an issue,' she said. 'The chef is drunk and he's chasing the waitresses around the kitchen trying to kiss them. They're now too scared to go back in.'

As I walked into the building I could see a full restaurant of guests who appeared to be chattering away quite happily, and with good reason, as the staff had been filling up their glasses to play for time. 'Keep the door shut,' I told Christine, 'and if there's too much noise coming out of the kitchen, start to sing "Auld Lang Syne".' I burst into the kitchen, where the chef was leaning against the prep table. I threw him into the dry goods store and had a word to him. Later I dragged him out into the yard and sat him in a chair. He was crying and snuffling and saying that nobody loved him, and his boyfriend had just run away with somebody else. By then Christine had got the staff back into the kitchen and they were starting to get some food out. Half an hour or so later and I was able to get the chef back behind his counter, considerably sobered up, and with no desire to chase the girls again. He didn't like girls anyway.

The first month or so I lost money, but then got things back on track and we started to make headway again. It was time consuming and most nights I would be down there, generally keeping an eye on things, and locking up at

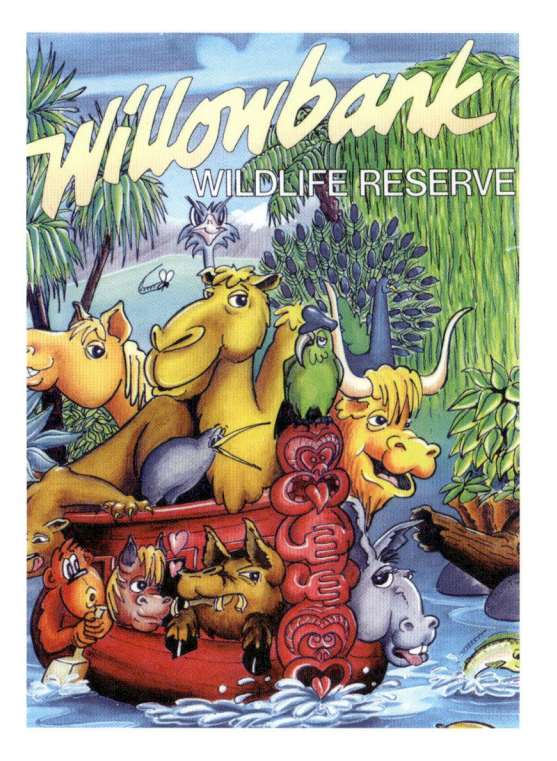

A commissioned illustration sums up the variety that was Willowbank at the time.

Seeing kiwi up close at night.

the end. I could easily understand the passion that good operators have for the food industry, and I found it quite exciting and requiring a whole range of new and different skill sets which, combined with artistic flair and creativity, make the experts very special people.

Integral with the restaurant were the nocturnal displays and tours. Most people never quite realise that a large percentage of wildlife actually prefers to come out in the dark. You see this only when you walk around with a torch or spotlight, or sit quietly under a tree on the edge of the bush or river at night, or maybe glimpses from your window while driving. A lot of birds are the exception, but then most waterfowl and many marsh birds are

CHAPTER TEN **CHASING RAINBOWS**

Above: Willowbank in darkness was a special sight.

Above right: Other creatures were also part of the Wildlife by Night experience.

always active at night. Kea certainly are, along, of course, with owls and kiwi. Most animals are out grazing in the protection of darkness, and most aquatic species are certainly busy then. You can create magic by using lighting effects, and training the animals to respond. The deer would put their heads through the windows of the restaurant, kea would be flying down to you, the kiwi would be out playing as you would never otherwise see them and the eels would writhe and twist in knots in front of floodlit viewing windows. The display also changed with the seasons. During the winter the mist would float up in ethereal streams from the water so that you felt you had stepped into the geyserland of some thermal resort.

When we first opened Wildlife By Night, it was slow. Some nights there would be no customers. Some nights there might be only one or two wanting a guided tour and I would go down, open up and take them around. My policy was always that we were open for business, and if someone turned up then they would be given an experience. Gradually it became busier and busier until there were hardly any nights, even in the depths of winter, that we didn't have customers. Locals would come with their friends, Scout groups would front up, and of course it really suited tourists, who came by the busload. It was a strong and innovative point of difference that made us unique in New Zealand. For me it was the high point in the development of the park.

Eventually I made enough money out of the restaurant to buy our 50 per cent of the company back and had full ownership once again. It had been an interesting ride that could have gone any way, but we were better for it, stronger for it and had no desire to repeat the mistakes of the past.

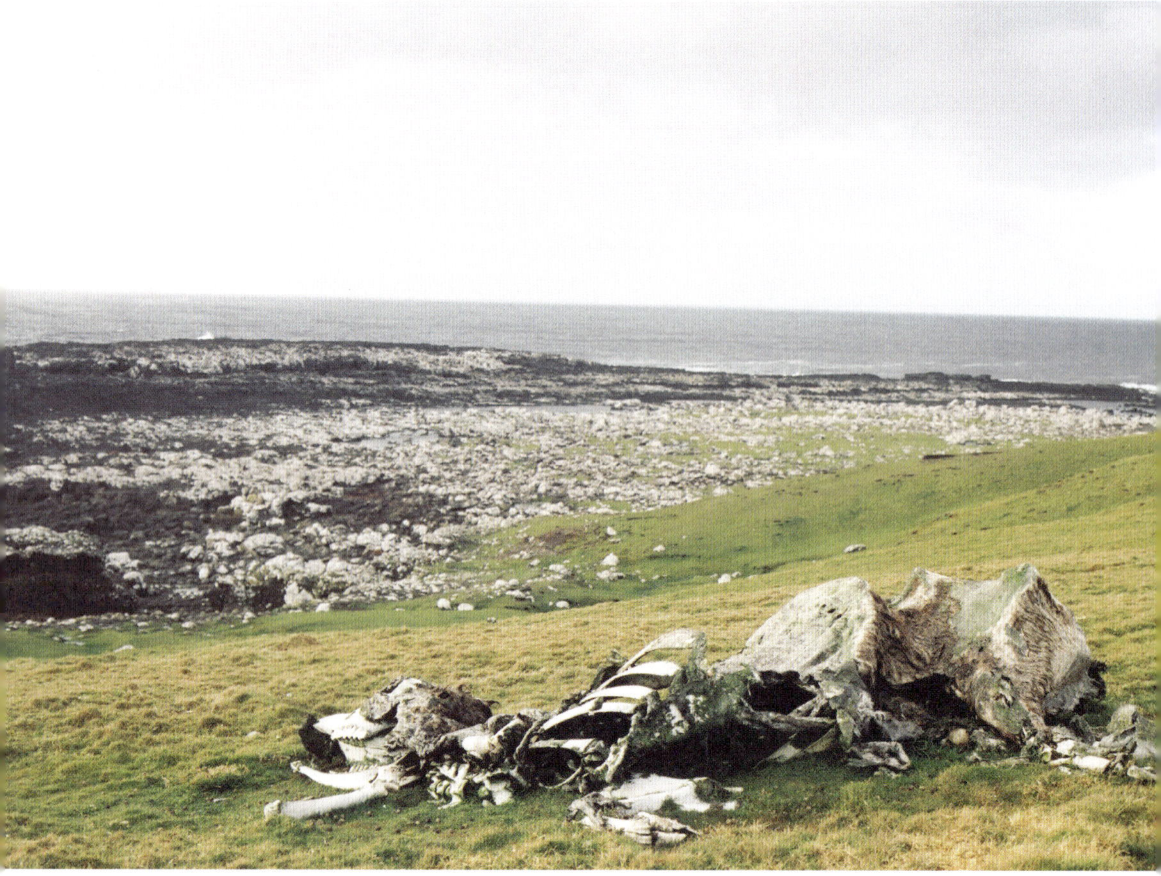

CHAPTER ELEVEN

THE SEAWEED-EATING COW

The wind buffeted in, hurling the savage sea against the granite cliffs of Enderby Island, with such a force that you would have to wonder how such a tiny speck in such a vast ocean could have withstood the elements for so long. The wind was an icy blast, for there was nothing between here and the Antarctic Continent but ocean and ice packs, which just last night had brought a flurry of snow around our camp. From where Dave Matheson and I were standing the landscape was open and desolate, a few twisted rata stumps clinging tenaciously to the peat, while the grass rose from the perilous cliff faces and up into the low windswept hilltops. In spite of the desolation, there was a grandeur in the landscape. It reminded me very much of the coast in the top of Scotland, except where in that country Highland cattle, purple heather and red stags predominated, here there were sea lions and penguins. Life tended to be short here, both for its inhabitants and the small number of human intruders who visited by choice or by misfortune. Below us in the foaming surf were the exposed teeth of the Derry Castle Reef, so named for the ship wrecked there in March 1887 with the loss of fifteen men. It had swallowed numerous other lives with unremorseful ease, leaving nothing but a memory and the odd shipwrecked survivor, who lived to tell the tale.

A memory was just what we were looking at now: the bones of a cattle beast. They were starting to bleach in the elements, but were still being held together by tattered fragments of skin, enough to tell its sex, age, colour – and how it had died. Above and between the eye sockets, perfectly round as if drilled, was an obvious bullet hole. It was with mixed feelings that I looked

Opposite: The carcase of a cattle beast on Enderby Island seemed to tell a story of extinction.

at the remains, for these were the bones of no ordinary cow, they were the last remnants of a herd of what was said to be early shorthorns, which had lived here alone and isolated for almost a century. They were believed to have been exterminated, but there had also been rumours from fishermen claiming to have seen one that may have escaped. The killing had happened a year or so ago, and I was intrigued with the possibility that maybe one animal had survived. The answer lay in front of me, as clear as writing in a book. Hoof prints and fresh ones at that. Approximately three or four weeks old we guessed. But that wasn't all. Alongside the prints of the cow, we could also see, keeping close to her side, those of a smaller animal. A calf. It just had to be a cow who had delivered a calf after the killing. A sense of elation gripped me.

We followed the prints across the grass and they led unerringly to another old carcase. The two sets walked around the stark remains and set off again. A short journey later and they stopped again at another pitiful patch of bones. That cow led us from carcase to carcase, and my heart went out to this beast on its lonely and pitiful pilgrimage, as she checked and nudged yet again the remains of her friends, in the vain hope that just maybe they could provide her with some much needed companionship. 'Just give me half a chance,' I promised, 'and I'll come back and get you. No longer will you live here alone.'

The story really began in 1895, when the *Hinemoa* landed some nine cattle and twenty sheep on Enderby Island for W. J. Moffett of Invercargill, who had taken up the pastoral lease. (Three runs had been offered on the Auckland Islands in November 1894 and Enderby was the most northern.) Over the years the number of cattle seemed to stabilise at about twenty rather stunted animals, struggling to adapt to an environment for which they were never intended. Adapt they had, out of necessity, for even the grass that they yearned for was eaten to ground level most of the time by a fluctuating rabbit population. They lived on tussocks that they could grab on cliff faces without crashing onto the rocks below, and by learning to browse on shrubs and other vegetation. When all else failed and they needed bulk, then they would fill up on seaweed driven up onto the rocky shore.

Almost a century went by and apart from providing the odd bit of meat for a passing fishing boat, the cattle went unnoticed and unmolested. That is until DOC decided that they were having a negative effect on the environment, and really had to go. At the time of the first cull, in 1991, some scientists tried to take semen and embryos from the dead animals, in an attempt to retain some genetic material. They obtained no embryos and only some poor quality semen. That should have been the end of the story but since my 1992

CHAPTER ELEVEN **THE SEAWEED-EATING COW**

discovery I had had evidence that one, if not two, animals had survived, and a promise to fulfil. How to catch them was the big question. The solution came through a friend who rang me one morning and said, 'I've found you a chopper. Richard Hayes has a Squirrel rated for offshore use. He already has a fuel dump at Stewart Island and with his long-range tanks he can fly from there to Enderby. I've spoken to him, and he says it's quite possible to do the job for you.' This was just the break I had been hoping for. Richard, later Sir Richard and better known as Hannibal, had recently also had an approach from DOC to fly down and drop their poison baits for the rabbit eradication. If that was confirmed, he could do both jobs.

The weeks went by and DOC's involvement and support were in place, and we could also use their supply ship, the *Marine Countess*. The hold would then be empty and could be free for the cattle on the return trip, if we were successful. There was, of course, no guarantee that the helicopter would get down there, as any significant weather changes would prevent it from flying, and that was a real possibility in that region. The next best option was a tranquillising rifle and good old-fashioned hunting skills. To succeed, however, I had to be able to stalk to within a reasonably close range.

The fresh hoof prints of hope.

The *Marine Countess*, which normally serviced the southern coast of New Zealand, was about 30 metres long. She would be carrying five crew, vet Peter Trolove, who was accompanying me, and two DOC officers going down to study the effects of the wild pigs on the vegetation of the main Auckland Island. Straight out from Bluff we hit the open sea with a vengeance, as the Southern Ocean gave us a typical reception. It was with relief and rising excitement that, after a few days, we reached the calm waters of Sandy Bay, on Enderby, and dropped anchor a few hundred metres offshore. The whales weren't there to welcome us this time, but the four DOC personnel who were to poison the rabbits were very pleased to see us. They had been dropped off earlier, after hitching a ride on a foreign cruise ship. We spent the next few hours ferrying off supplies and then erecting a tent camp for ourselves inside the edge of the rata forest. It was wonderful to be back on Enderby, and I recognised a few old friends among the bird and animal inhabitants.

Later that day, we headed out to ascertain the whereabouts or otherwise of the cow we had come so far to find. I guessed that she wouldn't be far from where I had seen her tracks back in 1992. That's where her friends lay, and there was plenty of cover and protection from the elements, so it seemed a logical place to start. We climbed through the bush to the midline of the island and started to drop down the other side towards the Derry Castle Reef. It was a route I knew well, having travelled it several times before, and I was looking forward to the spectacular views of the surf pounding the coast and foaming over the infamous reef on the exposed tip of the island. We picked our way quietly down into a scrub-filled gully, stopping every now and then to glass the countryside for any sign of our prey. Suddenly, there in the distance, held above the scrub, were the unmistakable head and horns of a cow, who had obviously seen us about the same time as we had seen her, and with the same amount of astonishment. She eyed us for only a second, before, to my dismay, she put her head down, her tail came up over her back and she dived headlong into the tangled mass of vegetation and disappeared. I wasn't expecting such a violent reaction. No other inhabitants on the island behaved like that and before the shooting people had been able to walk around very close to the herd. It was obvious, however, that such acute reflexes had stood her in good stead in the past and there was no way that she was going to drop the habit now. She obviously had a bit of a grudge against humans. This behaviour certainly laid down some ground rules: I was now under no illusions about how she would view any attempt I made to capture her. The most exciting thing was that we had actually seen the mythical cow. She was alive and looked like having every intention of staying that way. Not wishing to aggravate the situation in any way, we backed right off and left her alone to settle while we contemplated future moves.

The next few days were very much a matter of waiting to see what options were going to be available to us. The *Marine Countess* had by now departed for the main island in the Auckland group, leaving us alone and isolated. Everything now hinged on whether the helicopter was able to attempt the flight down. While there was a chance of that happening, I had no intention of attempting any ground capture, but there was always plenty to do in just trying to live in a tent as part of the local community. This was made slightly more difficult by the presence of large numbers of sea lions in a high state of sexual excitement, hell bent on claiming any bit of coastal land

CHAPTER ELEVEN **THE SEAWEED-EATING COW**

as summer camp for their harems. Because, to us, the boundaries were indistinct, we got a lot of abuse and had to be quick on our feet travelling through these areas. Back from the coast, through the scrub and peat, ran streams and rivulets that went back and up a few hundred metres towards the tops. For whatever reason animals, especially young bulls, would travel up these water courses, sliding backwards and forwards, creating their own luges. It wasn't uncommon, half an hour or so from the coast, to trip over a large animal lying in the scrub meditating on its existence. Some of these routes became black greasy highways and all of this activity made clean water a valued commodity. We obtained this only by collecting rain water, which fortunately was a very constant commodity.

No matter where you put your tent, it seemed to be always in someone's way. Sea lions were continually passing through our camp, blocking the way to the toilet, or getting caught up in our tent guy ropes, with hardly even a look of reproach. One night I woke up with a suffocating pressure pushing me into the dirt, until I began to feel like an opossum who hadn't quite made it past the dotted white line. I punched with all my strength into the shapeless mass of blubber that was enveloping me, and was gratified to hear a woof and feel whoever it was shuffle off into the night to bed down with some more peaceable companions.

Sea lion pups were no respecters of our tents and equipment.

The sea lion pups were just delightful. Pup hardly seems the right word for an animal the size of a large labrador, but they had the same inquisitive and playful nature as any such household pet and got up to just as much mischief. They were all around us when we were cooking, continually trying to get into my tent, and indeed succeeded on a couple of occasions. It was imperative, whenever we were leaving camp, to zip everything up and tie what was left out of reach. They had the most beautiful round, black, limpid eyes that would gaze up at you so trustingly and they would think nothing of wriggling up to sniff enquiringly at your hand or leg. Any movement towards them, however, and they were away like a lot of gigantic animated caterpillars, and God help you if they thought that you had any sinister designs and they barked in distress. Most of a tonne of agitated mother would come crashing into view, venting her wrath in foul-smelling roars and barks so that you had no option but to vacate the camp until things quietened down again.

In spite of our entertaining neighbours, we still had a job to do, and I spent hours every day familiarising myself with the area where we had seen the cow and building up a general picture of her movements and habits. I knew now that she did have a calf at foot, probably female, and I could see that the cow was never totally relaxed, always looking up to find anything suspicious or out of place. She was going to be a hard animal to catch unawares and she and her calf were obviously inseparable.

The sun was going down on another day, and I left them to their solitude, and rather reluctantly slipped away to fumble my way through the bush, and in the dark back to camp. As I reached the DOC base I ran into Nic Torr, the DOC ranger, who said, 'All going well, the chopper should be here at about midday.' Great news. So much depended on the helicopter's arrival: should it not be able to get down, all the projects were at risk. Everyone was up early the next morning. Fortunately the weather looked unusually perfect and we had high hopes. The *Marine Countess* had arrived back during that night and was anchored in the bay. On board were large bags containing tonnes of poisoned baits and the hatch covers were off ready for unloading into the chopper. There was little we could do but prepare and wait. I made up the drugs that we needed, and loaded and prepared the darts. The guns were cleaned and checked. Ropes were coiled and recoiled. Leg straps packed and repacked. Eventually there was nothing left to do, and I forced myself to go back into my tent and stretch out, wait and conserve energy. It reminded me of days way back when I would rest and wait for a coming rugby match or boxing fight. All revved up and no place to go. Then unbelievably, out of the distance, came the characteristic wop, wop, wop of blades and we all tumbled out of our camps and watched with mounting excitement as the chopper swept in from the north and flared up into a landing outside our base.

Richard and Alan Bond climbed stiffly out of the machine, relieved to stretch their legs, followed by the backseat passenger, whose specialty was rabbit control and whose responsibility it was to supervise the poison drop. He had probably just finished his most responsible job. The long-range tanks on the helicopter consisted of a 200-litre drum of fuel strapped alongside the rabbit man in the back seat, with a pipe out the vent and directly into the main fuel tank. There was a hand pump attached. When Richard said 'Pump', he had pumped, knowing full well that his life depended on it, and

CHAPTER ELEVEN THE SEAWEED-EATING COW

never once did he complain about the ache in his arms. They were pleased to have arrived, and we were pleased to see them. So many things could have gone wrong.

We wasted little time. The extra equipment the machine was carrying was emptied out and it was rigged up for lifting. The first job was to remove the loads of poison baits from the hold of the ship and deposit them on pallets that were placed along the bush edge ready for spreading. It was done with clockwork precision and there were still a couple of hours until dark. Too late to start spreading bait, but an ideal time to hunt game.

Within minutes one of the back doors had been removed from the machine and our gear was stowed. Richard had brought his net gun. This tried and proven New Zealand-made piece of apparatus was in reality an old ex-army .303 rifle fitted with three short barrels that, when loaded and fired, propelled three weights in a triangular pattern. Each weight was attached by a short rope to a central canister that carried the net, which then spread itself like a parachute and, you hoped, enveloped the animal you were aiming at. It kicked like a mule and was a brutal thing to handle. I was only too happy to leave that part of it in Richard's capable hands.

Once we were in the machine Alan wasted no time in getting airborne. Peter and I were kneeling in the empty space of the back with the side door off. Richard positioned himself easily in the open doorway, with me crouched behind. It took minutes to reach the middle of the island, where I had seen the animals the night before. There was no sign of them as we slowly beat our way along the coastal bush. Then, out to one side, something caught my attention and my eyes flicked back to it. It was just a patch of white, and in a split instance I was sure that I could see the outline of a cattle beast against the dark bush understorey. Tapping Alan on the shoulder, I pointed back and down, and he swung the machine in an arc to follow the direction that I was indicating. Down we went and slowly worked forward, hovering over the bush. Nothing, and I could feel the questioning glances from Richard and Peter as we beat slowly over the rata forest. Then there they were. The noise of the machine proved too much for them: mother and calf broke cover from the bush and galloped out onto the grass. Smoothly and effortlessly Alan brought the machine down to a position between the racing animals and the safety of the bush, effectively keeping them away from their only real avenue of escape. Relentlessly the machine mirrored their movements, and like a heading dog almost gained an invisible control over the now panic-stricken beasts, running together side by side. By now we had covered about half a kilometre of scattered scrub and the terrain had flattened out with few serious obstacles ahead: the situation was as good as we could ever hope it to be.

With the cattle running smoothly together right under our skid, Richard was out the door with one foot on the skid and taking aim. I saw the gun jump in his hands and watched the net arc its way down, until it was suspended like an umbrella over the point he had aimed at. The net spread itself out, then dropped down into the perfect spot for the cattle to run into and enveloped both beasts, tangling them up into a crashing heap. But the net was small and relatively flimsy, certainly not made for holding cattle, and definitely not very frightened ones. With a swoop, the chopper flared to a halt and started to descend over the struggling mass. Richard disappeared off the skid and dropped, landing spreadeagled across the writhing chaos. Grabbing my pack of gear, I followed his example and fell to join the general melee, which then allowed Alan to peel off and drop the machine onto the ground a short distance away. As I recovered from the fall I found myself lying over the cow, while Richard, similarly stretched across the calf, was deftly strapping the legs. I roped and tied the mother.

There was no time for backslapping. It was a great result but we still had to get those animals securely locked in the hold of the boat before we opened the champagne. Within minutes the machine was back in the air and hovering over the animals. Alan and I rolled the cow into a cargo net, and slung the net on the hook dangling from under the machine as it clattered overhead, the downdraught only adding to the difficulties of movement. Up she went and we waved her away as she headed off over the horizon and back to camp. Within a very short time the chopper was back, the calf was similarly rolled into a net and clipped on underneath. We leapt aboard for the last time, the chopper lifted smoothly and we were away, out of the gully that had been the animals' home for so long, skimming the tops of the trees and finally flaring up and descending to the small group of men standing around the now recumbent body of the cow at base camp. The tranquilliser administered by the vet had had more than the desired effect. These animals had little resistance to drugs, and time and time again over the next few days we would learn that their tolerance range was way below what would normally be expected.

The next step was to get the cow and calf out to the *Marine Countess*, waiting at anchor offshore. 'If you want to ride the strop then I'll take you out,' said Richard, 'but hang on tight.' I would be hanging on for grim death. As soon as he saw me clambering aboard the vessel, Richard was underway with the cow slung under the belly of the chopper. Standing in the gloom of the hold and looking up into the sky gave me a good appreciation of the

CHAPTER ELEVEN **THE SEAWEED-EATING COW**

Captured – tying the cow into a cargo net ready for transfer to base camp.

accuracy and small margins experienced pilots work by: it looked a very small opening indeed to be dropping a cow through. Then I saw the chopper arrive overhead, with the cow, a shapeless black mass in the net swinging below. As easily as if he was posting a letter, Richard dropped the cow through the hatch opening and straight into the crate in which I was standing below. The strop was unhooked, the net released, and he was off, up and away for the calf. The cow, 90 per cent out to it, was in no position to be uncooperative. After removing her from the net, I put a halter over her head while I had the upper hand, and dragged her to one side, so as to make room for her calf, who duly arrived and was deposited just as easily. The crew dropped the hatch cover back on, leaving me with a bare light swinging from a cord from above, and suddenly my world shrank to a small hold, just big enough for a crate about 3 metres square and a stack of hay bales. In its own way it was comforting in its enclosure and the generated warmth, and for the first time I could sit back and examine the animals and think, 'Hell, we've actually caught them.'

Later that night I grabbed my swag, climbed down from the bridge and went across the deck to the hold. Stirring a bit of hay around, I settled in for the night, deciding that the three of us were going to stay together until we reached Bluff, and by the time we got there, we were going to be friends. As we became closer and I got to know them, I looked at the cow one day and told her she was my lady. So that became her name to me, Lady. The yearling I just called Molly. Plain and simple, it seemed to suit her.

We were, however, just one small component, albeit an important one, in an overall project to obtain data from around the Auckland Island group.

The DOC botanists still had a lot of work to do and needed to cover as much of the main island as possible. And so the days settled into a routine of the *Marine Countess* dropping them off in the morning at the head of one bay, and picking them up at some other remote but predetermined spot at the end of the day. In some ways it was not such a bad thing, as it gave the cows a chance to settle down to their new environment. None of us got much rest the first day or so. The cow was understandably wide eyed, her nostrils flared, greeting any moving object with a firm shake of her horns. The young one was more confused than relaxed, and its attempts to suckle its mother were more for comfort than for sustenance. In an attempt to calm the cow down, we gave her a small dose of sedative, but again it was enough to knock her flat again, and we became even more cautious about administering any drugs to her.

But she remained our biggest problem. She did not appear to want to eat or drink, and as the days went by I became more and more concerned. Every time the botanists were dropped ashore I would go as well with a sack to pick what grass that I could find, which was very little. Realising that the cattle were probably more used to browsing than grazing, I took to collecting some leaves and small branches off shrubs and other plants I thought suitable. I had to be a little careful here as it was very much against DOCs policy to remove or damage any vegetation on the island, and I made sure that no one was ever openly confronted with the results of my raids, as it would have compromised their position. But, as usually happens, goodwill and pragmatic reasoning prevailed, and as we pushed our way through the scrub they would often point to some plant and say, 'If I was a cow, that's the sort of plant that I'd want to eat', and continue walking while I took advantage of their sage advice. A few days later it was more relevant when someone said, pointing to some bushes, 'If I was a cow and had diarrhoea, then that's the sort of food I'd eat to cure it.' Everyone wanted those animals to make it, and every little bit helped.

The cattle were starting to be more relaxed in their surroundings, but still not eating or drinking properly. The DOC boys had by now finished their botanical survey, and we arrived back in Sandy Bay off Enderby for the last time. We dropped a final lot of stores and equipment for the party who were staying on, then lifted the anchor and headed out to sea, with our next stop Bluff. Knowing the next few days were going to be rough, we prepared the cattle as well as we could, by manually filling them with fluids, lightly sedating them and making sure that they were well packed with bales of hay and a deep bed.

In a strange way the rough sea was welcoming, for it signalled the

CHAPTER ELEVEN **THE SEAWEED-EATING COW**

beginning of the end of an action-packed adventure or a traumatic experience, depending on how you viewed it. It was suggested that, for comfort's sake, I move back into the cabin, and I must admit to being fairly tempted, but in the end decided that I had come this far and would stick to my post in order to see the final days through. A rope was run from the bridge to the hatch cover to give me something to hang onto when accessing the hold in rough conditions. Because the vessel had offloaded her cargo, she was very light and too buoyant for comfort. To compensate for this, the engineer had filled the adjacent hold with sea water, a practical move that certainly gave a much smoother ride. I fell asleep with the sound of water on the plates, such a short distance from my ear.

Slung underneath the helicopter, the cow is taken to the boat.

I dreamt of water, cows, islands and shipwrecked sailors, and the noise of the sea became more and more insistent and real. My dreams turned into a doze that bolted into full alert when I realised that the sound of the water was not only close, it was too close. It was inside with me; the hold was awash with the stuff. It was around the cows' legs, and although they were not unduly alarmed, with every wash and pitch of the vessel their eyes were getting wider and wider. I shot up the ladder, through the hatch cover, grabbing the rope and stumbling across the deck and up onto the bridge. The boat was on auto pilot, with Sonny the skipper curled up on the little bench seat that ran across the back. 'Get Roger the engineer,' he said as soon as I had told him that we were slowly sinking, and I fell down the stairs into the crew cabin below. To lose the cows now and start swimming this far from land wasn't high on my to do list. Fortunately the engineer felt the same. He flew out of bed, got the pumps going and soon the water level started to drop. An investigation the next morning revealed a lump of wood that had lodged in a valve and prevented it from closing, thus letting the sea in. The rest of the trip was relatively uneventful and a few days later we finally entered the sheltered waters of Bluff Harbour. Both animals were still alive and well and I was starting to relax just a little. There were, though, still some hurdles to overcome, one of the major ones being getting the animals out of the hold and into the trailer.

The wharf appeared to be bristling with people. Not only were DOC and MAF, the regulatory authorities, there in force, but there were also TV crews, newspaper reporters, the family of the crew, people with an interest, people just passing and people wanting to be there just because other people were there. For me it couldn't have been a worse scenario, because they had all come to see the cows, and it wasn't going to be easy to get the animals out of the hold, and certainly not with any dignity, as they had to be strapped into a cargo net and then picked up by the ship's Hiab and dropped into a crate on the trailer sitting alongside on the dock. Hoping for no mishap, I strapped Lady into a cargo net and onto the hook of the Hiab. I rode the Hiab onto the deck, then jumped ashore and into the crate to receive Lady who, for a once wild animal, was extremely good. Molly soon joined her.

We obtained some good quality clover hay, to which the cattle reacted like kids with chocolate. They relaxed, they ate, they drank and they slept. I also did all four. The next day we overnighted at Willowbank, where a MAF officer again checked the cows, and then came the long drive up the east coast of the South Island and a comparatively short sea voyage to Wellington, where we were met yet again by MAF and escorted to the quarantine centre at Silverstream. It was with mixed feelings that I left the cows there, not because I had concerns about their welfare but because I had become one with them, and the environment of sterilised concrete and tiles just seemed so alien from the remote isolation they were accustomed to. When no one was listening I told Lady not to worry, that I would come back for them both.

Massey University has always had a strong relationship with the Rare Breeds Conservation Society, largely based around some key personnel who recognised the value of the society's work. When the Veterinary Unit at the university offered to attempt to breed the cows by using some of the semen previously collected from bulls on Enderby Island, it appeared to be a wonderful opportunity to advance the project to the next stage, and so Lady and Molly were delivered there. A year went by with no result and no feedback. I proposed a time frame be put on their work, and if there was no progress then perhaps we needed to develop another plan. Another season went by with nothing happening, and then we received the a communication to say that the young heifer had died, of the scours (diarrhoea).

It would be fair to say that I was upset and Dave offered to accompany me up north in order to pick up Lady. One Saturday morning we headed off into a strong nor'wester and eventually arrived at Massey University in Palmerston

North, where we were directed to the veterinary faculty. Standing in a bare paddock fenced with electricity was a black and white mass of skeletal bones. I thought it was her, but still had trouble recognising her as my Lady. This had changed from an animal transfer into a rescue mission. I was speechless. This was supposed to be a top facility. It didn't take much to realise that the yearling had died through neglect and lack of husbandry. A couple of the animal staff and a college vet met us and helped us to load. The vet was obviously embarrassed, but seeing little point in stating the obvious, we set off with our gaunt cargo spraying diarrhoea like graffiti around the walls of the crate.

Back in Canterbury, we put Lady into one of Dave and Judy's home paddocks, and I got home to a fretful sleep. The next morning Dave rang. He had woken up and could hardly believe his eyes: the cow was red raw, skin and hair rubbed off, accentuating the protruding bones hanging off her frame. It took him a while to realise what had happened. At Massey she had been kept in a bare paddock with an electric fence. Not only did she have a massive worm burden, but she also had a huge louse problem that, until now, she had been unable to relieve. At Dave's she had a lovely great big macrocarpa stump in the middle of her paddock, and had rubbed herself raw trying to alleviate the itching. It was a tribute to Dave and Judy's stock management that when I saw her a month or so later, she was putting on weight, had a shiny coat and bright eyes and, best of all, had started to cycle again. Was there still a chance? If so, we had to pursue it.

So Lady went off to yet another facility, and after several attempts produced only one egg, which couldn't be retrieved. Lady had been impregnated by semen off the island but of the original semen collected from fourteen bulls at the time of the cull, only one was even vaguely suitable for such a liaison, and so yet again the project stalled. There is a perverse law in life that says something like, 'If you keep trying and don't give up, then something, somehow, will make it work.' This came about in our case via a phone call from the Agricultural Research Centre at Ruakura in Hamilton. They were doing some new and exciting research on in vitro work in cattle, had heard about Lady and wished to know if we might risk using her as an experimental subject. By now we all thought Lady had gone through enough, but the opportunity for her to still leave that legacy couldn't be denied, and so it was that I packed my bags and headed again for Dave and Judy's. Lady had grown by then and only just fitted into the crate. She was so heavy that every time she moved around the poor little Hilux rolled and wallowed drunkenly. 'Go,' said Judy. 'I can't bear to stand and watch that any longer', and so I set off, travelling in a rather rotary fashion in the general direction of Ruakura.

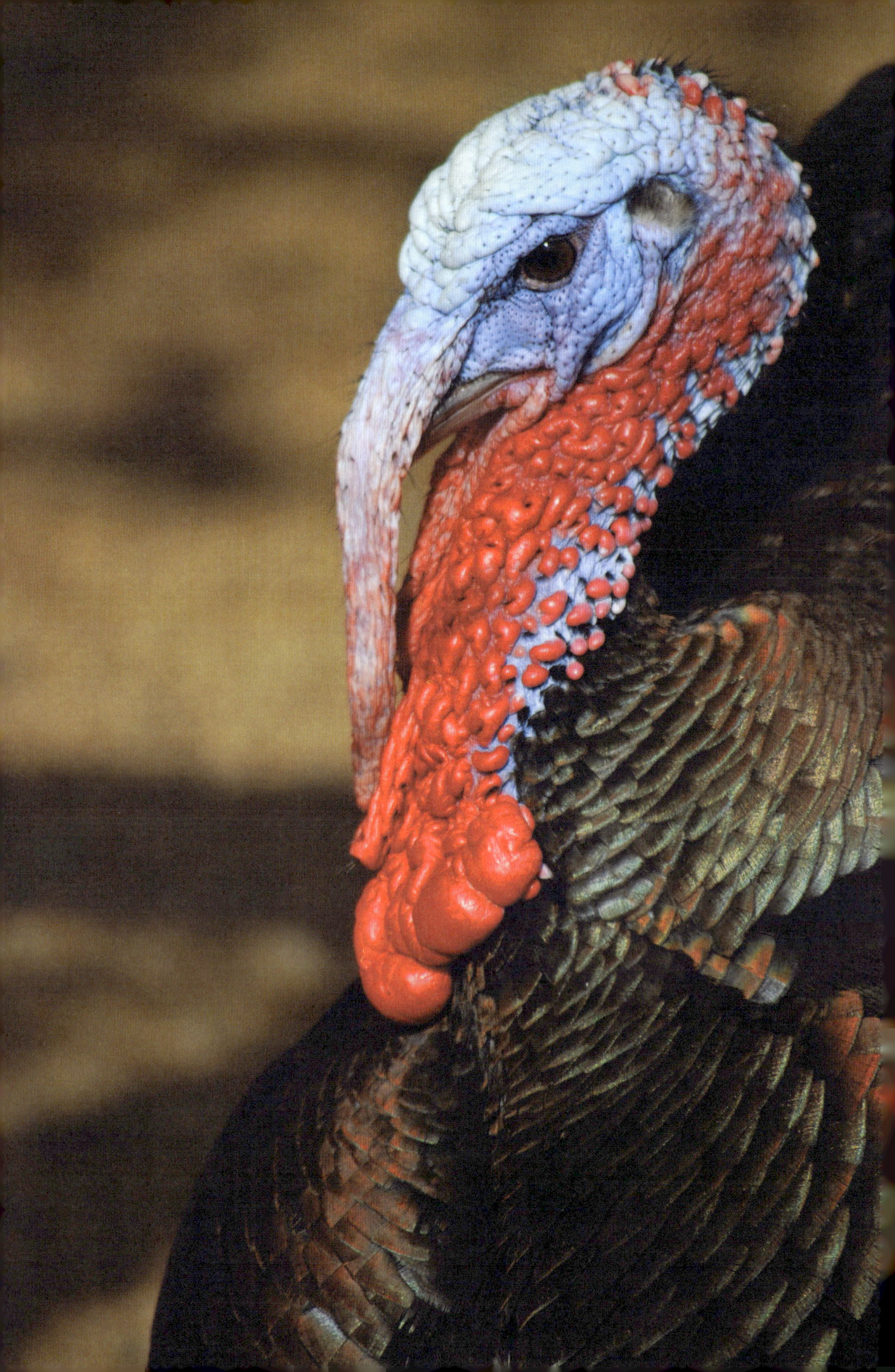

CHAPTER TWELVE

IF ONLY NOAH KNEW

It was a special occasion for me when eventually I pulled up at Ruakura and met some of the scientists who would be involved. We knew that it was going to cost us heaps of money, which we just didn't have, and things were becoming decidedly awkward until, fortunately, the committee running the Auckland Easter Show decided to sponsor it as a special project.

Using the best and most up-to-date in vitro techniques the scientists then tried numerous times to fertilise Lady with the one lot of viable bull semen, but without any success, and enthusiasm was getting very low. Then, almost miraculously, after thirty-five attempts, an embryo was created and implanted into a surrogate cow, and some months later a calf was born. This was a massive step forward. The little bull calf, named Derby, received huge publicity. As handsome as the last surviving male of a species should be, he was happy to be petted and feted, and revelled in the adoration.

It's all very well to be famous, but to be a stud bull, you needed to have a herd of purebred cows to play with, and we were far from having that – especially as the Ruakura team had decided that Lady's reproductive days were over, and that they had done well to generate Derby. It seemed, yet again, that we had come to the end of the road and had finally run out of options. We were making plans for Lady's return when we again got involved in some discussions with the reproductive team. Sitting in the wings was a special project they had been working on quietly: to be the first in the world to clone an animal. Fortuitously for us, they decided that if they were to clone any animal, then an Enderby cow would be a good and worthwhile subject. The work, however, was new and rather controversial, known to only a few. A number of embryos were generated and implanted, but for various reasons they all failed, until eventually it all happened, one embryo held and the first cloned cow in the world was developed out of Lady and born in July 1998. She was named Elsie (LC for Lady's Clone).

Although Dolly the sheep, cloned a few months before at Edinburgh University, had been the first in the world, Elsie still created huge international excitement. In fact, strangely enough, there was much more interest from overseas than in New Zealand. The project was written up in various prestigious journals and magazines, including *Time*, which gave Lady international coverage as the 'Seaweed-Eating Cow'. She had gone from an unwanted feral animal to be destroyed at any cost to become probably the most famous individual cow in the world, with an astonishing price tag. Everyone was extremely pleased, including the Auckland Show people, who were still largely funding the research. They asked if Lady and Elsie could be put on display as a main feature. There was, however, another serious side to all this, namely the polarised views regarding GE or genetic engineering. The risks to the animals were considered to be quite real, especially as the Auckland A&P Association received a threat of physical harm from one such group. The police were advised and the show organisers arranged for security guards to be alongside the animals both day and night. Fortunately the show ran without incident, and everyone seemed to enjoy themselves, including the cattle, who had their own special dedicated defence staff attending to their every want and need.

In actual fact the animals did two Easter Shows, and in between the research continued and the cloning techniques refined. Four more clones were born, but then the programme started to wind down because they had really achieved their goals, and then came a disaster with the death of Elsie, and the project went into a spiral and a state of limbo. The Easter Show people went on to fund and support other things, and Ruakura and the scientists moved to other interests. Arrangements were eventually made for the cattle to travel down to Canterbury and they duly arrived, a small group of five animals: Lady the matriarch, Derby the young bull and herd sire, and three cloned heifers.

The saviours who agreed to look after them were Dave and Judy Matheson. They both loved their cattle, and ran a large Simmental stud on their farm, which is also home to a range of birds, animals and other creatures. To visit there is to bring on an avalanche of welcome from the dogs, especially Judy's Doberman, massive, trying to be threatening and yet wanting to sit on your lap

CHAPTER TWELVE IF ONLY NOAH KNEW

at the same time. Greyhounds feature prominently, as Dave to a large degree specialises in them, but pride of place goes to a little Jack Russell bitch called Blossom, who was born totally deaf. She puts a lot of energy into barking, but as she has never heard what that really sounds like, she produces some pretty strange noises. Obedience is a bit hit and miss, depending on hand signals and well-aimed missiles, so results can also be very variable. Dave also likes his turkeys while Judy loves her Light Sussex chooks, horses and more. Dave is phlegmatic and takes everything in his stride, while Judy has zero tolerance for people and things that disrupt or annoy her. Normally things operate according to very sensible and fully understandable systems, but like all systems they can break down occasionally, as the bank manager found out one day.

Dave and Judy had quite a large development coming up, and as some modern bank managers do, to 'keep their feet attached to the soil', so to speak, this one came out to visit them. He had survived the initial meet and greet, had his shiny shoes sat on by the Doberman and brushed most of the hair off his creased trousers. The discussions were really going quite well. Dave, Judy and the bank manager were all sitting at the dining room table agreeing with companionable good humour and finalising plans, when Judy came out with a very loud and succinct expletive that had nothing to do with the business in hand.

Dave had two turkeys named Tom and Tina, a devoted couple who had formed a relationship, and Tina was currently proudly sitting on a clutch of eggs. Tom's hormones, however, were still rising, and with Tina otherwise occupied, he looked around the bush to see if there was anything he fancied, and spied a delicate morsel in the beautiful and innocent Henrietta, Judy's favourite Light Sussex chook. It wasn't a happy union. His weight and sharp claws and spurs created a tsunami of feathers, dust and lust that was all over in an instant.

One glance at the steely expression on Judy's face and Dave knew there were problems. Without looking, as she was, into the garden, he could hear in the background the squawks of a hen, the gobbles of a turkey and the yelps of excited dogs. As Judy steamed out, in spite of a very bad premonition he kept the conversation going, and indeed the bank manager, although a bit taken aback, was totally immersed and excited about ending his presentation. The effect was slightly lost when Judy charged back into the room, red faced and puffing with both exertion and rage. In her hands she held the tattered half-plucked body of Henrietta, which she slammed down on the table between the two men, pounding her fist down after it, scattering the biscuits. 'Your bloody gobbler,' she shouted. 'Look what it's done to my Henrietta', before

Dave Matheson with Derby, in a quieter moment.

leaving the corpse flattened between the milk and the sugar, and departing in a swirl of indignation and feathers, followed by a pack of contrite down-tailed dogs, and beating Blossom off with a pillow because she still thought the whole thing was all part of a great game.

Dave let the bank manager out the front door before the Doberman returned to sit on him again, and slunk out to the barn to commune with and

CHAPTER TWELVE **IF ONLY NOAH KNEW**

console his greyhounds, and try and prepare a defence for Tom the Turkey. The loan went through, but probably because the bank manager was either too scared to return, or more likely had gained so much kudos recounting the story at innumerable cocktail parties, that he thought it was well worth the gamble.

It was in this environment that the future of the cattle rested, and under the management of Dave and Judy they settled in and thrived. We had purposely brought all the animals in together to try and create a herd mentality, and see if that might spark some reproductive activity. Derby, as the herd bull, grew into the position. In spite of all being together and being interactive, only two females appeared to be fertile. Although two heifer offspring were born, it did seem as if we were heading again into a genetic bottleneck.

From a young age Derby had been petted and handled, so he was very quiet and easy to do anything with. Slowly, however, the testosterone levels rose, and when he was put in with his cows, his behaviour changed as he reverted to his wild heritage. Those original instincts, though, had been reshaped by his association with people whom he no longer feared, and the result was almost an identity crisis : should he be treating them as cattle like himself, or as something similar but different? He became very much a feral herd bull, jealously guarding his harem and territory. If he saw anyone, even at a distance, then his head would go down, he would paw the ground and he would maintain a nerve-wracking growling and bellowing. His paddock was his castle, and he landscaped it by digging out a great hole in the centre, and patrolling it zealously.

He got totally confused, however, when Dave shifted the cows into the next paddock. Should he leave his hole unprotected, or should he guard his cows? It took three days for him to make up his mind that sex was more important, and he finally left his hole and joined the cows in their new paddock. As time went on his behaviour didn't improve. He kept up a constant noisy grumble, killed numerous trees by debarking them with his horns, and if he couldn't find a tree to wreak his frustrations on, then he would destroy gates or just smash fenceposts off at ground level for the hell of it. He became increasingly hard to shift from one paddock to another, standing in the middle of the open gate and refusing to let any cows through.

One hot nor'west day Dave had had enough of Derby dictating the terms: he was going to go with the cows, whether he wanted to or not. The cows willingly walked into their new paddock, while Derby stood growling and eyeballing Dave. Having seen it done in the cavalry, Dave charged the bull on the four-wheeler, waving a length of alkathene pipe like a sword and

RESCUE ONE NEW ZEALANDER'S CRUSADE TO SAVE ENDANGERED ANIMALS

Lady, the matriarch.
Photo: Judy Matheson

shouting loudly. Two minutes later and he was standing on the other side of the fence, watching Derby rolling and pushing the bike, with its engine still going, all around the paddock until eventually it died and he lost interest. It went off for repairs but was never quite the same again. Derby was not only clever, but also cunning. He planned some of these assaults with military precision. As Derby looked on Dave as a potential rival bull, so he seemed to look on Judy as some sort of cow who really should be in her place, that is in his herd, but it wasn't a reciprocated feeling or one that Judy wanted to put to the test.

Derby was better than any guard dog and his reputation spread widely. Early one morning the neighbours on the other side of the road rang. 'That big black bull of yours was marching up and down the road bellowing. He came into our driveway and we've shut the gate on him, but now nobody can get out of the house.' Grumbling to himself, Dave pulled on trousers and

CHAPTER TWELVE **IF ONLY NOAH KNEW**

The growing herd of clones and progeny.
Photo: Michael Trotter

gumboots and ran down the drive to find a very wound up and voluble Derby putting on a great show for the neighbours, who were watching fearfully from the window. On impulse Dave walked up towards him until, seeing him, Derby swung around and stood pawing the ground, flicking strings of snot all over his face as he stood, head down. The neighbours became even more wide-eyed when Dave, who had recently watched *Crocodile Dundee*, with its famous water buffalo hypnosis scene, pointed two fingers at the raging animal and shouted, 'Derby, come here.' In the film the buffalo fell asleep, but in this case Dave walked slowly backwards across the road and into his drive, followed by Derby, shaking his head.

The neighbours were incredibly impressed, and the story went up and down the valley. 'That vet Dr Matheson, you should have seen him. Just pointed his fingers at this mad bull and the animal responded immediately and followed him home like a trained dog. Amazing the way he handles those animals.' What they didn't see was that, as Dave and Derby got out of their sight, Derby was slowly gaining and the pace getting faster with Dave back-pedalling as fast as he could, just enough to keep the bull coming but not enough to let him catch up. They both made it back to the home paddock at a controlled gallop that ended up almost traditionally with Dave going over the fence yet again, and Derby's gate being replaced, yet again.

Derby was by now becoming a problem; no one but Dave and Judy would ever have been able to put up with and manage such an animal. It was no longer considered reasonable or realistic to try and load him on a truck and send him to the yards or works. We therefore decided that we would have to humanely put him down in his own paddock. In the meantime, however, there were still a few options such as semen collection to consider, and also popping up was the man from the ministry whose job it was to test all cattle for TB. In due course he turned up in his overalls and gumboots, wanting to test the Enderby bull. 'You're welcome to,' said Judy. 'That's him in the paddock. If you want to put him in the yards and TB test him, then please feel free to help yourself.'

The man from the ministry opened the yards and strode confidently down to the paddock, closely watched by Derby, who had had his eye on him ever since the vehicle drove up. Clods of dirt were being pawed into the air, and snot and spittle flew as he shook the curls on his head, and roared his right to remain where he was. The man came back and leant on the fence in awe, before both his education and survival mechanism came to the fore. After studying the animal and thinking for a few minutes, he turned to Judy and said, 'He's from the Auckland Islands, isn't he?'

'Yes,' said Judy noncommittally.

'Well, there's no TB on the Auckland Islands and so there'll be no need to test him.'

Honour was satisfied.

Xcell Breeding Services are an animal genetic company that have supported the work of the Rare Breeds Conservation Society, and sponsor the Genebank project through providing storage and by doing collections and so on. They agreed to have a last try at semen collection from Derby, and so a week before he was due to be put down they arrived at Dave and Judy's and, surprisingly, managed to yard and sedate him sufficiently to be able to collect a number of invaluable straws. In so many ways it was a fortuitous act, for two days later the farm was unearthly quiet and something was definitely missing. Getting dressed and thinking the worst, Dave went outside and found Derby still and cold in his paddock. For whatever reason, he had died peacefully but his legacy was now established and protected, and tears were mingled with sighs of relief as peace settled once more on the valley.

The advances in animal reproduction continued and later, unexpectedly, another window of opportunity opened. All the original straws of semen collected from the island at the time of the cull had been kept in storage. In the past the semen from only one bull had been viable, but new technology meant that scientists from Lincoln University in Canterbury could revisit them and reassess their potential. Using newly developed techniques, they thought that they would be able to mature some of the sperm in the laboratory, and so another round of embryo transplant was initiated. The first six calves were born, and after some DNA tests, and to everyone's delight, it was found that there was a magnificent bull calf, as unrelated as possible to the existing cloned animals.

After years of frustration, disappointment, ecstasy and depression, not to mention huge sums of money and personal support and commitment, the little herd of cattle is now poised to become established. It's the only flock or herd in the world that has been established by cloning and in spite of many people's fears, there has been no indication that the cloned animals or their progeny were any different to any others in the group. But the battle to save the Enderby cattle is by no means over, and they must still be considered highly endangered.

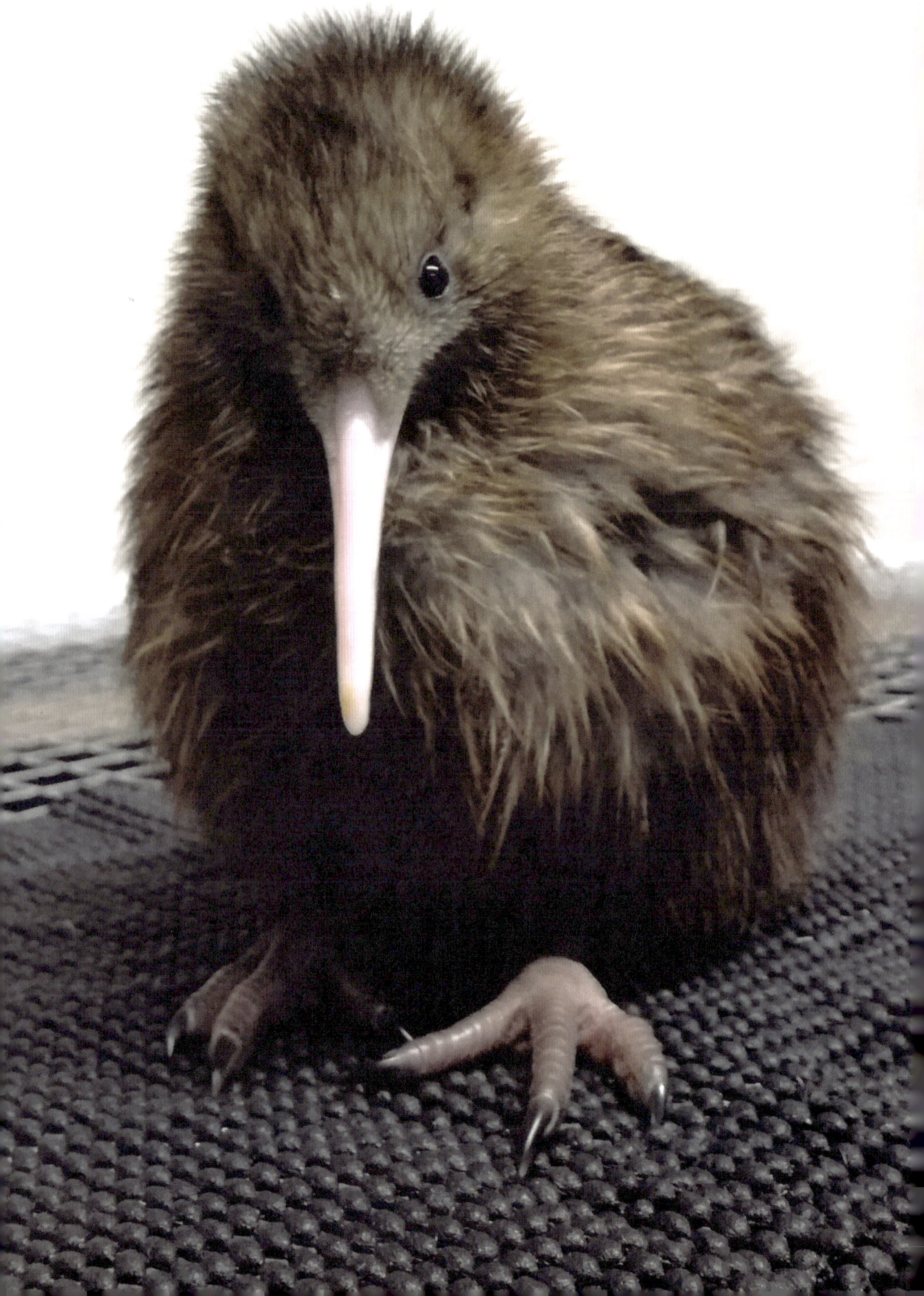

CHAPTER THIRTEEN

CAN DO KIWI

Turmoil goes hand in hand with running a wildlife park; each day is normally one of crisis management. There are so many facets to consider. You're running a reasonably large food and beverage operation, a retail souvenir operation, a front of counter/reception service, a promotions role, an education and advocacy role, a financial role – and that's before you even get to the animals. Over the years animal handling and welfare have changed considerably. When I started the park, if someone could shovel manure into a wheelbarrow and put hay in a hay feeder, then they were employable. If you built a box and put a wire front on it with a perch, then it was a perfectly acceptable cage. All that has changed. Now, instead of collecting animals, a lot of thought goes into selecting something, and justifying why it has been selected. You then design the enclosure, build the enclosure, landscape the enclosure and its surroundings, put in the services that the future inhabitant and staff require, design and produce the advocacy for the enclosure, write up a staff manual that details all of the inhabitant's nutrition and welfare requirements, and only when that is finished does the display become live, with the introduction of the species concerned. Much more justification is required in order to hold anything in captivity, and that's a good thing. The staff are now highly trained and qualified and totally dedicated to the project. The staff have always been one of our major strengths and one of the biggest catalysts in Willowbank's development.

Life was never made or meant to be easy, however. After we had spent megabucks on our new development, I approached DOC for some kiwi. We had designed, built and planted the enclosure and were well and truly ready.

In previous discussions with DOC there hadn't been any great problems, but now the answer came back: none available. Every time I tried to follow it up I was met with a brick wall. I was frustrated and furious. We had spent all of this money on the understanding that kiwi would be available, and now, without explanation, they were blocking us. The only vague reason given was that they didn't like people making money out of New Zealand wildlife. The thought of some fat-gutted civil servant on a huge and safe salary making statements like that made me see red. I rang the right place in Wellington, made an appointment to see the right person and then flew to the capital with copies of the awards we had received, photos of what we had done and other appropriate information. I was duly shown into his office, which was the biggest and most impressive I had ever seen. He listened and understood. We talked and then he stopped me in mid-flight. 'Don't worry, I'll get it fixed for you.' Next week we had kiwi.

They were a pair of North Island brown kiwi, one who had originated from the Bay of Plenty and the other from Taranaki. For some reason they were never given any proper names, they were just Mr and Mrs Kiwi. They were released into an outdoor enclosure that we had built for them, with a front and a back section. At night they were let into the front section, which was kept reasonably open and with a low artificial lighting level. That was where the people viewed them at night, when they were out probing and just doing their normal thing. Kiwi had never been displayed like this before anywhere in New Zealand and it was an outstanding success. Instead of huddling behind glass in a dark soundproof room, as was the case with most organisations, these birds were in their natural cycle and exposed to the noise and elements. People thought that they would run away and hide with the close proximity to humans and no glass, but that didn't happen. At times they were so close that you could easily touch them should you wish. When we shut down the park at the end of the night, we would open the gate into the back section and they were free to wander in the bush as much as they liked, before putting themselves back into one of their two boxes in the morning. It was an easy, low-stress system for both the birds and the staff.

A few months later, Big Lisa, the caregiver at the time, came racing up to me in great excitement. She had seen an egg in one of the boxes. Few kiwi had ever bred in captivity and so this was a milestone event. What to do about it? There were two options: we could take the egg and incubate it, or we could leave it and chance nature to take its course. I chose the second alternative and, to our delight, Mr Kiwi started sitting firmly on the egg, so we crossed our fingers and left him to it.

CHAPTER THIRTEEN CAN DO KIWI

Kiwi are strange in all sorts of ways, and reproduction and rearing is one of them. They have two working ovaries, while other birds have one. They lay a huge egg, almost a third of their body weight, with a paper-thin shell. They normally have two or three burrows, and will sleep in one, lay the egg in another and use the third as a holiday bach. After a day or two, the male will start incubating and sits on that egg for around eighty days. He will get off each night for several hours at times, in order to have a feed and do whatever kiwis do, and because the egg is so large it does cool down but not to a dangerous level. Sometimes the female will lay another egg about a month later and, rarely, sometimes a third one. It's one way of keeping the old man at home: Mr Kiwi once sat continuously for six months because Mrs Kiwi kept dropping an egg in his nest.

All going well, the little chick hatches, and again it is special. While most neonate birds are born with fluff and are obviously babies, a kiwi is born fully feathered and looks just like a miniature adult. This we knew, but we were thrilled when, about three months later, we found a brand-new little baby kiwi in the burrow. There's no parenting among kiwi. The father and mother have nothing whatsoever to do with their children, who must make their own way in the world. This is the point when they're most vulnerable and easily predated. Again assessing our options, we removed the baby into a safe rectangular box that contained a small nest box and had a dirt floor for him to probe in. We were taking no chances.

That little baby was a great success, and we were very proud of him until the person co-ordinating the kiwi programme requested it be transferred to another institution who had lost theirs. That was a bugger, but we bred another, and then another, and so on. Each time the chicks were taken from us, until I realised that one day we would lose one of our pair, and our chances of getting a replacement wouldn't be very good. So I dug my heels in and started to keep some back and build up some breeding stock. Once we had some stock on hand we could then swap them for other birds in order to make up more pairs. We got up to twenty-nine kiwi and were by far the biggest holders and breeders in New Zealand. They were also the only kiwi that were breeding while being on display.

Because we were displaying the birds only by night, many people, particularly tourists with tight time frames, were unable to see them. I didn't like the conventional nocturnal houses with the glass fronts that removed all relationship with the birds, and kept trying to think of affordable alternatives. One day I was looking at an advertisement for an open-fronted kitset barn – hard to get a functional building much cheaper than that. Then I wondered what would happen if I bought two and put them together face to face: surely that would create a big dark building. If you put a pathway through you could fence it and it would be just like covering over some of our outdoor enclosures. No glass. The Willowbank Wildlife Trust had by now altered its name to the New Zealand Conservation Trust, and with their help we designed and built New Zealand's first open walk-through nocturnal house. We didn't use the kitset barns, but instead found some telegraph poles and second-hand steel rafters and started putting things together. With trustee Dave Yates' digger we could landscape inside, and $40,000 and a few months later we were ready. The year before, in 1996, Princess Anne had agreed to be the patron of the trust, and knowing she was about to visit New Zealand we asked if she would agree to open the Nocturnal House, which, rather to our surprise, she did.

It was an interesting experience going through a royal visit. All invitees and people who might be on the property had to be cleared by security. Then the property and surroundings were checked, and just before the visit they even had divers in the stream checking under all of the bridges and walkways. Although nobody saw them at the time, marksmen were placed in strategic positions. You never quite knew what was security and what wasn't. The old man walking up the road swishing his walking stick through the grass could easily turn into a swirling dervish at the slightest provocation.

The day of the visit arrived and on time the entourage turned up, and Princess Anne stepped out, to be introduced to a handful of key people. Mark and I then led her on a walk through the park, followed by the rest of the guests. All went well until we entered the kea aviary and I could see that she wasn't comfortable with birds. Also in the aviary I had placed a large Arapawa Island billy goat called Shakespeare, thinking that with the English association it would make a good talking point. When Shakespeare saw us coming, he jumped down off his rocks and, like a troll guarding his bridge, came striding across it towards us, heading straight for the Princess Royal and her bouquet of flowers. With horns almost a metre across he looked fairly formidable and the leading security agent had no idea what to do. He had his hand inside his coat but could hardly pull the pistol out of his shoulder holster and shoot him. He looked very relieved, therefore, when I stepped forward, grabbed Shakespeare by his horns and passed him on to another unsuspecting agent who was following along behind. The next animal to almost wreck the party was a kererū or wood pigeon who decided that the Princess's high hairdo resembled something like a nest and tried to land in it. She ducked her head and threw her hands up at the same time as mine turned

CHAPTER THIRTEEN **CAN DO KIWI**

Mark, Princess Anne, me and Kathy during the royal visit to Willowbank.

the bird away, but she was definitely not amused. However the opening went well, the kiwi all displayed as they should have and we retired to the main building for a cup of tea.

There were the usual words of welcome and then we brought in the present we had decided on. On the assumption that Princess Anne probably has a dungeon full of unwanted gifts given to her over the years, and knowing that she was very fond of the Gloucester Old Spot pigs she had back on her estate, we had in a wheelbarrow a couple of cute little kune kune piglets. The

203

A present for a princess. Helen Peterson presents the piglets in their wheelbarrow.

look on her face was priceless, and you could see she was thinking, 'How do I get out of this one?' We let her off the hook by saying that if she agreed we would look after them for her, an offer that she took up graciously and with a big smile. So it was back to conversations and drinking cups of tea.

She was easy to talk to, and we were chatting about the importance of earthworms, when over her shoulder and out in the middle of the deer

CHAPTER THIRTEEN **CAN DO KIWI**

The Willowbank kiwi had more royal visitors in November 2016 when King Willem-Alexander and Queen Máxima of the Netherlands came to the reserve. Nick Ackroyd makes the introductions.

paddock I could see people running. It was some of the staff, all dressed up but the girls with their skirts up around their waists, and racing for the boundary fenceline. They hit this and disappeared, and I resumed our earthworm discussion, puzzling over what was happening. It turned out that the piglets had escaped and done a runner across the deer paddock, through the fence and up the road. As the staff reached the fence they were suddenly confronted by black-clad balaclavaed men dropping out of trees and out of bushes, bristling with arms. They explained what was happening and there was a lot of talking into collars: 'The royal pigs have escaped. Leaving our post providing assistance.' So everybody set off up the road, the pigs having a great time, followed by the staff and both parties being chased by the security men. Everyone was finally apprehended and returned to where they should have been.

The Princess Royal was forty-five minutes late leaving, which, according to her secretary, was unheard of. She was either having a jolly good time or had little desire to be at her next appointment. As the chauffeur closed the door, Mark leant over with his hand on the roof and said, 'Tell your mother when she next visits New Zealand to come and have tea.' With that parting comment and a wave she was gone, but still sends a Christmas card every year and in 2008 she opened our Kiwi breeding centre and viewing area.

DOC really didn't know what to do with me over the Nocturnal House.

Strictly speaking, our permit was for open natural viewing and I had stretched things a bit by putting that inside a building. In the end they did nothing, waiting for something to go wrong so that they could close it down. But the birds liked it, the customers liked it and the concept has now been copied by other zoos and parks.

We were now holding quite a large number of kiwi, and really thought that we had managed to achieve a lot, when we were dropped a bombshell. It had been decided that there should be no mixing of North Island brown kiwi that, like ours, came from different areas. They separated the North Island kiwi into five different groups, something I've never been able to understand as it's an artificial, human separation, and the isolation of those groups is caused only by deforestation. Before that they all mingled and lived happily as one big population. Our success was used against us. In spite of the fact that DOC had chosen the original birds for us, we were now accused of breeding a lot of hybrid kiwi and creating a major problem for the industry. The word hybrid was used extensively and publicly mainly, I think, because it sounded like a very bad creation, but in fact the kiwi we were breeding could in no way be considered hybrids which, by definition, are a cross between two different breeds. Ours may have been of mixed lineage but they were, and always will be, pure North Island brown kiwi, in spite of some experts who should be writhing in embarrassment. So we were told to stop breeding, something that went against the grain but in view of the current climate we had little choice.

Then came another totally unforeseen disaster. The story began with a special project in which we had been involved. A number of kiwi each year are accidentally caught in leg hold traps and become amputees. A kiwi relies on its legs, and it's hard to rationalise a one-legged bird, but when a lovely one-legged female was brought in we couldn't turn her away and she became our problem. Eva Ting, a staff member, picked up the challenge. If people could have prosthetic limbs, then why not kiwi?

The Britten family were good friends of my father and their son John was an exceptional and visionary entrepreneur. Using mainly nothing but good New Zealand ingenuity, he developed and raced one of the fastest motor cycles in the world and his engineering shop in Christchurch was a magnet for free-thinking brilliant individuals. One of those was Wayne Alexander, a very special person with very special talents. Despite having lost both legs to frostbite in 1992, mountaineer Mark Inglis wanted to climb Everest. Wayne spent months designing and developing prosthetic limbs that would do that job. Having designed and built them, he then accompanied Mark on his ascent in 2006.

CHAPTER THIRTEEN CAN DO KIWI

It was to this man that Eva turned for help. It was offered freely and compassionately, and for two or three months Wayne worked on a suitable leg for our kiwi. The process was both macabre and fascinating. He started off with moulds and bits of rubber and leather, and the last models were hi-tech titanium, with a lot of research into jointing, padding and fastening. It was such an interesting programme that a TV network decided to make a documentary on it. Just as things were coming to a conclusion, however, the park manager at the time decided to treat all the kiwi for internal parasites. This was a prudent and common practice, but the worming drug used, though fine for any normal bird, was toxic to kiwi. Although he got expert advice beforehand, nothing triggered an alarm bell. But the result was catastrophic: nine birds died, including Mrs Kiwi and the amputee. Everyone was devastated. Tears flowed as we adjusted to what had happened and then we really got hammered. The TV people, who had suddenly lost their happy ending, tried to retrieve a bit of footage by promoting and accentuating the deaths. In the news media DOC acted horrified. A huge loss to the kiwi population, they said. A national tragedy. It was no good saying, 'Hang on a minute, mate, according to you these were hybrid birds that you didn't want.' When the dogs are in biting the underbelly, then there's little you can do.

We survived but with a lot of internal scars, and a lot of cynicism, and then DOC decided that maybe all our hybrid birds could be released in Pūkaha Forest, which just happens to surround their Mount Bruce National Wildlife Centre. Mr Kiwi went up there, remated and continued to produce chicks. He has left a wonderful legacy even if it's not recognised by those who should do so. Having put so much into North Island brown kiwi only to be beaten about the ears at every opportunity, we decided to shift our focus to South Island species, which were highly threatened and largely forgotten, with few caring a toss about them.

The New Zealand Conservation Trust (NZCT) identified the great spotted kiwi as the species they would like to focus on. In order to do that, together we built a large modern hatching and rearing facility just for kiwi. It comprised an entry area, where footwear was removed and people were gowned up. It then went into a kitchen/reception room and on to a preparation area. All new eggs that came in were examined and hygienically cleaned before going into the next section, which was the incubation room. Here the eggs were weighed, details noted and placed in their own individual incubator. After hatching, the chicks were taken into another separate area that contained individual brooders, which held them until the staff were confident that they were feeding properly and doing all the right things. We had three such

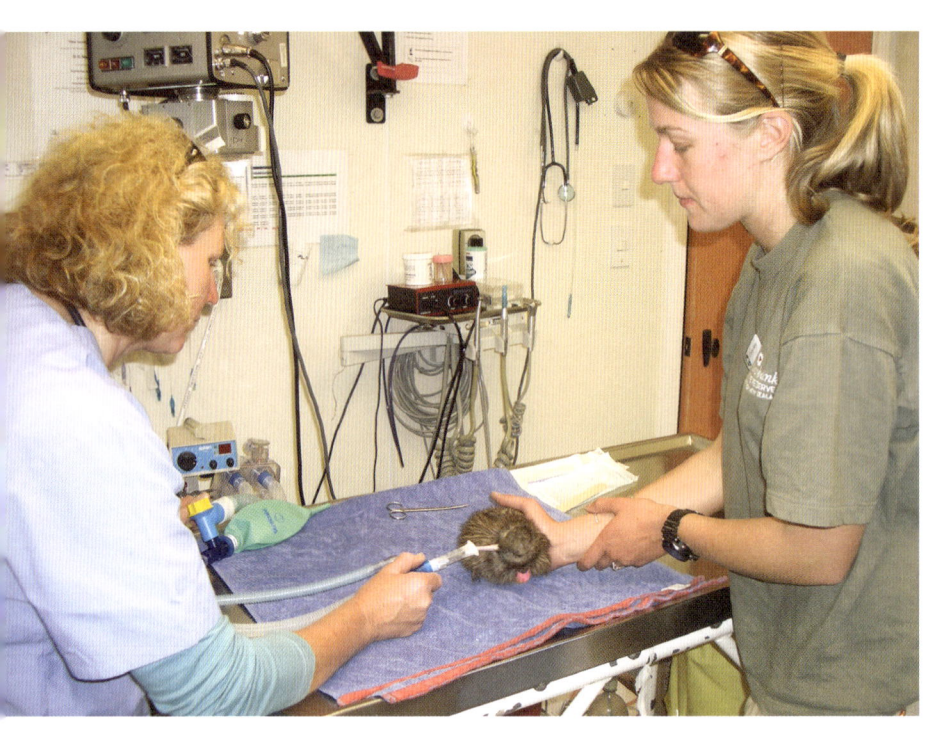

Anaesthetising a kiwi in our specialised wildlife hospital.

brooding rooms so that species could be kept apart and disease isolated. An additional one was for wild chicks that might be brought in, since they were a potential source of infection and had to be strictly isolated. They then moved to another section consisting of a building with covered runs going off it. Finally we had large outside runs to expand out into if required. It was a comprehensive facility which, when operating to capacity, required up to five staff to manage it.

DOC was just starting an operation nest egg programme for the Okarito kiwi or rowi. This particular species was estimated to be down to around 200 individuals, and with pretty much 100 per cent predation of any newborn chicks was on the brink of extinction. The Operation Nest Egg Programme or ONE, involves several stages, revolving around removing the eggs and hatching them artificially, then rearing the chick until it's old and wise enough to look after itself and escape predation. First, parties of people go out into an area and sit on mountaintops or other exposed areas in the middle of the night and listen for the call of the kiwi. When they hear one they mark the compass direction on a map, and by comparing such directions between parties, get an indication of where the bird actually is. Once the rough proximity is established, a dog and handler are brought in to locate the bird and place a transmitter on any males that are caught. From then on the movements of

CHAPTER THIRTEEN CAN DO KIWI

the males can be monitored, either on foot of even sometimes by air. The transmitter has an extra function that sends back a signal that indicates when the bird is stationary for any length of time, which gives a good indication that he's sitting on an egg. Because freshly laid eggs are very difficult to hatch, the rangers will wait until they've been incubated for about three weeks, then walk into the area, retrieve the egg, place it in a small chilly bin and carry or fly it out. From there it travels by road or air to Christchurch, where we take over and it's admitted into our facility.

We were thrilled to have the opportunity to work with the DOC team at Okarito, and over the years developed a very good relationship and have hatched and reared a large number of birds for release. There were always bumps on the road and hurdles to overcome, many unexpected. One year, for instance, we had an outbreak of salmonella. It was a strain not found in the wild and no birds could leave until they were tested clear. Despite bringing in experts from all over the country for advice, we still don't have any idea how the infection got into the facility. It was a mammoth task stripping everything out and disinfecting but we finally managed to get rid of it. The experience made our systems even more robust, but it created a lot of pressure as we were then holding over sixty kiwi on site, waiting for release. When the birds leave Willowbank they are placed on predator-free Motuara Island in the Marlborough Sounds, in order to learn to live like a kiwi in a semi-protected environment.

Unfortunately for DOC, island life didn't always prove to be quite as idyllic as it should be and a number of kiwi perished or disappeared. It isn't unusual for a baby kiwi to come out during the day: some were lost through misadventure and others when a hawk discovered this unexpected source of plunder. The cost of each bird at this stage has been estimated at being around $5000, so it was becoming an expensive feeding station. This situation put the department into a quandary because half wanted to shoot the hawk out of the sky, and the other half said that you can't interfere with nature.

A few years into the programme and a new wildlife facility opened up at Franz Josef, on the West Coast. DOC gave it a lot of support and as a result shifted the programme from Willowbank to there. The facility would do the hatching and DOC themselves would do the rearing. It all sounded really good, but after a year a lot of problems had arisen and we were asked to go over and give some advice at a meeting, which we did. The next year there were more problems and again we went over to help. The third year and they asked if we would consider taking back particularly the rearing part of the programme, which we were happy to do. A pleasant outcome, too, was that

RESCUE ONE NEW ZEALANDER'S CRUSADE TO SAVE ENDANGERED ANIMALS

Four Okarito kiwi chicks cuddle up in a box.

they then agreed to reimburse us for some of our outlay. Until then we had been covering everything, with a yearly cost well in excess of $100,000, so in a roundabout way we were now much better off. A bit further south another kiwi sub-species, the Haast, was also down to about 200 birds and struggling to maintain itself. We ended up doing quite a bit of work for that programme as well. You can spend your life working in conservation and never know if you've made any difference. These programmes were exciting because you could measure the success by the number of birds and we now know that the populations have pretty much doubled because of the effort being put in.

    The South Island is also the home of the largest and most impressive kiwi in New Zealand, the roa or great spotted kiwi. Now found mainly in the high country in a few areas of the northern half of the island, it isn't an easy species to study and is probably the least understood. A young female was brought in to us. Her name was Mohua, and she had lost the tip of her beak, which had broken off when it got caught in the lid of a box during a translocation. As a result she was unable to feed herself and couldn't be released. Some wanted

CHAPTER THIRTEEN **CAN DO KIWI**

her euthanised, but instead she came to us to be looked after. For months she had to be hand fed every day, but then the edges of the beak slowly grew and by careful trimming we managed to get it serviceable again so she could eat by herself, although it continues to need regular attention.

A small ONE programme was started with the roa, using eggs from up the Hurunui in North Canterbury, Arthur's Pass, the Paparoas on the West Coast, and finally from a small population in the Nelson Lakes. Again it was an exciting programme, as these birds were quite different from the other species to handle, and because so little was known about them, we were discovering things all the time. The programme has never really developed much because, for some reason, DOC have little interest in pursuing it. They really do not know the true numbers of roa, but they are generally recognised as being low and declining at an estimated rate of 3 per cent a year. That figure has been trotted out for at least ten years, and nobody seems to worry. When I first got involved with kiwi, it was thought that the North Island brown could be heading for extinction. Since then numerous community groups have been formed, all conducting their own trapping and restoration programmes. They have totally reversed the tide and now actually play a much bigger part in their conservation than DOC. The North Island kiwi is reasonably safe compared with the South Island species, and yet all the money and support goes into the North Island birds. It seems to be more a case of being seen to be doing something than actually doing it. Many of those involved in the decision-making appear to be more wrapped up in the DNA profiles and breeding co-efficients. The instructions come to mate bird A with bird B, and you know it won't happen because they hate each other's guts. You can't breed bird A with bird B, because they came from a different area. We keep playing God and forget that these things are just part of nature and all we're doing is preventing the process of evolution. Until recently Mohua, our lovely great spotted kiwi, wasn't allowed to be displayed to the public and we weren't allowed to obtain a mate for her.

Fortunately in the past a few people have bucked the trend. Otorohanga Kiwi House has always been a major contributor to Kiwi conservation, and its founder, local chemist Barry Rowe, did a lot of pioneering work. He wasn't allowed to have any kiwi, though, so eventually he went out and got his own, and went on to create one of the first successful breeding establishments.

Probably much naughtier was Elwyn Welch who, back in the 1950s, decided that the best way to save the takahē was to get some eggs and hatch them. He travelled down to Te Anau with some broody bantams in the back of his car, went up into the Murchisons and took some eggs. These went back

Shaun Horan with Mohua.

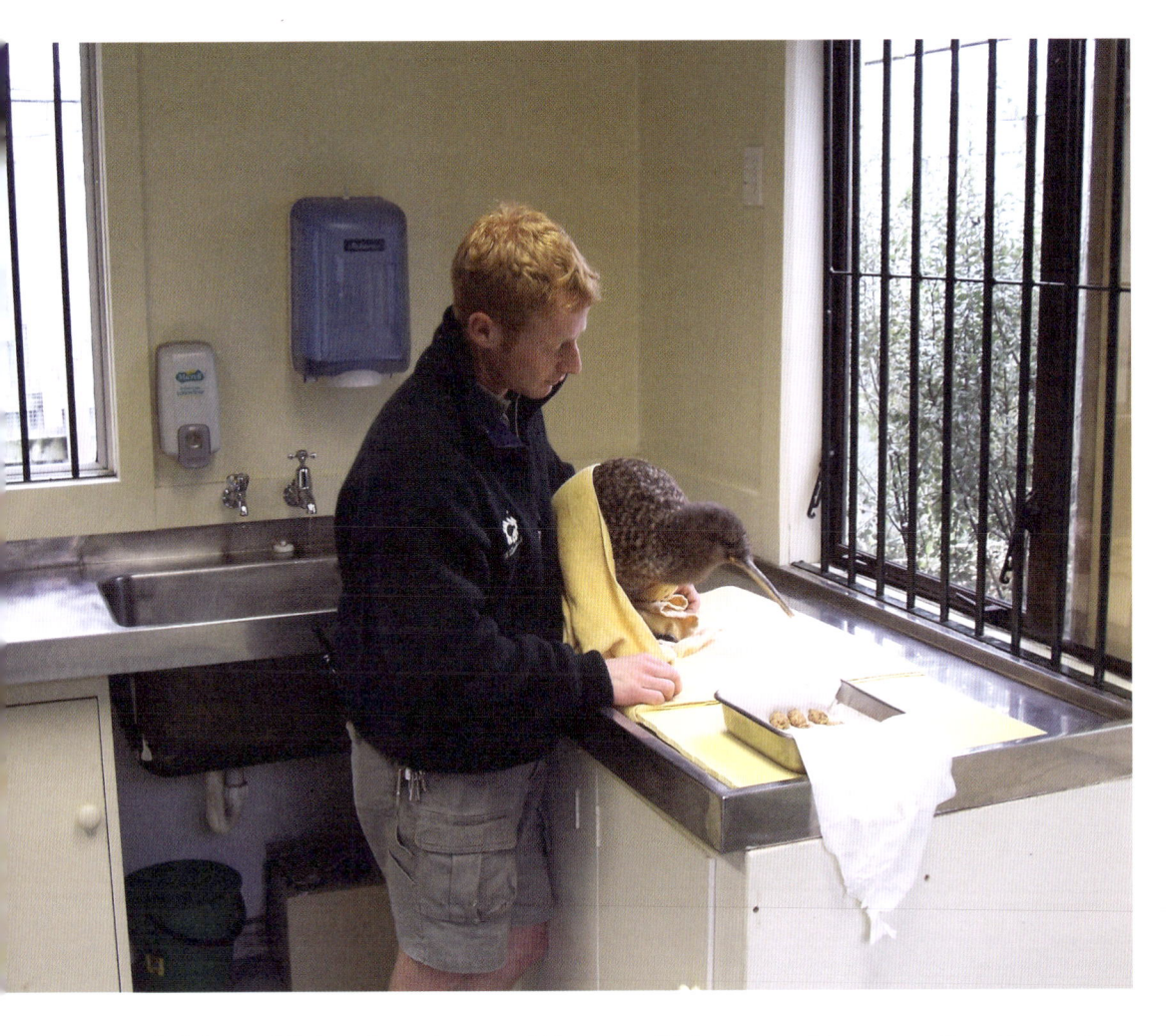

to a fledgling wildlife park starting out of Masterton. He kept everything very quiet until eventually they did hatch. It was then widely reported, and cars queued up for miles to see these birds. He received such acclaim that the Wildlife Service found it difficult to do anything, and the facility went on to become the National Wildlife Centre at Mount Bruce, where they congratulated themselves on their achievement.

Kiwi belong to a small group of flightless birds called ratites, which also includes emus, ostriches and the now extinct different species of moa. Not being able to display real moa, we decided that an ostrich would be the next best thing. Ostriches aren't to be taken lightly. They're massive birds with powerful legs, and a kick that even a lion will respect. A friend of mine collecting some goats from an ostrich farm heard the following story. The next-door neighbour was a large, loud and uncouth person who, as

CHAPTER THIRTEEN **CAN DO KIWI**

often is the case, owned a tiny fluffy dog, which kept coming through the fence and annoying the ostriches. Over breakfast one morning the farmer saw the male ostrich walking around the paddock with two little things sticking out both sides of its beak. Puzzled, he went out and risked going up to see what it had. To his horror, he saw it was the two back legs of the little dog, still wriggling, and so jumping up he managed to grab one and pull the creature out. He ran to the fence with it, put it down on the grass and was giving it mouth-to-mouth when the owner turned up. When he heard what had happened, he turned red with rage, marched up to the ostrich and unleashed a mighty haymaker punch into its chest. For the ostrich, grumpy at losing its breakfast, this was the last straw. Leaping in the air, it flattened the owner completely, and the farmer had to leave the dog and drive the now furious bird away. An ambulance was called and the owner was stretchered off, clutching his dog, shaking his fist and saying, 'I'm going to sue you.' The dog survived and the owner sold out, leaving the ostriches in peace again.

Right: New Zealand's first kiwi encounter free of glass and walls under construction.

Ours was a huge male, who for some reason the staff called Bubbles. Ostriches have a nutty elegance all of their own. Graceful in repose, they can suddenly fling themselves into a whirl of feather dusters and turkey drumsticks, controlled by a brain slightly larger than that of a barnyard fowl. Anything to them is vaguely edible, and they can hinge open their beaks to swallow the strangest things such as tennis balls, with ease. In spite of his loopy and unpredictable behaviour, Bubbles was a great favourite with us all. He loved the leaf blower that we used every morning, and would chase and dance in the clouds of leaves as they were kicked up around him. No one ventured into his paddock, however, without taking serious precautions.

RESCUE ONE NEW ZEALANDER'S CRUSADE TO SAVE ENDANGERED ANIMALS

Above: Nick Ackroyd shows a great spotted kiwi to a group of enthusiastic visiting children.

The years went by and age started to catch up with Bubbles. Sometimes he needed a hand to stand up, and the vets who were monitoring him warned that nothing could be done and it was purely a matter of time. Bubbles' future was discussed quite openly at staff meetings and eventually we decided that his quality of life was fading and his time had come. Because trying to restrain an animal like Bubbles in order to euthanise them can be very traumatic, it's often kinder and quicker to use a firearm. We could afford to wait for the right moment, which arrived early one evening when the park was empty and the staff had gone home. A perfect time to do a

CHAPTER THIRTEEN **CAN DO KIWI**

Tim Gamblins with Bubbles the ostrich and the leaf blower he loved.

job that no one wants to know about. Bubbles was sitting quietly by the fence, eyes closed and skin pale. I had a gun in the car; he would be totally unaware of anything. I loaded the gun, walked up, put it through the fence and cocked it. Slowly putting it to my shoulder, I took aim and curled my finger around the trigger. Suddenly Bubbles' eyes shot open and he leapt into the air and took off as if he had received a massive electric shock.

After that, Bubbles never looked back. He was completely rejuvenated, never had another sick day and confounded everyone by living happily for another year until we had a huge storm that blew over a large tree in his enclosure. He was found dead at the base of it, not through any injury, but presumably because his heart had finally given out. He was put to rest, a much loved if enigmatic animal. I guess that if there was a lesson here, it's about the power of the mind, and the dangers of appearing ill.

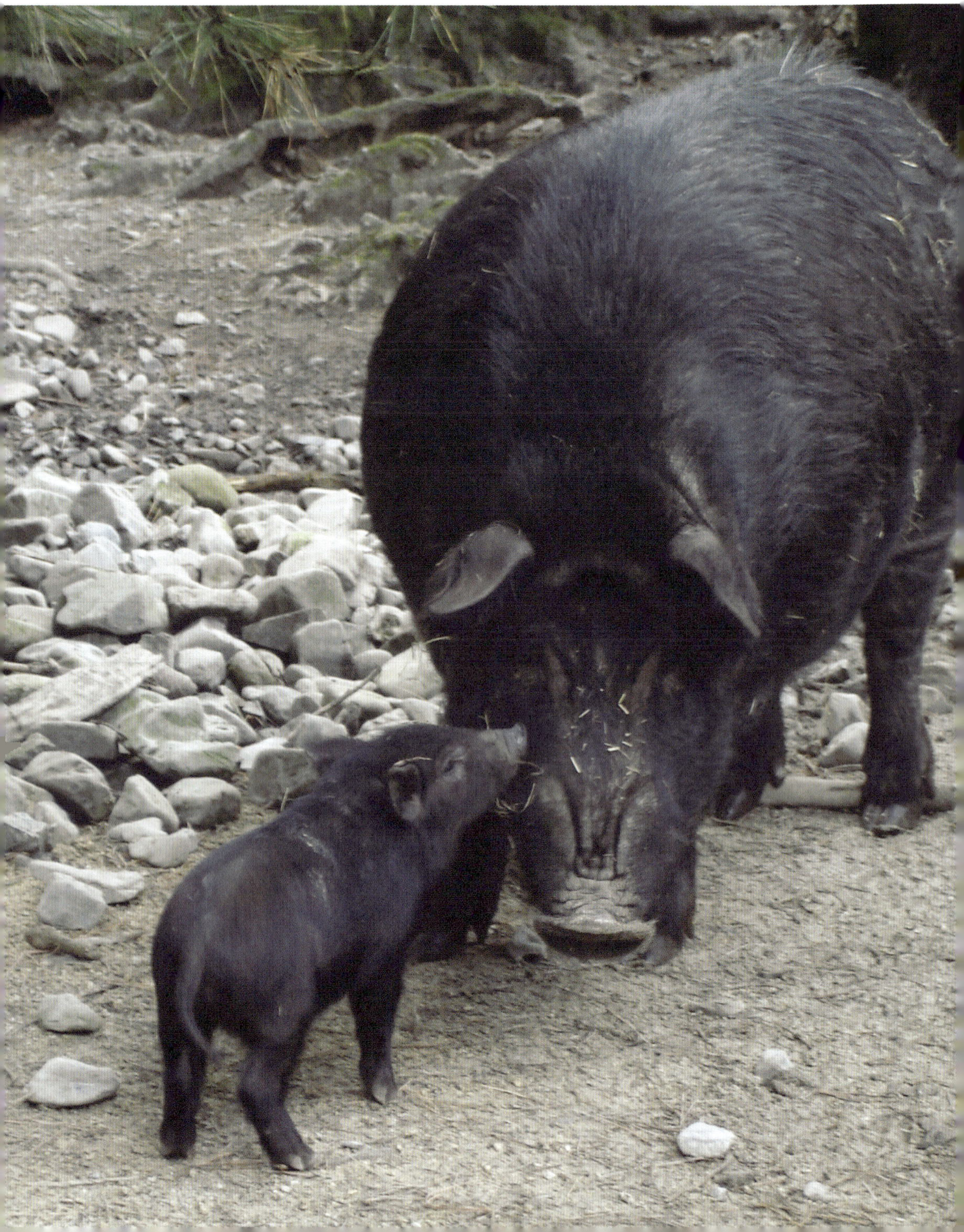

CHAPTER FOURTEEN

A PIG OF AN IDEA

The beat of Latin American music thumped through the sultry heat of the night, and below me in the darkness of the Takaka Valley a crystal clear bubbling river flowed down into tranquil Golden Bay. It was a magical night, velvet star-studded sky merging into the outline of the hills behind me. In the fading dusk a huge bull yak had stood looking down on me, his massive horns and outsized shoulders making him look like a cartoon image of a wrestler. Behind me the lights of the house glowed warmly, inviting me back inside. With some reluctance I headed back from the peace of the night and into the house, spilling over with people. I was at Bencarri Farm, the home of Mathew Benge and his partner Ruth Carrigan — hence the name — who operated a wildlife park at Kotinga incorporating a range of animals, and an eel-feeding experience in the river itself. It was Mathew's birthday, and I had come up from Christchurch to help with the celebrations.

They knew how to party in Golden Bay, I'd have to hand them that. Out on the enclosed verandah was set up an ancient dentist's chair, all porcelain, dark wood and shiny metal. A feature in its own right and one that brought back some unfortunate memories of the past. It was manned by a team of partygoers, representing a medical team from the TV series *Shortland Street*, whose aim was to ensure that everyone carried the same social diseases, and so there was no reason to be shy and hold back. One by one everyone was press-ganged into the chair, and had to submit to the ministrations of the female doctor, who had a sheep drench gun in her hand attached to a bag of tequila over her shoulder. After biting on a slice of lemon and then licking

Opposite: An Auckland Island piglet at Staglands Wildlife Park listens to words of wisdom from its father.
Photo: Gail Simons

some salt off the web of your thumb, you were laid back in the chair and administered as many squirts of tequila as you could reasonably take. I had passed the test, hoping that no one else carried any germs that I didn't, and so with now some immunity could watch other poor souls submit, some passively, some struggling all the way. I have to admit it was a hell of a way to start a party.

The guests were a diverse lot – recovering addicts and prostitutes, plus several who looked as though they were well on the way to becoming one or the other; men holding hands and giving shy glances; artists, poets, deadbeats and the wealthy. Ruth, immaculate in full evening dress, and Mathew, in tails and bow tie, circulated graciously among them. More like a Mad Hatter's dinner party, I thought to myself, and slipped through the crowd and into the relative calm of the living room. John Simister and his new partner Sarah Purdy were there, talking to a man who stood, back to the fireplace, with his feet apart, and eyes that showed the signs of many years scanning horizons. A cowboy or a sailor, I decided. Julian Matson was his name, and he turned out to be the latter. The initial small talk developed into an in-depth conversation, especially when I discovered he had spent some time in the sub-Antarctic, and in particular the Auckland Islands.

'Now there's a place I'd like to go back to,' I said. 'There are some pigs down there that DOC are wanting to eradicate, and we need to get some off the island first.'

'That's not too much of a problem,' he said. 'I'll take you down.'

Boozy talk at a party, I thought, but as the conversation developed, I began to change my mind somewhat. He just happened to be the captain responsible for the vessel *Sea Surveyor*, which was a survey ship, ideal for such a job, and coincidentally could be made available just after the coming Christmas of 1998. By the end of the evening we had talked through all aspects of a plan, had two more shots of tequila, had obviously known of each other for twenty-odd years and life had no barriers.

Come the next morning, and my sea-going mate had sensibly gone. A prostitute was asleep in the dentist's chair, and Ruth and Mathew were last seen dancing on the lawn like will o' the wisps, to disappear in the growing light of the dawn. It was a long and reflective drive back to Christchurch, with plenty of time to dwell on the previous night's events. I've always marvelled at the way opportunities present themselves if you stay focused on something. What had previously been a potential project had become a possible project. The conversation with Julian had removed many of the previous obstacles. Could we put the final pieces together, and make it work?

CHAPTER FOURTEEN **A PIG OF AN IDEA**

The first pigs had been liberated on Auckland Island in 1807 by Captain Abraham Bristow of the *Sarah*, which meant they offered a window into history now over two centuries old. The Rare Breeds Conservation Society, asked to comment on a proposal to eradicate the pigs from the island, had expressed the wish to obtain a viable breeding group. DOC had agreed and I had been asked if I would lead an expedition in an attempt to catch some. We put in an application for a Lotteries grant and a few months later we got the welcome news that it had been approved. In the end it was not enough, and so we advertised for people to come, and chose six to be paying working passengers, making a team of twelve. Added to that was a three-person film crew from *Country Calendar*, who were thrilled at the opportunity to do a programme and pay for their share of costs. There was also to be a DOC officer on board, who turned out to be Wayne Costello, whom Dave and I had met while catching rabbits.

First we had to establish the essential core of people without whom we weren't going anywhere. That in itself wasn't too difficult. There was me as expedition leader, and Dave Matheson as veterinarian. We then needed two experienced hunters with dogs. Hunters, hearing about the trip, had written and rung from all over New Zealand. They all had the best teams of dogs, ones they had bred themselves from a long line of cracking pig dogs, or they had paid thousands of dollars when they bought them off a top breeder, and they had all caught huge boars that no other hunter had been able to get near. There were, however, a couple of hunters I knew of, Brent McClintoch and Bob Page. Brent was a farm manager from Marlborough with whom I had hunted several times. He was quiet, reserved and totally dependable. Bob had spent his life as either a commercial fisherman/diver or a hunter. Hunting and especially pig, was not a sport for him but his life, 'what he did'. He was a rugby player of some renown. One day he was late for practice and the coach demanded to know why.

'Well,' said Bob, 'it's like this. The dogs were onto a good pig and couldn't hold it. I've spent all afternoon chasing the bloody thing but got it in the end. Came straight here.'

'You'll have to get your priorities right,' was the reply. 'It's either rugby or pig hunting.'

And so Marlborough lost one of its best players, who was also picked as being All Black material.

Those priorities didn't change. My friend Rick Denton had recently had a ring from Bob's wife, asking if he had seen him.

'No', said Rick. 'Why?'

'Well, he told me he was just going to take his young team for a run yesterday afternoon, and I haven't seen him since.'

It turned out that Bob had indeed taken the team out for a run, but it was a good day and they all went further than they intended. Then they got onto some really good pigs and the young team were coming into their own. Time passed, as it does, and darkness fell and there were still dogs out hunting. Bob got back at noon the next day with a great grin and some proven dogs. That marriage lasted about as long as his rugby career.

These two were my perfect pig hunting partners and the deal was done.

We not only needed a vet, but also a human medical officer and Dave's wife Judy, experienced and no nonsense, was perfect for the job. Everybody had to submit all their medical details before we left. A full medical kit was then assembled, including everything from body bags up. Just prudent preparation.

Slowly the team came together. From the outside it may have looked a bit of a Dad's Army, but under that patina was shiny steel. No one had to prove why they were there. They had been there, done that and we just needed to link together as a group. We had several meetings together in Christchurch to go over the plans and allow for eventualities, of which there were several. The list was endless and kept getting added to as the time got closer.

Our main plan for capture involved the use of dogs. Generally speaking, no dogs are ever allowed in such an area. DOC were very supportive but we had to adhere to the standards they laid down: the dogs we were hoping to use on the island had to be assessed by one of the department's dog handlers, who would measure the level of control between the handlers and their animals. This is good standard practice, and normally such dogs go through a long and regimented programme before any such approvals are given.

In the end we had six dogs certified, along with the handlers. Bob's were a mixed bag. Boof was a largely white seven-year-old battle-scarred bull mastiff cross, who, according to Bob, had so few teeth left that he had to suck on pigs' ears rather than hold them. Red was definitely of mixed and undeterminable breed, and a hard dog at five years of age. Boof was the one with the brains; Red provided the muscle. The third member of Bob's team was Beau, a brindle greyhound cross and the youngest at three years of age. An impetuous hard-working dog who covered heaps of ground, he complemented the other two well. Brent had just two relatively small, solid, black bull terrier crosses called Sas and Bull. They were highly experienced, nuggety little dogs, happy to find or hold, as long as they were hunting. The sixth dog was one of a Rick Denton's, a delightful little

CHAPTER FOURTEEN   **A PIG OF AN IDEA**

Bob Page with Red.

tan-coloured bull terrier called Tank, who was general back-up and also certified for my use.

The weeks and days passed, and it wasn't long before we were getting down to countdown time. Then, on the appointed day, one by one the vehicles arrived in Invercargill, and for the first time we had the whole team together and could meet one other. The city had decided to put on a mayoral reception for us, to which we had all received formal invitations. Since none of us had dress clothing, we all went along in our best casual attire. Invercargill Mayor Tim Shadbolt was there with a number of councillors, plus some local dignitaries. There were nibbles and speeches, and drinks produced from circulating trays of wine. With a free bar running, it was a convivial group. We finally managed to extricate from the function, and wandered our way home through the deserted streets that were a bit of a shock to some of the North Island contingent, who were used to the hustle and bustle of the larger cities. You could stand in the main street and fire a shotgun up the middle of it, without fear of hitting anyone.

The next morning, 12 January 1999, Bob and Brent were the first two away, loaded with dogs, meat for the dogs, food for the pigs and so on. They needed to be there first as a local TV crew had asked to film the dogs in particular boarding. As is standard television practice, they had to do this over and over, but by the time the dogs had walked on and off the gangway several times, they and their handlers were starting to question why they were doing it, while also suffering the inane questions of an eager young journalist. Looking up at Bob, the reporter asked, 'Tell me, Mr Page, what makes you think that these particular dogs are capable of capturing the pigs down on the Auckland Islands?'

Bob's answer was to point to his dogs and say, 'That one's seven years old, that one's five and the other's three. They never live that long if they're not good enough.'

'But how can you make them good enough?' was the next rather naive question.

'There's a heaven for dogs, and for me, three pair of boots a year, boy, three pair of boots a year. That's what it takes,' replied Bob as he disappeared up the gangway for the last time, followed by his faithful team.

The *Sea Surveyor* was a relatively squat boat, with a purposeful look about her. She had a worryingly blunt bow, that didn't bode well for a smooth passage, but that aside she was roomy and comfortable. Last-minute medical and waiver of responsibility forms were signed in case of accident, the good mayor came down to say goodbye, the crowds waved from the docks, the ropes were cast and we were away.

If most of the party had known what lay ahead, however, there would have been fewer smiling faces. Dinner was being cooked as we sailed down the harbour and served as we hit Foveaux Strait. The tide was running and that notoriously lumpy piece of water was just as bad as I would be expecting on a bad day. The meal had just finished and I was sitting at the table with my back braced against the hull. On the other side of the saloon I could see the

CHAPTER FOURTEEN **A PIG OF AN IDEA**

porthole rising and swinging wildly, until it plunged down into the swells and green water filled the glass. The ship plunged violently, then rose high in the air, flinging Ross Fraser across the saloon and onto our table, breaking the leg of his chair on the way. Within a matter of minutes it had become mayhem. Food was hastily picked up, cleaned up and put away. Many stumbled to their bunks; others found their miserable holes and fought their own private turmoil. We ran into Port Pegasus on Stewart Island that night, and sheltered until the storm had passed us by. When comparative calm had returned, we lifted anchor and with more stolid resignation punched our way south. For most it was a brutal introduction to the aptly named Roaring Forties.

Dawn had just broken as we sailed past Enderby Island and the headland on which my last challenge had finally been secured, the now famous seaweed-eating cattle. Sandy Bay drifted past, the focus for the rare rabbit hunt. An emerald bay with striking white sandy dunes across one corner, it was the only such geographical feature in the whole Aucklands group. Enderby and Rose Islands faded into the dull light of the rising dawn as we sailed past and we began to pick up the headlands of Port Ross which, weather permitting, was to be our base. There was a hut at Deas Head, just inside the Port Ross Harbour, and we headed for and anchored in the inlet. After the sea voyage we were looking forward to getting out and walking on some dry and stable land. If we were pleased to be out, the dogs were ecstatic. Like many of us, they hadn't escaped lightly the traumas of the sea journey and were also suffering from the effects of seasickness. Indeed it was to be a couple of days before some of the party, canine and human, were recovered enough to take an active part. Bob's Beau was one such casualty.

We quickly set up a shore camp, and while that was being established, and although time was getting on, a group of us headed off up the harbour in the two runabouts, laden with men and dogs. The sea was coming up and the soaking spray powering over the bow of the Zodiac was turning us blue with cold and making us stiff from chilled muscles. Gratefully we saw a line of possible access to the tops where a slip had come down and turned the boats into the shore. We were soon in the shelter of the bush edge, where we lifted the boats out and tied them up to a tree. It was our intention, if possible, to climb right up into the tops of the island in order to establish if there were pigs at that altitude, or indeed, where they were. With that vital information we could effectively plan the next few days. Pleased to be in the

The inhospitable cliffs of Enderby Island.

calm of the bush, we began working our way up through the rata forest. The exertion got the blood flowing and soon we were just comfortably wet, and more than a little excited, for there were definite signs of a pig having recently travelled the bush edge. Slowly we ascended through the changing layers of vegetation until eventually we heaved ourselves through the last tangle of interlocking branches doing their best to ensnare us, and into the beginning of the tussock-clad top faces. Although we had found some pig sign, it had decreased, and become older, as we got higher. There appeared to be little reason that a pig would want to live up there at that time of the year, and so we rather reluctantly headed back down.

Back on the shore, after a quick conference, we decided to separate into two teams. Brent would head north up the coast with his dogs and helpers, while Bob and his team would work the coast south. Terry Nelley, Wayne and I were backing up Bob, and we thought that we had the best deal, because we had seen the fresh pig sign earlier and knew that meant we had a reasonable chance. Waving them 'good luck' as they motored off, we set ourselves about 100 or so metres back from the coast and worked our way along it. Bob was in front, with the two dogs, Red and Boof, fanned out, one on each side. Working independently, they hunted left and right, and after about five minutes of being away, would suddenly appear again and turn up at Bob's side. A quick look at the boss, a nod and they would be off again, searching their allotted sides.

Time went on and distance was being covered, when Bob commented that Red hadn't come back: he must be tracking on something. Boof turned up a minute or so later and Bob gave him a pat and kept him alongside. We stood in the trees and just waited, listening. Suddenly a sharp bark split the air like an electric spark. Boof took off like a rocket and it was all on. 'Go,' said Bob. 'He's got one.' Adrenaline pumping and the hunt was on. Terry and I tore through the tangled mass of trees, fighting through the undergrowth and clawing our way around the twisted trunks The sound of the melee ahead kept shifting as the pig moved and our breath was becoming shorter. Soon there was a huge commotion going on down at the water's edge as Terry and I arrived simultaneously, with Wayne in close pursuit behind. The dogs had a large black boar among the rocks and an epic battle was taking place. He was in his prime and certainly taking no nonsense from the dogs, spinning like a top and lunging at them with his short, razor-sharp tusks. Fully aware of the boar's capabilities, the two dogs worked as a team, one distracting him while the other waited patiently for that inevitable opportunity to get a 'hold', without being ripped to pieces in the process.

The boar broke from the dogs, plunged into the sea and climbed up onto a rock. From there the dogs also had to swim and climb, and their quarry was now well positioned and in a mood to generally dictate the play. Since Terry and I both carried short aluminium catching poles with a noose at the end, I suggested that we try and get one over the boar's top jaw. This wasn't

The tricky task of getting the boar off the rock.
Photo: Wayne Costello

particularly hard as he was happy to chase and snap at anything, and soon Terry managed to get his noose over and draw it tight. As soon as I saw that he had a hold, I jumped into the water and was able to grab a hind leg and swing and drag the pig onto the shore, trying at the same time to beat off the dogs, who were keen to have the last say. Flicking the boar on his side, we immobilised his front end by laying a heavy boot firmly across his neck, to keep that long, lethal nose on the ground. We put some strong tape around his muzzle, taped his jaws closed and also covered the tusks. We also tied his legs and, once he was sedated, we could finally sit back and look with a certain amount of pride and exhilaration at our first capture.

So this was the famed Auckland Island pig that we had come so far to see and collect. A jet-black young adult boar, he was in relatively light condition for his size, probably weighing around 50 kilos. His tusks weren't long, about 60 millimetres, but that was a pretty dangerous length. As pig tusks grow and curl backwards, they can become quite useless, especially in a very old boar. These were viciously sharp and a good length to hook and open up anything. His nose was certainly long, and his whole head and body were narrow, culminating in a long almost donkey-like tail that hung straight to the ground, unlike a normal pig's tail with its characteristic curl. He might not win first prize at an A&P show, but he was our pig and we were absolutely delighted.

A call on the radio soon brought one of our paying guests, Graham Thompson, racing over in the Zodiac, and we were quickly loaded up and on our way back to camp. Halfway back and we heard over the radio that Brent's team had also caught a pig, a small black sow, and so for our first day on the island it looked like being a pretty good start. We had a breeding pair, no injuries and the weather was holding. Back at camp a working party was building cages out of the sheets of mesh we had brought over with us. Dave gave the captives a full vet check, treated any injuries and they were released into the cages with their beds of shredded paper.

The next day we were back in the boats and heading up the harbour to the site of the ill-fated agricultural and whaling Hardwicke settlement, established at Port Ross from 1849 but closed within three years. There was little left of the township. The cemetery had been fenced off and the few tombstones that remained were protected from the effects of sea lions and other overweight, inconsiderate island vandals. Some graves were those of shipwrecked mariners who had drowned or died of starvation. Others barely had a chance to live their life. There were five weddings while the colony lasted, and sixteen known children were born; two of those remained behind in the cemetery. The houses had all gone, along with other town buildings, and even the sites themselves had long disappeared into the slow-growing bush. There was a tree that had some names carved into it, but otherwise everything had slowly been absorbed back into the land. We found a brick plinth just off the beach in close-by Terror Cove, the remnant of an 1874 German expedition sent to observe the transit of Venus.

That afternoon saw us out at the entrance of Port Ross itself, again split into two groups and hunting separate areas along the coast. Wayne, Terry, Bob and I made up one team, and on this excursion the *Country Calendar* film crew was also with us. It started off well. We had been going for only a short time when we got onto another boar, again black and feisty but soon captured and trussed up. A short carry to the coast, a radio call to Graham and it was on its way back to the *Sea Surveyor*. Elated, we continued on around the coast, then struck a little inland, but soon got ourselves tangled up in thick scrub. The further in we went, the less pig sign we saw, and so worked our way back closer to the coast itself. We continued on through the tangled rata, heading out now towards a headland. We eventually broke bush and stepped out onto a rocky shelf, with a fringe of grass, where we dumped our swags and sat down for a rest. For the Aucklands it was a tranquil scene. From our vantage point we could see the *Sea Surveyor* heading east across the bay and further down the coast. The day was warm, and we sat with our backs nestled into the rocks for shelter from the wind.

With Terry Nelley in the almost impenetrable rata bush.

Suddenly there was a bark from the bush, a sound that brought Bob instantly upright with an oath. There was no time for discussion. Running and diving between the trees, we eventually tracked down the source, about 100 metres up the coast. By the time we arrived there was a whirligig of pig, dogs and hunks of vegetation, accompanied by a medley of squealing screams, yelps, barks and the crashing of shrubbery. Red and Boof were hard onto a good-sized black and tan boar, who was more than capable of looking after himself, and there was nothing silent about this one. It was a bit of a stand-off, until Terry and I arrived, which shortened the odds against the boar. This was particularly because Terry who, being shorter than either Bob or me, was almost as quick as any dog, could run through the tangled bush like a ferret and possessed the temperament of a fox terrier who likes nothing better than a good scrap.

CHAPTER FOURTEEN A PIG OF AN IDEA

Our standard technique in such circumstances was to wait until the dog was addressing the front end of the boar, jump in and grab a hind leg, then lift the animal's rear off the ground and roll it onto its side. The theory was good and worked well providing you got the hold quickly and didn't let go, for pigs can spin around and exchange ends in a flash, and you won't talk yourself out of that situation. While trying to get some control over the pig itself, you also then had to deal with the dogs, who hadn't heard the whistle go: for them the game was still well and truly on. There was every likelihood of being bitten yourself, as the dogs, once fired up, had little understanding of anatomy, or awareness of where the pig began and you ended. Indiscretions were common, but you never really knew if they were by mistake, or driven by a sense of humour and settling of old scores. It was only ever Bob's arrival that brought some serious discipline back into our canine gladiators.

On this occasion, Terry got that vital back leg, which then allowed me to grab a front foot, and between us we rolled the pig onto his side and held him with a boot implanted firmly but delicately on his neck. It was only once we had him in this position and, with a certain amount of difficulty, had driven the dogs off, that we could consider trussing him up.

'I should have guessed that bloody dog was onto a pig. When we were lying there I saw him tracking along the shore and into the bush with his nose to the ground,' said Bob. It was Red, the dog who never slept, who had picked the boar up. Red was an unusual dog. Until he was given to Bob, he was going to be destroyed because of behavioural problems. His innate distrust of people meant that if you went to pat him you risked losing your arm. He was content in his own company and working for his master. As the days went on he relaxed a bit and became more used to us. When travelling in the small boats he would sometimes lean against you for support, or back into you for warmth and protection from the spray, and even tolerate being rubbed with a hand. He would never stop working, however, and this wasn't the last time he would wander off by himself while everyone was resting, and find a pig on his own

He had certainly done a very good job on this occasion. Our captive was a fine boar, whom we studied with great interest and growing excitement. He was black and tan, this fellow, and with an impressive nose that seemed to go on and on. We had anecdotally heard of pigs on the island having noses a third the length of their bodies, and although this wasn't quite that, it wasn't too far away. For the animal's size, the head and body seemed very narrow, and the eyes appeared to be too close together. The general appearance was that of a high-shouldered animal tapering off at the rear end, with the now characteristic donkey-style tail. Some documents have suggested that this could be an Asian wild pig characteristic coming through from the first release. It was obvious that this pig had spirit and wasn't to be messed around with, a trait that endeared him to Bob, who fell instantly in love with him, and called him Boris. Boris was put over Bob's massive shoulders and carried triumphantly back to shore to where our gear lay, still scattered among the rocks.

An hour or so later the *Sea Surveyor* reappeared over the horizon and dispatched a boat to pick us up. It had been a good day. We had caught three boars to add to the one from the previous day. Brent and his team had also caught three pigs, sows, all of which were successfully recovered. We accordingly became known as the boar team, while they became the sow team, which introduced a bit of friendly rivalry into the project. Back at base camp the pigs were all examined and treated by Dave for any injuries and released into their cages, which were covered with tarpaulins to protect them from the weather. They immediately burrowed into their shredded paper and looked as content as could be expected except for Boris, who ground his tusks and flew at anything that approached him, with that deep 'whoof' of an angry pig, leaving no one in any doubt as to his real feelings. It was no good explaining to him that this temporary pig motel was preferable to dying of poison or from pneumonia and starvation. The others seemed relatively relaxed, but Boris was different – a truly wild animal with pride and courage.

The mighty Boris on Bob's broad shoulders.

Since our theory that the pigs, at this time of the year anyway, were mainly to be found along the coast and headlands, seemed to be holding up, we stuck with the game plan the next day. True to form, the sow team captured a sow, while we captured another boar that we had found feeding on a dead sea lion. Most unusually, the weather was still holding, which gave us the opportunity to work headlands and small bays that normally would never have been accessible. There were seldom beaches to land on, normally

CHAPTER FOURTEEN A PIG OF AN IDEA

just a rock shelf slippery with seaweed to leap onto from the boat, before making our way into and through the bush. We had to keep an eye out at all times, for weather changes could be very sudden, and there was always the danger, should that happen, that a boat would be unable to pick us up again. There's little doubt that most of the areas we got into were most unlikely to ever have been visited by a human being.

Nothing could ever be taken for granted, and the speed with which a situation could change was soon very graphically illustrated. Brent's two dogs, Sas and Bull, were certainly proving their experience, making up in speed and enthusiasm for what they lacked in size. They took this from their master who, when hearing a bail was on, had no qualms about throwing himself blindly over the scrub and into the melee, to back his dogs up and sort it out. One day Brent had been a bit slow or the boar he had bailed a bit quick, because it spun around and opened up the calf of his leg. They still caught the boar and tied it up, then looked at Brent. A pressure bandage from the first aid kit was put on to stem the flow of blood, the pig was picked up and everyone withdrew to the ship. A good, private country boy was Brent. He had spent his life with men and wasn't going to bare his body to any female, even if she was a nurse, so it took a few shots of rum before he would relax enough to allow Judy even a cursory peek. What we didn't know at the time was that he had a phobia about his own blood and needles. Fortunately he took one look and promptly passed out, which enabled Judy to clean and secure the wound with sutures as best she could. It wasn't a good place to put in stitches and expect them to hold if he was to continue hunting, for the skin would be stretched and pushed with the muscles working under it. Fortunately it wasn't in a cosmetically obvious place, and only time would tell if it became infected, or if any other complications would develop. When he came around again, he alleviated the pain with a bit more rum, and the pig was from then on known as 'Brent's Boar'. It was a good opportunity to explain to the sow team that they should leave the boars to the more experienced hunters, which only made Brent more determined to keep hunting, and he was away again the next day, even if it was with a slight hobble. No way was he going to let the team down.

One of our objects was to get pigs from as wide a range of places as possible, so as to maximise any genetic diversity. Although we knew there were probably fewer pigs down the other end, I decided that we would pack up and sail down to Carnley Harbour, leaving a couple of people at base camp to look after the animals that we had caught up until then.

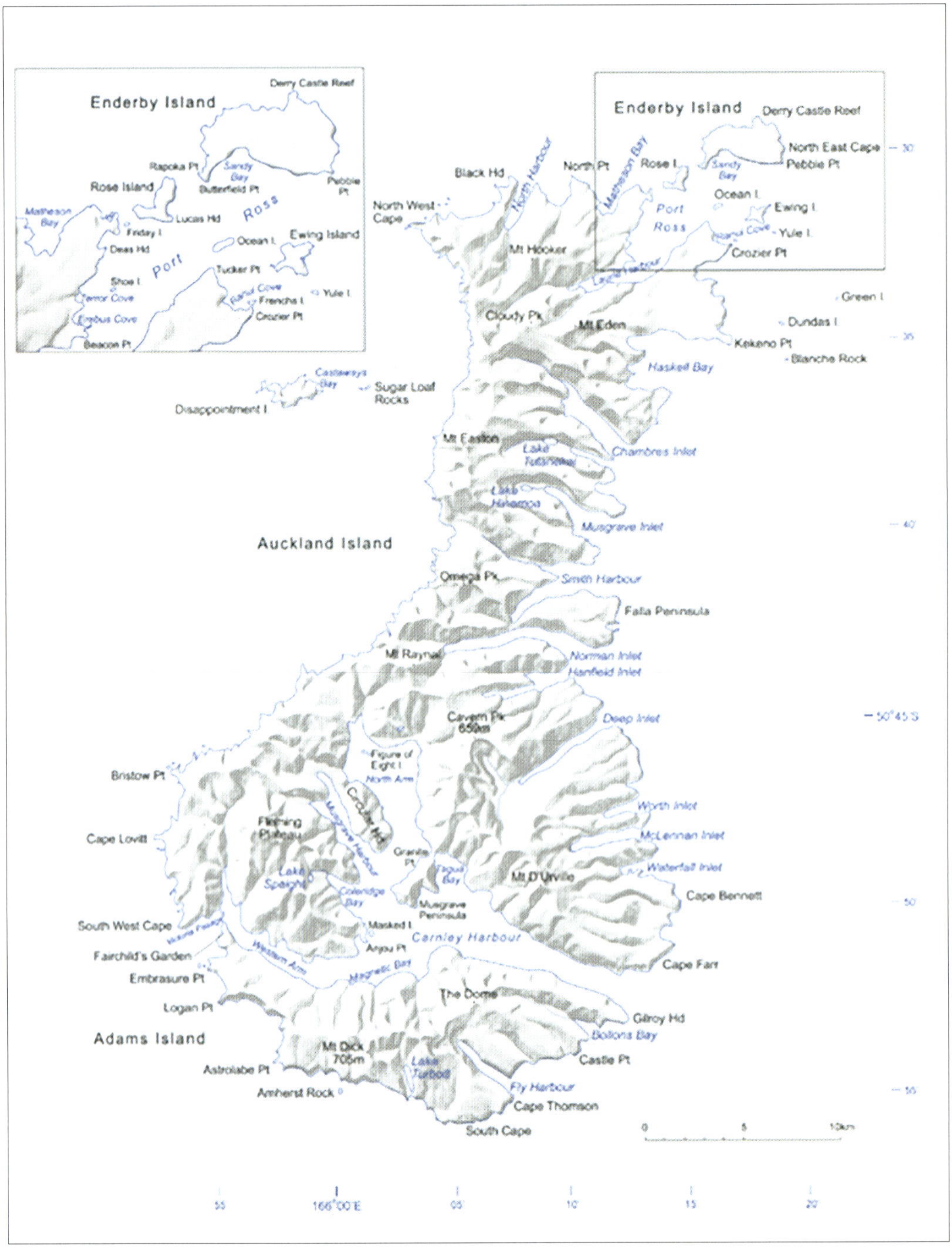

Enderby Island
Derry Castle Reef
Rapoka Pt
Sandy Bay
Butterfield Pt
Pebble Pt
Rose Island
Matheson Bay
Lucas Hd
Ross
Friday I.
Deas Hd
Port
Ocean I.
Ewing Island
Tucker Pt
Shoe I.
Terror Cove
Erebus Cove
Frenchs I.
Crozier Pt
Yule I.
Beacon Pt
Enderby Island
Derry Castle Reef
North East Cape
Pebble Pt
Rose I.
Sandy Bay
Matheson Bay
Port Ross
Ocean I.
Ewing I.
Yule I.
Crozier Pt
North Harbour
Black Hd
North Pt
North West Cape
Mt Hooker
Cloudy Pk
Mt Eden
Green I.
Dundas I.
Kekeno Pt
Blanche Rock
Haskell Bay
Castaways Bay
Sugar Loaf Rocks
Disappointment I.
Mt Easton
Chambres Inlet
Lake Hinemoa
Musgrave Inlet
Auckland Island
Omega Pk
Smith Harbour
Falla Peninsula
Mt Raynal
Norman Inlet
Hanfield Inlet
Cavern Pk 650m
Deep Inlet
Figure of Eight I.
North Arm
Bristow Pt
Circular Hd
Fleming Plateau
Musgrave Harbour
Cape Lovitt
Lake Speight
Granite Pt
Tagua Bay
Mt D'Urville
Waterfall Inlet
McLennan Inlet
Worth Inlet
Coleridge Bay
Cape Bennett
Musgrave Peninsula
South West Cape
Masked I.
Anjou Pt
Carnley Harbour
Cape Farr
Fairchild's Garden
Western Arm
Magnetic Bay
Embrasure Pt
The Dome
Logan Pt
Gilroy Hd
Bollons Bay
Adams Island
Mt Dick 705m
Castle Pt
Astrolabe Pt
Lake Turbott
Fly Harbour
Amherst Rock
Cape Thomson
South Cape
0
5
10km
30
35
40
50°45'S
50
55
55
166°00'E
05
10
15
20

CHAPTER FIFTEEN

HAIR OF THE DOG

'Funny about old Boof's tail,' said Bob. 'It used to be quite long and always got in the way. He lost it after a hard-case pig hunt.' We were gathered around the saloon of the ship and Bob was launching into one of his innumerable stories that flowed in a seemingly endless array, ranging from classic bar-room brawls to face-to-face encounters with white pointer sharks while diving for crays off the Chatham Islands. Most of the stories were hilarious, but when reciting pig hunting episodes his whole face would light up with excitement and his clear blue eyes would shine with enthusiasm for a sport he loved with a passion few can understand.

'We were onto this huge boar. Chased him before and never got him, but this time they had him bailed up under a waterfall. Time I got there they had been on him for a while, and I could see that old Boof was getting a hell of a tough time. We were all pretty knackered and so I blew the boar over with the 30-30 and dragged him out. Boof was lying on the rocks looking a bit queer. I rolled him over and his guts fell out. Poor bugger didn't look too good but I got my needle and thread out and shoved them back in and stitched him up. We were all a bit knocked around so we had a bit of a rest for a while, and then I gutted the pig, threw it over my shoulders and gave the old boy a whistle. It was a hard thing. He stood up to come, wagged his tail and the top half fell off. Bloody pig had bitten right through. He walked out all right, but it took a while for him to get back to full strength again. Second time I've had to stitch his guts in.'

For many people this would seem an horrific experience, and they would

Opposite: The Auckland Islands, an archipelago of New Zealand, lie 360 kilometres south of Stewart Island.
Source: Department of Conservation

RESCUE ONE NEW ZEALANDER'S CRUSADE TO SAVE ENDANGERED ANIMALS

Wayne Costello with the inimitable and legendary Boof.

have difficulty in comprehending the harsh realities of the sport, but the dogs had as much fervour as their masters. Boof was almost a legend. Heavy-set, with a grizzled face and a body covered in scars and lumpy with scar tissue, he had slit eyes that followed every movement and his nose was always testing the breeze. He would forever work upwind, testing every wayward scent, and a pig had to be pretty smart to get away unnoticed. He was slower now, and it sometimes needed a younger dog to catch and hold until he got

CHAPTER FIFTEEN HAIR OF THE DOG

there, but he was a wily old animal, with a lovely temperament that made him a firm favourite of everyone in the party.

We were moored in Waterfall Inlet, which is really the only true all-weather safe anchorage on the island. In many ways it was an idyllic spot, an almost circular little anchorage at the head of the bay, with just enough room to get a boat in and moor it safely. We had come south that day and, stopping at various spots, managed to collect another three pigs. On the way we searched the coastline, taking advantage of the good weather to find evidence of any shipwrecks, as we had been asked to do by DOC. We found it in the form of a huge spar off a sailing vessel that had been washed up and was lying on the edge of the bush. We took detailed measurements and photos, which were later sent to the Maritime Museum in Auckland.

Brent's leg was still hanging together, even though his lips were pressed tighter than they should have been at times, but there was no way that any bloody girl was going to have another go at him. He was quite happy to swallow antibiotic tablets by the handful, preferably washed down with a glass of rum after a successful pig hunt. Any further interference was non-negotiable: he was here to do a job and he wasn't going to let this spoil it.

Sticking out of the water we came across a few timber relics, all that remains of the *Grafton*, which was wrecked in January 1864. The peninsula is named after the captain, an American seaman named Thomas Musgrave. He must have been a very resourceful and practical person, for his handling of the situation was superb. He kept his crew occupied at all times, first building a hut for shelter, then making concrete out of burnt sea shells and starting on a project that saw them remodel the little dinghy they had managed to save and turn it into a 17-foot long boat. To achieve this they made their own forge and bellows out of seal skin, and using that manufactured a saw out of a barrel band, along with nails, spikes and so on from other bits of steel. They also maintained regular entertainment sessions, teaching sessions, brewed beer out of the megaherbs, manufactured soap, mortar and sealskin garments and had a kākāriki as a pet. Musgrave kept a regular journal, written in seal's blood, which was later published as *Castaway on the Auckland Isles*. His entry for Sunday 26 March 1865 read: 'The sea booms and the wind howls. These are sounds that have been ringing almost constantly in my ears for the last fifteen months, for during this time I dare venture to say that they have not been hushed for more than a fortnight together. There is something horribly dismal in this boom and howl, sometimes it makes my flesh creep to hear them.' Musgrave eventually sailed his home-made craft back over 400 kilometres to Stewart Island and led an expedition back down to rescue the

The pigs in their crates ready to be unloaded at Bluff.

rest of his men. Their survival story was in direct contrast to another group of people who were shipwrecked at almost the same time, at the opposite end of the island. With an indecisive captain, and virtually no leadership, the survivors disintegrated, and in their miserable existence largely perished.

We had to go as far as we could go, and that was into the headwaters of Carnley Harbour and up to where the German steamer *Erlangen* had famously hidden for five weeks early in the Second World War. After leaving Dunedin for Australia on 26 August 1939, a few days before war was declared, she had insufficient fuel aboard so moored behind Figure of Eight Island in the North Arm of Carnley Harbour. We could still see where the bush had been cut over to provide fuel for her escape. Other crew members made sails and the vessel made it to Santiago in Chile. There was a lot of other history in this area, some known and some not. We hunted through the site where, in 1900, George Fleming built a homestead and yards, and landed some 2000 sheep. It was a complete disaster and all the animals died within a few years.

We managed to catch another little black sow in the bay up North Arm, and were very happy to know that we had two boars and a sow from this

CHAPTER FIFTEEN **HAIR OF THE DOG**

end of the island as well. Daylight the next morning saw us up anchor and head away back up the coast. As the seas were relatively calm, we managed to hunt several of the bays on the way up and arrived back at Deas Head that evening. We had now covered the length of the island and in conditions few people experience. Whichever god or saint was looking out for us was doing a pretty good job.

Our arrival back into the harbour was cause for some celebration and Nigel the ship's cook was invited on land for some dinner. He arrived carrying a cabbage under his arm named Myrtle, who was his dinner companion. Brian Fowler had had dinner cooking for quite some time, and as was his wont, it required a reasonable lashing of red wine, which needed to be tasted regularly to test its continued suitability. This procedure required companionship from the hut, and as the night passed the party progressed and it was much later that I found my way to my solitary tent tucked up in the trees. As I wormed my way into my sleeping bag and stretched out, smelling the peaty smell coming up from the damp forest floor, mingling with that of equally earthy-smelling well-used socks and shirts, the singing and thumping continued to emanate from the hut, where it floated across the water and mingled with equally happy sounds coming from the ship swinging on her anchor in the light of the moon. I reflected on stories of the early inhabitants on the Aucklands, how they brewed their own beer, had their Saturday night parties and generally manufactured their own fun and entertainment. I had always found some of it a little hard to imagine, but then my last image as I went out of the door of the hut and into the night was of Brian and Terry holding hands and dancing a polka together.

There was yet one other area where I was keen to get a pig – around on the other coast at totally the opposite end of the island to Carnley, at a place called North Harbour. Also the scene of past shipwrecks, North Harbour was a narrow relatively exposed bay, and certainly not a safe anchorage. A sailing ship would have extreme difficulty beating her way back out of it and its marginal shelter provided only a brief respite before an inevitable end. There used to be a small herd of Auckland Island goats living in some of the rocky faces, but they had been exterminated some time ago. After a quick check with the dogs at the head of the bay established that there were no pigs there, we lifted the anchor and withdrew. On the way back, we took the opportunity to revisit Enderby Island. It was interesting to see the changes since the rabbits and cattle had been removed and how the megaherbs were recovering.

Anchoring again at Deas Head, we began to prepare for our departure, as we had decided to run for home the next day. The weather was still holding in our favour, and now that we had a reasonable number of animals – seventeen, all fit and healthy – it was imperative to get them back to New Zealand alive and in as good a condition as possible. All were black except for three who were tan and black, and there was a slight bias ratio towards boars.

Our luck was still holding: it was another settled morning, ideal for loading, and we struck camp immediately. Both pig-hunting teams were out hunting at first light and working the as yet untouched area around the hut, which we had always intended to leave either until the final day, or as a bad weather option. The pigs in their crates were fed and watered for the last time on the island, and the long job of ferrying everything out began. Poles were slid through the pig crates and one by one they were carried away from the hut and slid down the steep bank to the rocks exposed by the tide below, and then onto a waiting boat. It was a mini porcine Dunkirk, achieved only with some difficulty and accomplished with more injuries to the people concerned than the animals themselves. The hunters returned, having had no luck, crammed down a quick breakfast and the packing up continued. With the last of the pigs now gone, the ground under where the cages had been was restored, and the finishing touches put on cleaning the hut and its surroundings. All ready to go and then, no Boof. He had gone, vanished into thin air.

The diesels on the boat had been warmed up and the last of the gear was being stowed, while Bob yelled, whistled and listened along the shore. Suddenly there was a shout: 'I can hear him. He's onto something.' Brent was there in a flash, letting his team go, and Red also joined the fray. They seemed to go in a great circle, and half an hour later were back in the bush a few metres from the hut. All, that is, except Boof. 'Where's the old fool gone now?' grumbled Bob as he started whistling and shouting all over again. Time passed and still more time, and no sign of the dog. We certainly couldn't leave without him but fortunately all the dogs wore electronic tracking collars and so we assembled the tracking gear and picked up a faint signal towards the top of the harbour. Wearily Bob and a couple of others climbed into a boat and, armed with the tracking gear, headed back up the bay. About 4 kilometres later they were opposite the signals, and finally called Boof down to shore, his stump of a tail wagging furiously, and mighty pleased with himself. That was Boof's last hunt on the island and, as always, he had given it his all. Bob reckoned he had a pig but the old boy just wasn't fast enough on his own to catch up. Firmly chained to the boat, he was brought back to the ship, the anchor was lifted, the decks vibrated as the screws bit into the sea, and then

CHAPTER FIFTEEN **HAIR OF THE DOG**

Judy Matheson giving antibiotics to a boar.

smoothed out as the vessel slowly picked up speed, and ploughed her way through the first ocean swell of the voyage home.

The pigs were travelling well, and the weather was as good as anyone could reasonably expect, and with a following sea the ship's motion was much smoother. The cages, which had been made to fit through the hatch cover of the hold, were stacked snugly around the walls, and on top of each other, with tarpaulins underneath. The pigs were dry, warm and appeared little affected by the noise and movement of their new world. We stayed overnight at Port Adventure on Stewart Island and daylight saw the anchor being hoisted for the last time. We headed up the coast and finally across the strait and into Bluff Harbour. It was a tired but exuberant ship that finally threw the lines ashore and tied up once more at the wharf. There was a small welcoming crowd and, as large as life as only he could be, there was Tim Shadbolt. The man certainly had dedication and energy and his consideration was widely acclaimed by all on board.

The pigs now had to be our priority. As soon as everything was secured properly, a tarp was put down on the deck and the cages began to get passed out of the hold, in a laborious and rather unsavoury fashion. It was important to get them on deck, for the day was hot by Southland standards and the loss of movement of the ship also meant the loss of cooling air in the hold. With the best will in the world, getting them on deck was to be an awkward and slow process. By this stage there had been an inevitable build-up of waste material, and as the cages were tilted on their ends to be passed out of the hatch, then those carrying the weight below were rewarded in an unenviable fashion. When the loading was finally completed, the last cameras whirred, and the truck and a small convoy headed out to the quarantine, located just out of Invercargill.

It was now up to Ross Fraser and his team of volunteers to manage the quarantine, which in theory should have been a matter of weeks. Instead it became an absolute mission, and tested everyone's patience and enthusiasm. The testing procedures went on and on, and then the ministry invited the pig industry to comment on the animals' release from quarantine. That opened up another can of worms, as the Pig Council vehemently opposed them being released in case they carried some unknown disease. The whole thing became a stalemate and the months turned into a year. The costs were escalating unavoidably, and although there was a lot of community support, it wasn't enough to continue running the operation. Money had run out, the strain on the caregivers and families was starting to tell when, out of the darkness and to save the day, came Tim Shadbolt who started to use the mayor's discretionary fund, in order to support the pigs, without his council necessarily knowing about it.

At the other end of New Zealand, living in Auckland, was Professor Bob Elliot. Bob had one of those brilliant, enquiring brains, and a strong will to help humanity. His research had led him to believe that he could manufacture a cure for diabetes by using the insulin-producing cells from pigs. The research had ground to a halt, however, when it was discovered that all known pigs carried a porcine retrovirus in their cells, which could be passed on to humans. So all transgenic transplants using pigs had stopped worldwide and this had brought his research to a dead end. Reading about the pigs being held in quarantine in Invercargill, however, made him wonder if, because of their long isolation, they might never have been exposed to this virus. Samples were taken from the animals and sent to laboratories all around the world, and the results came back. Yes, they were free from the virus – the only known pigs in the world that were. It was a game changer.

CHAPTER FIFTEEN **HAIR OF THE DOG**

Invercargill Mayor Tim Shadbolt surrounded by his beloved Auckland Island pigs in 2010. He was a huge supporter of the pigs in Southland.
Stuff / Southland Times

It now became essential that the pigs remained in a secure state of isolation, because once they did leave and became exposed to viruses, they would lose all their value. To overcome this, a purpose-built facility was erected in Auckland and later another one out of Invercargill. All of this cost a huge amount, putting a published value on each animal of up to $450,000. These were now the most expensive and valuable pigs in the world.

The technique that Bob Elliot developed was to take the insulin-producing cells from the pancreas of piglets and encapsulate them with an alginate made from a seaweed. This was a key part of the process, as the coating allowed nutrients in, and insulin out, while blocking the immune system from recognising that the cells were there. The seaweed was a special type found in only two places in the world. One place was in Northern Scotland, and the other, strangely enough, was Bluff Harbour. You would have to assume that it hitched a ride on the bottom of a ship, possibly even the one that brought some Shetland cattle out in those colonial days, and maybe the precursors of the Enderby cows. Whatever the real story, it was a strange coincidence. The process gained medical approval, the trials were extremely successful and the patients were largely cured. Bob continued his research, and found a number of other potential uses. So what began as a simple pig rescue ended up as a multi-million-dollar project, with international ramifications. In spite of all of this, however, the government is researching ways to completely exterminate the Auckland Island pigs, which will effectively close the door on a fascinating piece of New Zealand's heritage, and possibly the opportunity to change the lives of millions of people.

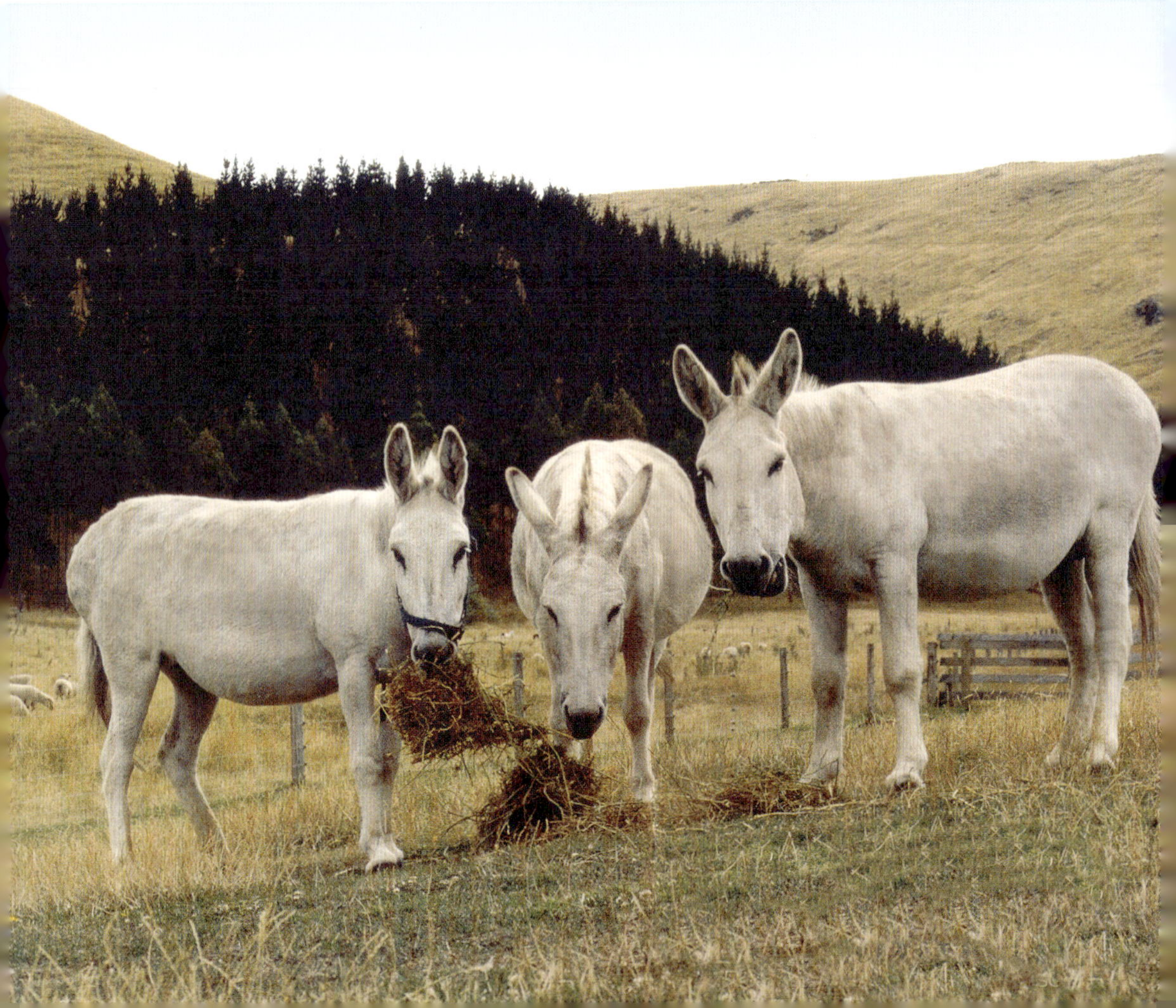

CHAPTER SIXTEEN

A DONKEY DEBACLE

It was a typical Canterbury Show Day. Hot gusty nor'west winds, a press of perspiring people dodging cowpats, flatulence and vendors as they got a thumbnail experience of rural New Zealand. It was later in the afternoon that Dave Matheson, Brian Fowler and I wandered somewhat aimlessly among the exhibits. Being part of the Rare Breeds Conservation Society, who were exhibiting at the show, we were semi-official, and having been involved in various projects and escapades together, were relaxed in one another's company. Now filling in time viewing some of the other exhibits, we wandered out of a marquee munching emu burgers, and were looking with fond eyes towards the beer tent, when a familiar face beamed out from the crowd. It was Mathew Benge from Takaka, who had recently travelled down to the Auckland Islands with us on the pig-hunting expedition. As usual he gave the impression of being as solidly attached to the ground as a D8 bulldozer, while having the wide open relaxed grin of a Mexican bandit holding a royal flush and a fully loaded shotgun. You never knew quite what to expect from Mathew, and this occasion was no different.

'Pleased I ran into you guys,' he said. 'There are some donkeys that need to be caught on the Galápagos Islands. What do you think?'

What did we think? The beer tent certainly increased in importance as the only makeshift office available and we all adjourned to it to hear the detail and discuss the implications of such an unrealistic and improbable venture. According to Mathew, he had been approached by a member of the Galápagos Conservation Trust, Tui De Roy. Tui had been raised in the

Opposite: Ponui Island donkeys are a New Zealand breed that was introduced in 1880, then roamed wild on the Hauraki Gulf island.
Photo: Michael Trotter

Galápagos, spent her wonderful formative years there and had gone on to become a world-renowned naturalist photographer. She had heard about the pig expedition, and wondered if a group of New Zealanders who could do that would be prepared to go to the Galápagos Islands to attempt the same thing with some donkeys. As with most of these projects, this was a case of the wrong animal in the wrong place at the wrong time: the donkeys needed to be culled for the overall benefit of the islands.

To ask if we wanted to do such a thing was like asking if the Pope is a Catholic, but even the logistics of attempting it were daunting, to say the least. We all discussed the project at some length, and as the show drew to a close, and with it the beer tent, we all convinced ourselves that it was a jolly good idea, and indeed there was a certain duty and even a responsibility to conservation to do so.

As I started to explore the concept further, I found it strange that many people had not even heard of the Galápagos Islands. To someone who as a boy had lived within Charles Darwin's experiences on the voyages of the good ship *Beagle*, this was incomprehensible. It was, after all, the wildlife of this remote and harsh group of islands that helped Darwin to formulate his theory of evolution. It appeared that everyone knew about giant tortoises, but as for them coming from the Galápagos, along with blue-footed boobies and other peculiar things, then forget it. The islands had been a favourite stopping off point for sailing ships, which used to load their holds with as many tortoises as they could. Stacked upside down in the cool and dark, they would last weeks, if not months, without food, and so were a ready source of fresh meat during those long voyages. It was such a lucrative trade that it was thought that the original donkeys were brought to the islands in order to transport the tortoises to the waiting ships.

One of the key people in helping to develop the project was a woman living in Ecuador, named Lynn Fowler. Lynn had been brought up on the islands with Tui De Roy, and had done her thesis on the giant tortoises. Not only was she the English-speaking contact with direct links into the Galápagos National Park Service, but also the one driving the project to save some of the animals. At the end of it all, she was going to hold them on her farm in Ecuador and maintain a breeding group. In addition, she wished to accompany the expedition herself, along with her two children. The donkeys were located on Isabela, the largest island in the group. This was one of the most pristine areas in the Galápagos, and only a very small number of people were given approval to land there. It was uninhabited, except for a village of Indians in the bottom corner. According to Lynn, the donkeys were often just

CHAPTER SIXTEEN **A DONKEY DEBACLE**

Above and right: We were focused on donkeys, but the Galápagos Islands are home to a range of unique wildlife, including these marine and terrestrial iguanas.

245

in the bush around the shore, and it shouldn't be too difficult to approach them. Her knowledge of the area and participation was the essential component needed to justify the success of such an operation and the National Park Service eventually approved the project.

A permit was eventually issued for six New Zealanders to link with her and a park warden, in order to capture and remove donkeys. For several reasons this wasn't suitable. If we were to go, we needed enough capable people to be able to achieve our aim and not have to rely on unskilled people who might happen to be over there. Six wasn't enough to capture, train and look after any number of animals, should we succeed. We therefore put the expedition on hold for that year and applied for new permits.

The months again went past, and the Galápagos started to drift into obscurity when almost unexpectedly the new permit arrived. It was for twelve New Zealanders, and came with the paperwork needed to get whatever tranquillising and capture gear that was required onto the islands. Knowing how difficult it was to get any sort of approval to set foot on the Galápagos, this was an almost unprecedented step. We now had to develop a team who not only had the requisite skills but were also prepared to pay both all their own and the expedition expenses. Broadly speaking, there would be two main parts to the operation: first, catch your donkey, and second, get it to a stage where it could be led and generally handled. It was obvious that we needed a capture team of experienced hunters, followed by knowledgeable animal handlers who could also manage the husbandry of the animals as they were captured. There were no fences, pens or yards, and park protocol meant that we couldn't built such structures anyway. We were going to have to rely mainly on tethering any donkeys we caught, which in turn meant constantly monitoring, shifting and supplying them with water.

The catering requirements for the humans were just as complex and necessitated a chef de camp, for we anticipated long, hard days and would be wanting plenty of fuel. The chef has a pivotal and vital role. He or she organises the running of the camp, provides a means of communication, and in some cases entertainment, defuses arguments and helps to keep the team together. Brian Fowler had filled this role before and was an obvious choice. Medical expertise was also essential, for both the animal and human participants, and fortunately again the veterinary role was filled by Dave Matheson, with his wife Judy as the medical nurse. Terry and Heather Nelley, from past trips, weren't going to be left behind. Slowly, in fits and starts, the team came together.

The food logistics took a new turn when the park people informed us that all loose food, such as cereals, had to be frozen for several days before being landed on the islands. We overcame that by the use of a cruise ship, *Polaris*, that was in the area and offered its assistance. One thing they couldn't help with, however, was our personal diet. A list of fruit and vegetables with pips and seeds was circulated: we couldn't eat these before departure, in case some exotic germ plasm piggy-backed a ride through our digestive systems and created yet another problem. Water wasn't normally a huge consideration on such a trip, but where we were going there was none. To cover ourselves we needed eighty 20-litre containers of it, or about 1.5 tonnes. We could buy water on the main island of the Galápagos, but containers were in short supply and had to be purchased and shipped out from Ecuador before we arrived. When the local Ecuadorian contacts suggested a good diet would be tuna and rice with cereal thrown in, it became obvious that there was more than a little difference between our dietary expectations and theirs. I suggested, as politely as possible, that New Zealanders, by reason of their isolation, had developed into a meat-eating nation, and although this was no doubt unhealthy, it was essential for the mental and physical stimulation that would be required.

Final details were stitched together that eventually culminated in us all meeting at Auckland airport, ready to board a plane to Tahiti. Some of us who had flown up from Christchurch had already gained an insight into some of the problems that could make our travel quite tiresome. We had been quite open about the fact that we had drugs, ammunition and firearms with us, not to mention a wide range of knives, electronic communication devices and a range of other bits of equipment that give airlines headaches. Although we had obtained all of the required paperwork and excess baggage notifications, leaving Christchurch was a mission as we had to unpack and repack a lot of equipment in order to satisfy a testy official. We therefore planned a more traveller-friendly approach. We would all approach en masse at the last minute and only Judy and I would do the talking. We would hand over all the paperwork and passports together. We would load the gear quickly and efficiently, at the same time keeping up a running conversation with the people behind the counter. Eleven hours from Auckland and we were practising our new immigration/customs evasion skills in Tahiti. They worked like a charm, and again ten hours later when we arrived on Rapa Nui, Easter Island, where we waved our way through a smiling and relaxed group of officials and blinked our way outside into the tropical sun. Garlands of flowers were placed around our necks and we felt that indeed we must have arrived in a South Seas paradise. At that stage we had no comprehension of the tragedy of Easter Island.

In our three days there, with the help of our guide, Victor Ika, we explored our way around the island. The first thing we noticed was the complete lack of wildlife. No seabirds calling around the coast. No birds flitting in the grass or perching in trees – largely because there were no trees. Everything had gone, taken for food or firewood or other reasons. The second thing we noticed was the feeling of sadness and depression. There were no children laughing in the streets of the villages, the inhabitants appeared sombre, as if the weight of the island's history had taken the joy out of the land. The huge, world-famous moai or statues were awe-inspiring, and, with no real answer to their purpose, still an enigma. Erecting each one must surely have cost many lives. Overexploitation of the island's resources and inter-tribal tensions had been followed by the cruelty of slavery when the Europeans arrived.

Victor, island born and bred, and of royal lineage, had an obvious passion and love for the place. Like many from the island, he had gone to school in Chile as a child, and then on to university in Paris. He spoke seven languages fluently, but his roots were firmly set in Rapa Nui. There were many similarities between our own Māori culture and that of Easter Island, similarities that Victor knew about and was keen to explore. He showed us statues that had been swept aside by tsunami and strewn like flotsam along the coast, and the remains of villages, boat ramps and altars. We saw stone walls made of huge slabs of stone fitted together with a precision that defied explanation, and listened and watched in admiration as Victor stood bareheaded in the mist and rain, singing the songs of his ancestors among the ruins.

We almost added to the tragedy of Easter Island ourselves. Street lights and health and safety were non-existent, and walking back to our accommodation one black night I disappeared down an uncovered manhole. It was a bad fall, slamming my thigh into the upper edge of the hole, and miraculously not breaking it. Later that night when I tried to stand the pain shot up my body and I collapsed onto the edge of the bath, breaking some ribs and demolishing the shower curtain. Nothing could be done. The next day we did a lot of walking, and although the injury was painful, it kept me moving. Over the coming days the bruising emerged, and the back of my leg was black but still workable. I've had several broken ribs before and they're never fun, especially when you cough. Duncan Ensor, who made up one of the hunting parties, was no better. In a simple trip and fall, he had partially dislocated his shoulder and was in considerable pain. While getting packed, however, he twisted it, yelped like a pup and largely put it back into place. Things were improving and before anything else could happen we caught the plane to Santiago, and then Ecuador.

CHAPTER SIXTEEN A DONKEY DEBACLE

Lynn was there to meet us at the airport, surprised at the speed with which we came through customs, and even more surprised that we had arrived with all our gear. Normally some went missing, never to be found again. 'Trust no one, and don't turn your back on your bags,' she said. 'Stay together, watch for the razor gangs, don't wear any jewellery and carry nothing of value in your pockets.' So welcome to South America. Forming a scrum, with the women in the centre, we headed for a hotel by bus and the final preparations before flying out to the islands and the task ahead.

Only one passenger plane serviced the Galápagos, and only personal luggage could be taken, so it was by deception and bribery that we slipped some of the equipment onto the flight the night before we were due to leave, as we had a lot of gear. Dave, Lynn and I went on to buy some extra drugs that Dave needed, then headed off to the waterfront to find the ship that we hoped to use should we be successful in capturing any animals. The waterfront of Guayaquil was not a place for fresh-faced young tourists. Blowsy prostitutes lounged on street corners, or if they considered it to be their normal location, carried their own stool to claim a form of ownership. The streets were one car wide, and around the docks themselves were deeply rutted mud, lined with primitive houses where people conducted the basics of living on the edge of the very street itself. Eventually after several wrong turns that had taken us through the seediest areas, we arrived at the right dock and found the ship being refitted. She was a snub-nosed little vessel, which in a storm would roll like a pig in the mud, and only several flakes off being a rust bucket. As Lynn said, 'It will be an adventure in itself coming back in that.' We climbed the rickety ladders up onto the deck and met the first mate.

Accommodation for the donkeys turned out to be the bow – no stalls or walls. 'Tie them to the rail in a row,' he said. 'Been transporting stock for years like that.' I guessed if we had to we could do it with some modifications, and not daring to look at our accommodation, I went back to join the others. Since the local people all seemed to come up to my chest level, I shuddered to imagine the height of the cabin, the length of the bunk and the depth of the cockroaches, and decided that, all things considered, when the time came it would be preferable to sleep on deck with the donkeys.

After purchasing extra supplies, we were back at the airport and finally on our way to the Galápagos. The method of boarding was unique, to say the least. Boarding passes were issued, but no seat numbers, so when the door out to the runway was opened, there was a mad rush across the tarmac and a free for all fight up the gangway. The locals, of course, were savvy. Loaded with all of their newly bought household goods minus only a few live chickens,

RESCUE ONE NEW ZEALANDER'S CRUSADE TO SAVE ENDANGERED ANIMALS

On our rotting wooden ship.

they determinedly led the charge for the best seats, followed closely by us, and trailed by a large contingent of tourists, largely American, who stumbled owlishly behind and sat uncertainly where they could. Being classed as an 'official party' meant that we got cheap air fares to the island of Baltra, and landing dispensations, which made things very easy on arrival.

Once settled in our accommodation, we began organising the next stage. We had to buy fresh food and wash all carrots and potatoes of any dirt or other contaminants. Our water containers were there, ready to be filled and trucked down to our departure point. Dave, Lynn and I went off to park headquarters in order to check in and generally introduce ourselves. Lynn knew her way around and appeared to be on friendly terms with the park staff we met, so it was a relatively easy exercise for Dave and me. Everyone seemed relaxed, and we also met the ranger who would be accompanying us. Alex was his name, and he was considered to be their number one hunter.

Since we were leaving late afternoon the next day, trucks were called and everything taken down to the docks, where the boat we were to travel on had pulled up to the wharf. With everyone pitching in, within an hour the boat was loaded and the gear stowed, and we were waiting for Alex and departure time. I idly passed my eye over the boat, but quickly decided that this wasn't a good idea. The wooden upper decks had rotted to the point where the frayed or knotted ropes that held the vessel had dragged gaping holes in them. There was no life raft and a quick look at the life jacket situation showed that the crew had a better faith in God than in any artificial buoyancy. The sleeping arrangements were such that we all thought it was preferable to sleep on the open deck. With Alex's arrival, the remnants of rope that held us to the safety of the land were parted and we headed off across a velvet sea to the island of Isabela.

The next morning the sun slowly rose like a golden globe over the horizon, lighting up a pile of bodies strewn all over the deck as if after a late-night party. As the heat warmed the stiffness out of their limbs, they slowly drew themselves out of their sleeping bags like a lot of caterpillars hatching from chrysalises. Breakfast consisted of lumps of bread and jam and piles of sliced watermelon. We had just finished cleaning up when a huge whale shark went past, a massive creature like a mini-whale. Although I knew it was harmless, my eyes again went around the rotten holes and rusting appendages, and searched the horizon for storm clouds. Fortunately there were none, and by early morning the only line on the horizon was Isabela. Eagerly our eyes absorbed the detail, as the reality of what we had come so far and worked so hard for became more and more distinct. As we moved steadily closer, the smudge became a volcano that merged into coastline that spread out of sight on both sides. This was no small island, and it would get bigger by the day as we grew to know it. Slowly the old diesels beat their way along the coastline, which had obviously been formed by lava flows coming from the crater rising up steeply behind. Spiny scrub and cactus grew on the lower sections, except where recent fingers of lava stood out like coal-black glaciers winding their way down from the crater. No such thing as a white sandy tropical beach here. The coastline was all lava outcrops and jumbled rocks.

The boat crew were aiming for a wide open bay, but Lynn redirected them further up the coast and eventually we arrived at our embarkation point, a very small bay about 200 metres across, slightly protected by short low headlands that provided basic shelter to a small gravel beach. An anchor that looked just about big enough to hold a dinghy was thrown over the side attached to a rope made up of about six different pieces knotted together. We had, apparently, finally arrived at our destination. Within minutes of the engines having stopped their endless rhythm and silence falling over the bay, we were ferrying load after load of gear and equipment onto the beach, then carrying it up into a small patch of scrub at the top end. While the crew and Alex watched from the deck drinking coffee, in an hour we had everything ashore and a base camp well under way. Judging by their comments, our teamwork was obviously a far cry from the parties they had dealt with in the past, but we were keen to get going. As the tents went up, some boots were being put on and three parties went off in different directions for a quick scout.

Together Dave and I sat on a bare knob and with binoculars slowly glassed the surroundings. Below the ocean glistened blue and the waves sipped gently at the shore. My gaze wandered up the coast to the inlet in which we had landed, and I saw with satisfaction that there was no sign of our camp and all the stores were hidden up a dry riverbed. Our presence had to be hidden from the sea, so that no passing Indian fishermen saw it. Not only would they 'borrow' anything that they found, but they were also inclined to be less than hospitable to people intruding into what they saw as their patch. Above us, clustered in a tree, sat a group of Galápagos hawks. They had no fear of humans and were quite happy to perch just a metre or

Relaxing on the beach among our food and supplies. The many containers were full of the water that was our lifeblood.

so away, squabbling gently among themselves and craning their necks to get a better view of the soft flesh below. You got the uncomfortable feeling that they were waiting for, and rather hoped that you might have, some form of nasty accident, so they could check out your body parts more closely.

The heat was oppressive. As soon as you left the shore it closed in around you like a suffocating mass, a deadening presence that sucked all the energy and enthusiasm out of your body, leaving you feeling like a much-used bathroom sponge. Water was always at the front of your mind. Not only did you need to drink, but without water your life expectancy was very short.

It was a thoughtful walk back to camp, and when we checked with the other parties, the stories were similar. The terrain was hard to walk on, everything prickled, stung, bit or generally made life tough, but worse was the fact that there were no donkeys, and no one had seen any old sign either. Lynn shrugged and Alex pointed up the hill towards the top of the crater, into the gathering mist, and I thought, 'Bloody hell, this will be no walk in the park, and nobody told us that.' We considered our options and laid plans for the next days. Brian served a magnificent evening meal, after which we all retired to our respective tents, which were dotted around the countryside so far apart you would think that we all detested each other, but it just suited us.

It was well before dawn when the first of two parties set off. Their job was to head for the crater and a hut that was up there somewhere, and then do a preliminary hunt. The third party, comprising Dave, Judy, Sarah Purdy and me, were basically packhorses carrying supplies. Lynn and her children were also heading up taking a different route. Heather, Sue and Brian were to wait at camp for developments. The first few hours away were a straight grind up the edge of a shallow ravine. Although not steep, it was a continual stiff pull, and the heavy packs made everything just that much harder. The exercise was taking the stiffness out of my leg, but the weight of the pack kept pulling my damaged ribs apart, which caused a rather strange grating feeling, but when I thought of Duncan's dislocated shoulder, I decided not to complain too much. When we reached the base of the crater we skirted around, but it proved really hard going and little ground was being covered with big venting of frustration. The going was rough and unstable, and the tangled network of scrub held us back, forcing us to crawl and clamber. We had but a rough idea of where we were going, having only a sketch drawn by Lynn from memory.

At four in the afternoon we decided to head directly to the rim. It was pretty much straight up and as we neared the top we could see the daily mist or garúa starting to close in. After what seemed an eternity, we were finally able to look down into the expanse of the crater, long dormant but still with towering clouds from a number of fumaroles wisping up into the air. We had no idea where the hut was, but guessed it would be south. A scheduled radio time came up, and we made a call, hoping for, but not expecting a reply. Our spirits lifted when Terry's cheerful voice came through, offering to come and meet us. By then the garúa had thickened, and was swirling around in thick grey tentacles, and the temperature was dropping swiftly. If not for that call, we would have been unlikely to have made the hut that night, for the trail led through many steep bluffs and by then visibility was almost nil. It was a relief to finally walk into the hut and drop our packs.

Having settled ourselves in, it was time to compare notes. One thing had become obvious to us during the day: we had gone ashore at the wrong embarkation point. For whatever reason, Lynn had ignored the proper one and directed us to the old one she had used in the past. If we wanted to get donkeys and move them down, then we needed to move camp. Alex contacted by radio some locals who had a fast boat and would be able to do that for us. First, however, we had to find Lynn, who was up the hill somewhere with her children. With radio communication established, we decided that I would return to camp and plan for a shift, which could be actioned when Lynn had turned up.

The garúa, which comes in every night, is a vital and important part of the ecosystem since it provides a lot of moisture, and keeps the upper part of the volcano a verdant green. We were 5 kilometres from the equator, and yet when surrounded by this mist we were freezing, wearing heavy polo fleeces and with our hair and eyebrows white like snow. As the day warms up the garúa disappears and the heat comes in to fry you. The effect of this, however, is that, for the summer, all the tortoises and other wildlife head for the volcano rim and crater, where there's plenty of water and food. So while there were no tortoises back at camp on the shore, the mountainside was dotted with hundreds. A huge specimen, whom we nicknamed George, lay against the toilet door, stopping the early risers getting in. These creatures are like bulldozers on auto-pilot, walking straight through anything in their path. They can smell water from a huge distance and demolish everything in the way to get at it. The whole hut was surrounded by 2-metre chain-link fencing and a solid gate to keep the tortoises away from the water collection area off the roof, and should you erect a tent, then it needed to be behind barricades of strong logs or similar, otherwise you would awaken to a heavyweight destruction party passing amiably through it.

The next day Alex, Sarah and I, with light packs, headed off back to

CHAPTER SIXTEEN **A DONKEY DEBACLE**

The famous giant tortoises and, in the distance, the fumaroles across the crater.

camp. Alex showed us a new route and we got lost, but it was easier than the night before. About two hours from base we came across some flattened grass that marked the campsite that Lynn had used the previous night. She had cached gear in order to lose weight and dumped empty water bottles. That, and the short distance they had covered, told us a lot and had to be a cause for concern. The others at camp were pleased to see us. Alex, with the help of some pelicans, caught some fish for dinner, and I played with some baby seals in the surf. We did the dishes by placing them just above the water mark on the beach, where hundreds of gaily coloured hermit crabs would scurry out, all wearing a variety of ridiculous shells on their backs. They furiously shovelled minute scraps of food into their mouths until the plates were spotlessly clean. As arranged, a radio call came through, from Jeremy Maguire, a Willowbank staff member on the trip. They had seen several donkeys, but had not been able to capture any yet. Lynn and her children had not arrived at the hut and anxiety was mounting. How long could they last if they ran out of water? Not long, we decided, and Alex, who was fast learning

On the chilly heights indispensable chef de camp Brian Fowler gets to know a tortoise.

to use a good Kiwi word starting with f, expressed his frustration and concern in a mixture of Spanish and odd English punctuated by plenty of f's, before taking to his tent under a scrub bush in an attempt to sleep.

Sunrise saw Brian getting Alex fed and stocked up with sustenance and water for his day ahead. With another meaningful comment about 'F'ing Lynn', he strode off up the hill again for the third time in as many days. A call came through later in the morning to say that Dave was now on his way down. We were a bit quiet as we gathered around the open kitchen that evening and were thrilled to see Dave stride in as darkness was setting. The news wasn't all good. The hunters were putting the tranquillising darts into the donkeys all right, but for some reason they were having no effect. He needed some more from base to try another combination, but it didn't look

CHAPTER SIXTEEN A DONKEY DEBACLE

great. On the positive side, Lynn had finally arrived at the hut. By a quirk of fate, she and her children had found a container of water that somebody had left tied up in a tree. That had probably saved their lives. Because of the drug problem, moving camp just now wasn't an option and so we decided to pack up and all go up the hill tomorrow to see what the result of the new drug combination might be.

It was dark when we surfaced in the morning and Dave headed up the hill first, on his own and travelling light, to get the new drugs there as early as possible. The rest of us tidied up, made sure the camp was invisible, then followed him. He had found a new route that was much easier than the one that we had first been told of, and using that we made the hut by early evening, to be met at the door by Dave, wearing a bow tie. It was his and Judy's wedding anniversary, and we had a third of a bottle of whisky to celebrate it with.

The next morning, Dave made up another combination using the new drugs that had been brought up, and the hunting parties were away. This time I went with Duncan and Hamish Mackenzie, who was a high country lad like Duncan, and Nik Merrilees, an old staff member of mine, and we made our way around the volcano and dropped down into its base. They had established a fly camp there, and it was a perfect spot. There weren't hundreds but thousands of tortoises, of all sizes ranging from soup plates to about a metre long and almost as high. As you passed groups of them, they would gaze short-sightedly at you, then decide to be on the safe side and pull their heads in. They couldn't do this, however, without getting rid of some air within their shells. Like a lot of tyres deflating, they would start to give out a long hiss and slowly, as the compression within eased, their legs and necks would retract and finally their heads.

Donkeys were certainly there too, but surprisingly hard to catch. There was always a jack on guard and they didn't miss a movement. If they saw a human body, they would start running, which meant that, far from being able to walk around and throw darts at them, we had to hard stalk them. They had without doubt been hunted before, which made our task considerably harder. It all became a bit irrelevant because still the drugs didn't work. We caught one old jenny by hand, but she wouldn't have been worth taking down.

The next day I was sitting on the rim with binoculars, surveying the scene below. It was a fascinating little kingdom down there in the base of the volcano, with grassy flats and rocky islands interspersed among the fumaroles. There were thousands of tortoises plus a number of donkeys. Now if I could find a ravine or something, we had the manpower to maybe drive them into it and block off the entrance. As I was searching, some of the others came up and said, 'Lynn's called the boat. She wants out of here, so Alex says we have to pack up and go.' To say I was furious was an understatement, but our choices had been taken from us. The boat was on its way.

On our last night we cleaned up camp and had a final party on the shore while waiting for the boat. It arrived about midnight, still floating, much to my amazement, and soon we were heading back to Santa Cruz and the docks at Puerto Ayora. We had a few days to fill in before our plane tickets were valid, but lots of gear to clean and tidy up. Dave, Lynn and I went to the park headquarters to meet again with the director, Pierre. I was a bit apprehensive about his reaction, given our failure to achieve our goals, but he appeared relaxed and more than happy. I think Alex must have reported back to him in a favourable manner, as he was more than pleased to help in any way. It had taken two years to get the first permits to go over, but he said we had an open invitation to return at any time. His sister, who turned out to be the local vet, turned up to try and throw some light on the tranquillising problem. She had brought a drug, 2 millilitres of which would have definitely worked. It was the one we had used extensively and when we told her that we had put 27 millilitres in one animal, she couldn't believe it. By then we had come to the conclusion that the drugs must have been affected by the heat. Sitting in a black plastic container on the tarmac in full sun would have been enough to destroy any potency.

Pierre and his sister suggested that we try hunting some animals on Santa Cruz; she even offered to come along. Alex was still keen for a hunt, and there's nothing Terry likes better, so the four of us crossed the island on a truck at dawn the next day, before taking a longboat around the coast to a spot known by Alex and his brother, who joined us. It was hard walking, let alone stalking, and the donkeys were very flighty. As a last-minute attempt,

Sue finds a friend on the way to the top of the volcano.

CHAPTER SIXTEEN A DONKEY DEBACLE

one of the villagers turned up with what they called a donkey dog, and off we went again, only this time it was more like a classic Kiwi pig hunt. The dog got onto a mob of donkeys, but the jack, instead of running away, turned around and attacked the dog while the rest of the group ran off through the trees and away. So in the gathering dusk we had a real circus going on, with the jack running strongly, then turning and chasing the dog as he tried to get a bail on, barking all the time while Terry and I tried to follow at a run. It became a total waste of time. Eventually the dog was called off by firing a couple of shots into the air and we made our way through the darkness to the beach and the boat. It was our last attempt at any capture, and it had been a long fourteen-hour day, but when Terry and I took our boots off that night we felt we had done pretty much everything we possibly could. As we said goodbye to Alex for the last time and thanked him for his help, his reply was the ultimate compliment: 'You are not gringos, you are hunters.'

In our final days we enjoyed the stunning and unique wildlife of the Galápagos: large black sea iguanas, blue-footed boobies, spectacular tropic birds, swallow-tail gulls and, of course, the finches that Darwin made so famous. We returned to New Zealand, blown away by our experiences, but not proud of what we had achieved. The donkeys and goats on the Galápagos were to be culled and the international tender, unsurprisingly, was won by a New Zealand company: we're very good at that type of work. It was to be done by helicopter, and because New Zealand is a small country, I knew the owner.

'What are the chances of using one of your choppers to catch some donkeys?' I asked him.

'Absolutely no problem. I'll get on the phone and tell the boys to leave them alone. Just let me know when you can get there.'

Quick conversations with Dave and Terry and we were looking good to get back, but then communication with Lynn stopped. We all had the feeling that she had perhaps just used the whole thing as an excuse to get her children onto Isabela, so that they could experience what she had while doing her thesis. The donkeys weren't really that important to her. They've now been culled along with the goats, and there's little doubt that the island will be better for it. It was hard, however, to have 'could have done better' on your report when you knew that you had had it all sorted, and I felt the need to achieve something. I had made several frustrating trips to Australia. Frustrating because each time I was just able to get to the edge of the deserts or outback proper, and had either run out of time, or had a vehicle that was unable to go any further. I had always promised myself that one day I would go back and do it properly. Maybe now was the time.

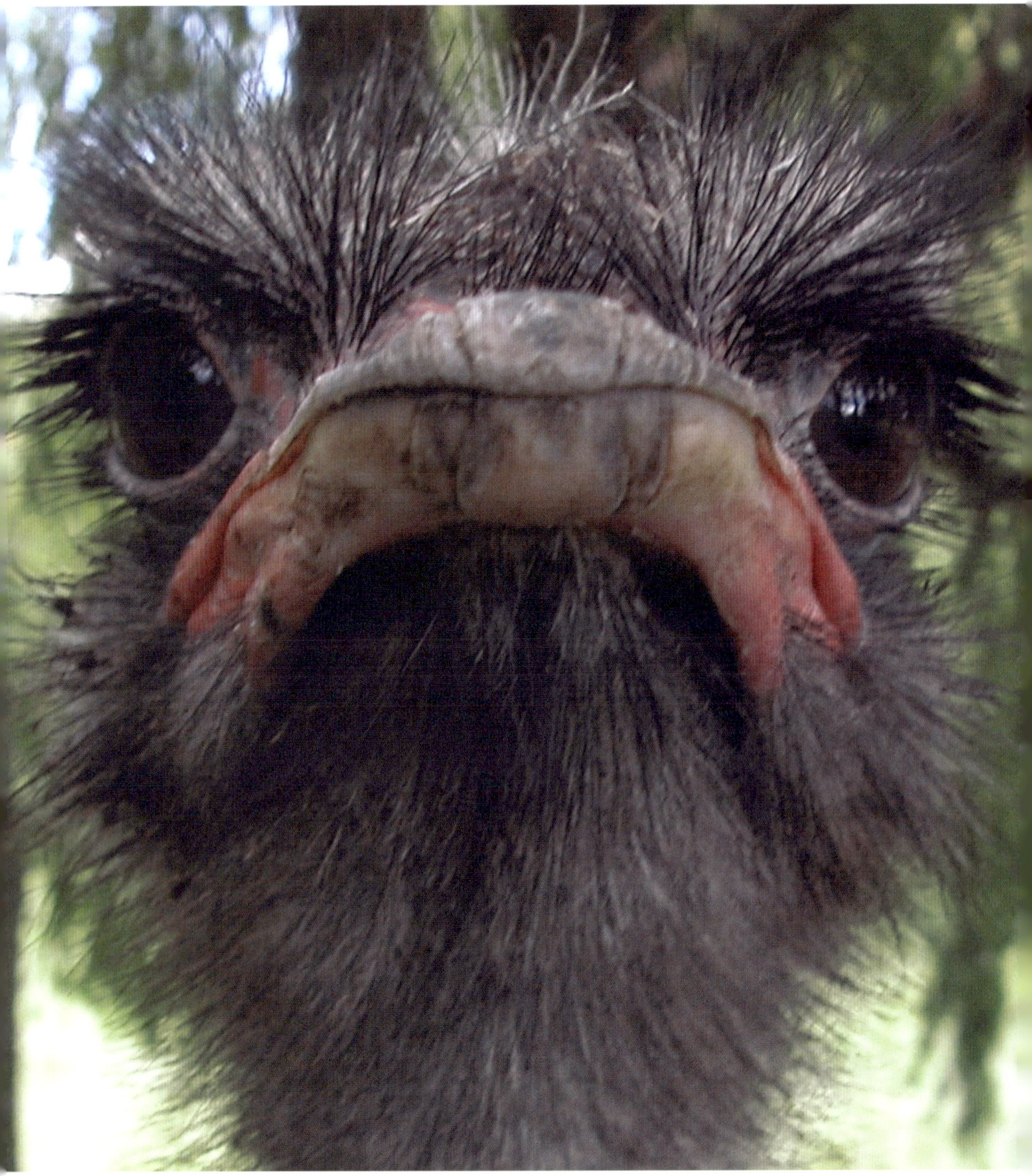

CHAPTER SEVENTEEN

OZ ODYSSEY

I had crossed The Ditch several times and been outback, but not outback enough. To tackle Australia the way I wanted to would require a whole new approach. This is a totally different environment with its own set of rules, and you can be in deep trouble if you don't respect it. Rental car companies aren't too happy about losing a car in a desert. I needed to find another way.

When he heard of my plans, John Simister offered to also buy a vehicle and accompany me. It's hard to take the British out of John: he wanted to do it in a Land Rover or nothing. He found a really good one in Christchurch and was on the verge of coming down to buy it, when he made the mistake of saying why he was making the purchase.

'Sorry, I won't sell you that vehicle,' said the salesman, who was a reputable major dealer.

John was gobsmacked. 'Why not?'

'Won't do the job. You'll never get that vehicle through Australia the way you're planning.'

He was a very honest salesman. The 'best of British' bubble burst for John, and I was back on my own.

The guy was, however, absolutely right, and there's a very good reason why you'll seldom see a Land Rover or a Range Rover outback. Almost without exception, the vehicles are 90 per cent Toyota Land Cruisers, and the rest Nissan Safaris. My choice of vehicle came down to which made life easier for spare parts, of which there were heaps in various stages of decay littering the outback. The next decision was whether to buy a vehicle in New Zealand

and ship it over, or just purchase one in Australia. This was a harder one. If my life was going to depend on it, then I really wanted to know my vehicle intimately. I opted to buy something in New Zealand and ship it over, then at the end of the journey bring it back.

I was lucky in that I liked Land Cruisers. I had had plenty of Hiluxes, but very much preferred the additional strength the Cruiser gave. For my lifestyle I almost always needed a truck deck, but the lack of space with a single cab was always a problem. At this stage Toyota had not come out with a double cab, and so I decided to get one made. But I also wanted a full-sized deck out the back, and that created some additional problems. Eventually I found a company that had converted several station wagons into double cabs, with a short deck on behind. That was a good start, but not good enough. A bit more research and I found a company in Australia that was converting Land Cruisers into six-wheelers, in order to get additional length. Now we were getting somewhere, but the conversion costs were eye-watering.

I glanced seriously at a Nissan Safari I owned, but although it was a really good vehicle, it had done a bit of work and was starting to show it. I was under no illusions that this conversion was going to cost me a lot of money, and although it went against the grain to chop a really good vehicle, equally it made no sense to put a lot of money into a well-used one. I went looking for a really good Land Cruiser station wagon and eventually found one that had recently been imported, was in pristine condition, was a manual drive, which is hard to find, and had never done much work.

The pristine condition bit got a bit of a hammering as the first cutting blades went through the bodywork just behind the passenger seat. That first cut meant no going back, and a few months later I had a double-cab Land Cruiser with a short bit of chassis sticking out behind. To get the extra length, the first option was to extend the chassis and move the back wheels, but that would make the vehicle act like a bus; it would take three attempts to turn around in even the widest street. I therefore went for the Kiwi No. 8 wire option. Through a good friend involved in a car-wrecking business I acquired the back part of a newly wrecked modern Land Cruiser. We chopped the chassis just forward of the back wheels and axle and welded the whole lot back on behind. The braking system was all reconnected to give six-wheel braking, which was a huge advantage, especially when towing. The additional back wheels were also put on air bags that could be operated from inside the cab. This allowed them to be raised and lowered, which meant that the original turning circle was kept and the whole thing acted like trim tabs on a boat.

The original back, with lights and tailgate and all the fittings, was

CHAPTER SEVENTEEN OZ ODYSSEY

My specially adapted vehicle was both transport and home.

replaced, and new sides made up so in effect it became a double-cab well-side truck. We fitted long-range fuel tanks with two filling points put back into one side. The other side had a lift-up flap that could be lifted on gas struts and contained a full tool kit, recovery gear, axe, shovel and other important stuff. The back had to be both long enough for my elongated frame to stretch out in, and lockable and secure. This was crafted for me by a neighbour down the road, Keith Birkett, who was an expert old-fashioned sheet metal worker. He also manufactured a pop-up top that allowed me bed space above all of my gear. Slowly the truck came together, with lots of refinements built into it, and in preparation for the trip I spent months poring over maps, reading about others who had spent time outback – and planning and dreaming.

Sometimes there's almost no end to the planning, and if you're not careful the action itself becomes secondary. There was a lot of paperwork to do, but eventually I had to bite the bullet and book the vehicle for transit to Australia. It was a significant day when I turned up at the shipping yard and drove it into a container. The measurements were exactly right. About 25 millimetres to spare front and back, and you had to climb out the rear window and into the back to get out, as there was no room for the doors to open. A couple of weeks later I followed the truck to Brisbane, where I stayed with ex-Willowbank staffer Gill Bayley and her wonderful, natural, full-on family. It was great to have a base and enjoy their hospitality, but I was keen to get the wheels moving. As the release papers for the vehicle were being signed, I was packing my gear and getting ready to leave. It was a big moment when I first turned the key and drove into the Brisbane traffic. I pointed the snout west and as straight inland as you could go.

Birdsville was the first goal, and I was going there as fast as I could. The first few days it was just town after town, with increasing gaps in between. It was a big night when, after about a week or so, I could pull off the road and camp for the first time. It started raining and it came down in buckets. The sand changed to the consistency of porridge. In places the wheels just disappeared into it as if it had no end to its depth, and that threw me right out of my comfort zone. In that sort of situation, should you stop or, worse, get bogged, the whole vehicle sinks up to the level of the running boards. I saw plenty of examples, which often took another two or three vehicles to tow them out. Despite a few nervous moments, I eventually made it to Birdsville, with the sun shining and the desert turning to sand once more.

Having a beer in the Birdsville pub had been a long-held aim. It was an establishment of some notoriety and I enjoyed a notice over the bar that said, 'If you wear your cap backwards, we will show you the shortest route back to the city.' This was where they hold the famous Birdsville Races each year – camel racing outback style. Beer over and provisioned up, a couple of days later it was time to turn my attention properly to the vast Simpson Desert ahead.

Half a day out Big Red, the highest sand dune in Australia, loomed forbiddingly above me as I drove west. The only way to the top was straight up and so I started to climb. I got about quarter of the way up before the vehicle shuddered to a halt. The soft, deep sand just sucked the life out of the truck. Working my way back down to the bottom, I backed off a bit and had another charge at it. To my dismay, this attempt got me about two-thirds of the way up before once more I was firmly bogged and stationary. This is starting to get embarrassing, I thought, as again I reversed down. The only good thing about

CHAPTER SEVENTEEN **OZ ODYSSEY**

Sitting on top of Big Red in the Simpson Desert.

it was that normally when you're making a fool of yourself several people are watching. This time the nearest person could be 100 kilometres or more away and I only had myself to either abuse or laugh at. This time I was going to make it. I backed up like a bull getting ready to charge at a particularly obstinate opponent, only I retreated a good 100 metres or so. Selecting the gear I now thought was right, I floored my foot and hit Big Red with all the horsepower I could muster and we made it finally to the top.

The view alone made the whole thing worthwhile. From that height you saw, far below, the endless lines of the dunes like swells in an ocean. There are over 1140 of these elongated dunes, the longest in the world. Between them were flat pan areas with occasional low scrub, and stretching out from me and angling down from the top and disappearing into the distance were the wheel marks of another vehicle. My elation once more faded into misery

RESCUE ONE NEW ZEALANDER'S CRUSADE TO SAVE ENDANGERED ANIMALS

Above: The sobering remains of houses in the cruel heat of the Sturt Desert.

Left: Distance measured Aussie style. Mount Dare is on the western edge of the Simpson Desert.

CHAPTER SEVENTEEN **OZ ODYSSEY**

when, after drinking in the majesty of the setting, I climbed back into my vehicle only to find that it had settled into the sand and was bogged again. Learning fast, I gently rocked it backwards and forwards, packing the sand and clearing it from in front with my hands. A final big rock and we were back onto those other wheel marks and away again. Welcome to outback Australia and the Simpson Desert.

I hadn't really appreciated the difference between the different deserts until I crossed into the Sturt Desert and went from waves of sand to flat hard rock interspersed with sand patches. There I came across the odd rocky ruin of a long-abandoned farming attempt, and all too often if I walked away from the remains of the house I would come across a grave or two, often of young children. You couldn't help but sit on the rocks in the shimmering heat and wonder at the blind optimism that led people to such a desolate spot. The Sturt Desert was memorable for the mirages that floated just above the horizon, hazy in the reflected heat. It wasn't hard to imagine trees and lakes. Surely all you had to do was drive to them and plunge in.

The Sturt wandered itself down towards Adelaide, and from there I took the well-known Nullarbor route across the bottom of Australia, and then into the Victoria Desert. Days later I hit the west coast and made my way to Margaret River, an area that I had previously visited and enjoyed very much. Having got there it seemed to make sense to go down to Port Augusta, which is on the very south-west tip of Australia. That was a lovely little village, and I returned, via some verdant green hills, through a place called Dunedin, and up to Perth. It was a contrast to be in a place of trees and grass, and a great thrill to see flocks of white-tailed black Carnaby cockatoos, a species that I held at home, and is very rare.

Perth sprawled down the coast in suburb after suburb of houses all looking exactly the same. It was probably a pretty city but after a few days, during which I went to the zoo, I was pleased to get my wheels turning again. I had serviced the vehicle and was well provisioned, for the next leg was going to be one of the most challenging. My route took me through the famous and historic mining settlement of Kalgoorlie, which still had the air of a frontier town with wild bars and streets of brothels. Mining is still the most important industry in the region, and it was an odd mix of wealth and exploitation. Touching the Victoria Desert again, I went through the little town of Laverton and turned right into the Gibson Desert.

It was interesting, when going through such small towns, to see the mainly elderly inhabitants rocking on their chairs on the verandah and watching the world pass them by on the main street. I knew that all of my movements were being noted, and should anyone make enquiries about where I was, someone would remember a dark-green six-wheeler going past, travelling in such and such a direction. Often I would pull in somewhere in the outback and someone would come up and say, 'I remember you. You were parked by that billabong six days ago.'

Just past Laverton was a typical set-up: a roadhouse offering fuel and some supplies, along with basic accommodation and a bar with a restaurant. Such outfits would have a compound into which you were locked at night, sadly, to protect you from the local Aborigines, among whom alcohol was a huge problem. I saw many lying around in the scrub under pieces of plastic and bits of shredded mattress. Alcohol, it seemed, was everything to them and they would do anything to get it. I heard of people getting knifed for a can of beer. I had been advised to take, and offered, a handgun to put under the front seat, but decided that was going too far. I did have a pick handle on the side of the truck, and also a pair of nunchucks, two short pieces of hard wood connected with a length of chain. In the right hands, they were an extremely efficient piece of equipment.

As the sign suggests, outback pubs can be tough and difficult places.

You always took the opportunity to fill up to the max with fuel etc. and, if possible, have a shower and clean-up. At one roadhouse I needed diesel and there were pumps outside, with big padlocks on all of them. Coming from the blinding sun outside, entering the building was like going into a cavern dimly lit by TV screens and containing a number of local Aboriginal men. I fronted the bar, behind which was a large young European gentleman who, when he heard I needed service, swore eloquently, then reached up and slammed down big steel shutters to enclose the alcohol. We then went outside, he undid the padlocks and I filled up, the locks went on and it was back into the bar and shutters flung up so I could pay. And that was normal practice.

The Gibson Desert is bisected by a highway that connects the top of Australia to the bottom, through Alice Springs. So one day I could see these black dots crossing the horizon and as I got closer I realised that they were vehicles and later I came to a black ribbon of tarmac. It felt a bit bizarre to be one minute in an untouched world, and the next bouncing over the shoulder of the road and turning right towards Uluru, or Ayers Rock as it was then called, bound for a soft bed and the trappings of civilisation.

Uluru was impressive and I walked all around its great mass, but the best fun I had was at the organised chaos of the Alice Springs camel races. This was a real crack-up, not through any fault of the organisers, but because of the temperament of the animals they were trying to organise. The races began from a sitting start, which meant that all the camels had to be sitting down with their riders aboard and ready to go. This position was achieved only with much shouting from attendants, who were as colourful as their animals – wild-looking men sporting a range of whiskers. They seemed to have a love-hate relationship with their camels, who were gurgling and slobbering and making as little attempt as they could to obey their riders.

Once they were all deemed to be in some sort of accepted prone state, a horn was sounded, a rope barrier was dropped and the race was on. Some camels were slow to get up and one or two simply refused. Once they were standing, several turned in circles and it was a lottery as to which way they would actually run. Eventually most started down the track and the race was on, the ungainly beasts lumbering along in their two-sided awkward gait. Crossing the finishing line was an achievement in itself, but stopping the animals was yet another story. Camels and riders were being chased around the racecourse by their various attendants, while a new group would be brought in to start the whole process again.

A few days in Alice and I was geared up and ready to hit the road again. The next stage was my last full desert crossing, of the Tanami, which was different again: quite scrubby, with dry riverbeds marked by stands of river gums. Towards the end was a roadhouse called Rabbit Ranch, where diesel was around $8.00 per litre. It was run by an old couple whom you never saw. Everything was boarded up and there was just a small wooden hatch that was opened enough for you to pass your money over. The Tanami ended at the Halls Creek township, and again I turned right and headed for the Bungle Bungle Range in Purnululu National Park, a fascinating wilderness of rocky canyons, famous for its spectacular views. I had known Callum Fisher, a helicopter pilot there, for many years, as his mother Jenny had worked for me since the days when I owned a pet shop. Callum took me out in the chopper for a bird's-eye view of the national park, and then we finished off with a low-level flight, skimming the waters of a river where a number of crocodiles were peacefully sunning themselves.

The dust and craziness of the Alice Springs camel races was a memorable highlight.

I wanted to do the northern coast, but there is no such thing as a coastal road. Next best is the Gibb River–Wyndham Road, which varies in condition from passable to impassable, depending on the rain and depth of mud. Off this road were side tracks that led out to the coast of the Cambridge Gulf, and some of these I followed to some wonderful isolated places. There were large boulders along many of the tracks, which were often steep and needed to be negotiated with power on. The suspension was getting a fair hammering and the body was crashing down on the chassis, which eventually damaged some big cables and started a fire. Fortunately I was able to put it out relatively easily, but couldn't repair the damage. Luckily I could disconnect that system, and the vehicle was still drivable. The next town of any size was Derby, and a couple of days later I pulled in.

I was fortunate in that I had a friend there, Trevor Parr, who describes himself as a missionary doctor. He seems to delight in going to the worst of places to work, and at that stage was alternating between Africa and Australia's Northern Territory. As he said, 'In today's world, no one else will touch the work that I do. You're too liable to be sued. I have no money, and don't intend to have any, so they can sue me for everything they can.' In Africa he would be amputating limbs and putting shot and bombed bodies back together; in Australia he would be in the outback working with the indigenous people, stitching up wounds from knife and axe assaults, helping with births and performing caesareans.

My vehicle needed some repairs from the wiring burnout, and I found an auto electrician who was able to do the job for me. His name was Colin, and he had the vehicle for about three days, during which time I dropped past regularly to chat. It took the first day to learn that Colin was Aboriginal. Apart from his thick black hair, there was little to show of his ancestry. As we got to know each other, snippets about his past would come out. The government had set aside millions of dollars to provide solar power for remote communities. This was Colin's area of expertise and he tendered for the work, but it went to another contractor who was related to the communities concerned. Out of interest Colin checked on the work and found it fell well short of what should have been done, and as a result the families had not received the services promised. One day, Colin told me, walking down the main street of Derby, he saw the contractor and said to him, 'I do not see you. I do not see your family. You do not exist.' To me this seemed a bit bizarre, but for Colin it was quite normal, and he had never seen nor heard of that man and his family again.

Aside from his ebullient company, I learnt a lot from Trevor, His love for humanity and dedication to his work, for absolutely no personal gain, were inspirational. Few would have the courage to tread his path. As a parting gift he gave me his medical officer's card for the Northern Territory. 'It's got no photo,' he said. 'Just wave it at people if you have to. No one will stop you and you can go where you like. I don't need it. They won't stop me.'

It was with some sadness that I left Derby. I felt I could have stayed and learnt more from Trevor and Colin but I had to move on. I was off to Port Hedland and then up to the farthest north-west part of Australia. The two highlights there were the pearling luggers and their workers and history, and then the North West Cape, isolated, with stunning beaches, azure blue sea and rocky outcrops, and whales and other wildlife cruising past. That was as far as I could go that way, so I retraced my steps and after a week or so ended up in Darwin. That was a bit of a struggle because I had not seen a city since I had left Perth, and felt very isolated, insecure and vulnerable. I was happy to get back on the road and into the hinterlands of Katherine. Here in a dusty outback museum I saw a page of a diary, written in pencil, the words becoming more wavery towards the end. It had been found on a bunk in a hut, alongside the body of a young station owner:

Dear Jim,

    There is no hope. The water has all gone. The horses have all died. Please sell my saddles and anything else that may fetch a bid, and send the money to my mother in Cornwall.
Your loving friend
Bill

I sat looking at that note for a long time.

From Katherine I headed for the Kakadu and the top eastern corner. It was a spectacular piece of Australia, a combination of dry desert areas and lush swamp and river flats. It had an aura of primitiveness about it, and I couldn't help feeling that I wouldn't be at all surprised to find a herd of mammoth grazing on the verdant grasslands along with all the other storks, herons and swamp birds. It was deceiving country. I knew of some caves in some dry lands which I was keen to visit. I drove as far as I could, parked under some gum trees and headed off in their direction, but totally underestimated the heat and distance. I got within a short distance of them and knew I was going to get into trouble if I continued. I was developing all the symptoms of heat exposure and dehydration: a swollen tongue, blood thick as soup and a head of cotton wool. It was with considerable relief that I got back to the truck, where it took several more hours to rehydrate myself back to normal.

I never did get to those caves but explored many others and saw some fantastic Aboriginal rock art. What I had not appreciated until then was the X-ray effect they had reproduced in their drawings. Not only did they depict the outline of the fish or animal, but also showed the bones within. I also found clear drawings of the now extinct thylacine or Tasmanian tiger. I hadn't understood the extent of their range. The bulk of this territory was Aboriginal land, seldom visited by outsiders, but with Trevor's card and a friendly, confident attitude, I travelled largely untroubled to some extraordinary places.

I was sad to leave the area and point the wheels south to travel the east coast and down to Brisbane, stopping on the way at a place called Proserpine. Here I met up with Lesley Slade, who was a major breeder of Nadudana or miniature Zebu cattle. I had seen these animals on previous trips and was very keen to get hold of some. The simplest way would have been to import embryos, but when Lesley had taken some of her cows to a breeding centre in order to flush for embryos for me, she had no success. It was good, however, to see her and her animals.

As I travelled further south I encountered some lovely areas, but the tarmac and towns had limited appeal. My vehicle was travelling on a carnet,

CHAPTER SEVENTEEN **OZ ODYSSEY**

My quest for miniature Zebu cattle was fulfilled.

a document which in effect meant that it was only visiting and had to be returned. The carnet had a time limit and you weren't allowed to leave the country without the vehicle unless you had approval. At that stage we were making plans to shift the chimpanzees to Australia, and so, using as an excuse the fact that I was the only one who could manage those animals through such a shift, I got approval to leave the vehicle in Brisbane and return to New Zealand.

A couple of months later, however, I was back in Australia, strapped in the driver's seat and heading for Sydney. I was taking the opportunity to also follow up on some more of the miniature Zebu cattle that had by chance been imported into Australia. I had tracked down a breeder in the Snowy Mountains and arranged to buy four calves off him, two bulls and two heifers. These I put in the back of the truck and transported to a quarantine centre, in preparation for shipment to New Zealand. The road then took me to the south-eastern corner of Australia and I journeyed inland again, dodging forest fires in Victoria and driving up into the desert areas of Mungo Lakes and Lake Eyre. From there it was a straight run down to Melbourne and after a good clean down, the vehicle was driven into a container and taken back to New Zealand. In spite of the hammering it had taken, it remained a very good truck, and a favourite to drive.

My four months in Australia had been a physical, visual and emotional experience – long nights watching the stars, exciting encounters with wildlife, harsh conditions and remoteness, a lot of adrenaline-rushing moments, along with times of outstanding beauty and peace.

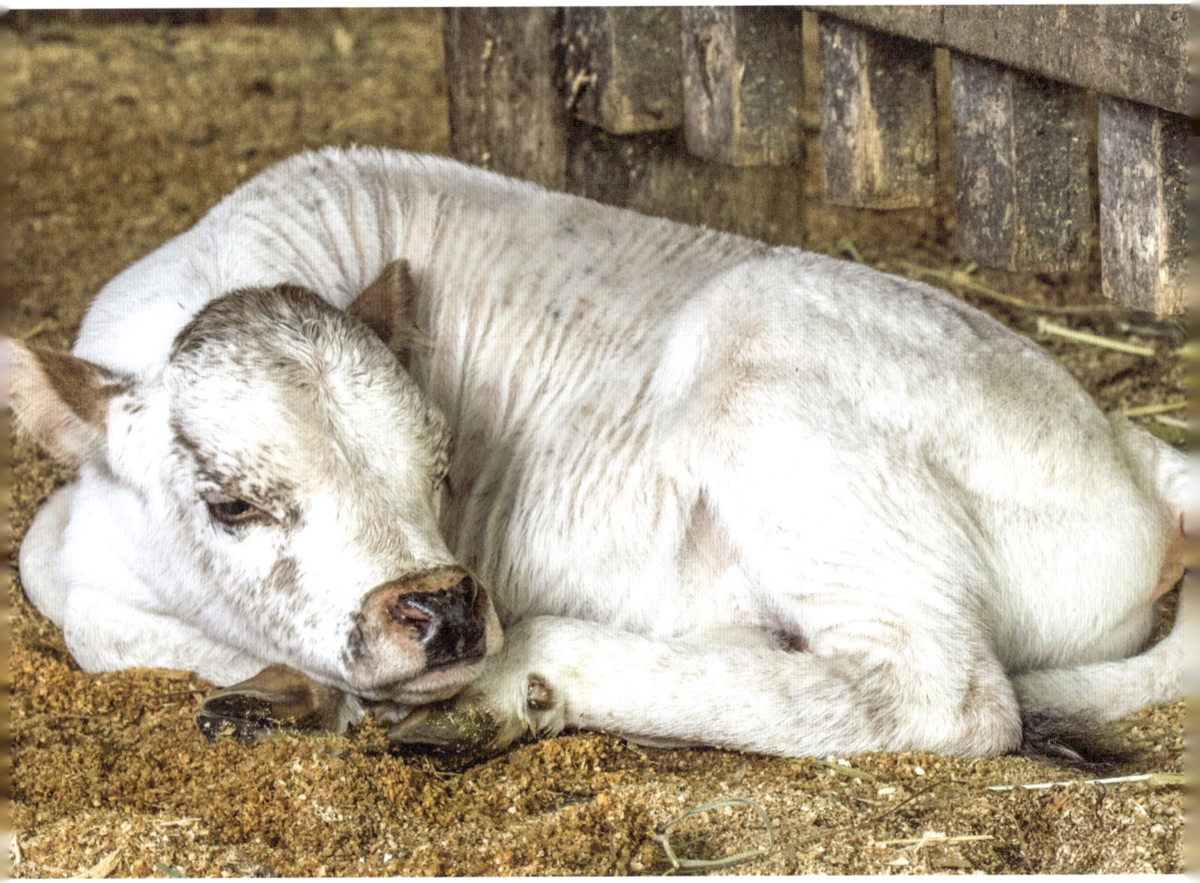

CHAPTER EIGHTEEN

THE WAY OF THE FUTURE

After Kathy and I separated I moved to a small cottage in Lyttelton Harbour and commuted to Willowbank each day. It was easier for me to move than disrupt the family, but it was a bit like hiding in a dog kennel, and odd not being able to walk out the door and play with the animals that had always been my life. I had my wee fox terrier dog Tussle, which helped, and we got to know each other fairly well. After a year or so I needed to move on and started looking for some land on which to live. My requirements had not really changed too much: it had to have some redeeming features I could work with, be private and, most of all, be affordable. Quite by chance I found a block advertised for private sale, which was unusual in those days. At Halkett, only half an hour west of Willowbank, 20 hectares on the banks of the Waimakariri River, secluded and at rock-bottom price, it had a large number of pine trees on it, with a water race and a bit of a pond. The vendor had run it as a pig farm and got himself into financial difficulties: I was able to offer him a quick sale, deal done.

My family came out one Sunday to see my new purchase, and it couldn't have been a worse day. A strong nor'west gale was lifting the river sand and dust from the Waimakariri River and the property itself, creating dust storms that made the whole thing a most unpleasant experience, even in my biased view. My poor father said later that he thought the land I had bought at Willowbank was the worst he had seen in his life, but he reckoned this one topped it. I must admit it looked pretty rough. The pigs had done a great job of turning it into something that resembled a First World War battlefield, complete with trenches and virtually no vegetation. Before the pig farm, however, it had belonged to a naturist club, whose members had been looking for new, more discreet premises as their old place was becoming a bit public. It was well suited to that purpose, being way down a remote shingle road and bordered on two sides by Catchment Board land. It was the club that had planted the pines, in a bid for more privacy, and dug out the sort of pond for swimming. After I had bought it, a friend roughly worked the land up to begin with, almost losing his tractor in the holes as he went, and I got a digger in to enlarge the pond and do some landscaping. By this time I had moved from Lyttelton to Coalgate and was living with a friend, Sue Meager, and her two children, Shelley and Kirsty. Sue, whom I had known for a number of years through endurance riding, had moved up there after her separation. Because it was conveniently close to my land, on every spare day we would be at the property, cutting down trees and peeling off the bark. Cut to length for poles, they were stacked and dried before taking them to a treatment plant. I got a permit for a barn and using the poles started building. Six months and $13,000 later, we had a thing that in theory was an enclosed barn, but we called it a cottage, and moved in.

There was no power up the road, and I didn't want to build anywhere near the road in any case, and so we had to look for alternatives. Solar power was really the only answer, but in those days it was relatively new technology and very expensive. We ended up buying four 60-watt panels, but that was only a start. The first winter was the worst. We spent it huddled in heavy jackets, woolly hats and gloves around a wood burner I had installed. The window frames were sealed with bits of newspaper and we cooked on a gas stove. Using four long poles, I built a high water tank tower and created a waterwheel out of a couple of old steel wheels, mounted on a shaft with bearings and a pulley. This sits in the water race and drives an old windmill pump, which then gravity feeds water from the tank around the whole property. You're often happier when you have little, and there was lots of laughter in that little cottage. My poor father still couldn't understand it. One day he put his arm around Sue and said, 'What has he brought you down to?'

It was only ever to be a stepping stone, however. We had plans for a house drawn up and the following year managed to put the foundations down. I purchased a second-hand chainsaw mill and started cutting beams. This became a routine for the next two years. I would cut a tree down one day and limb it up and cut it into the lengths I wanted. The next day I would take it to the mill, piece by piece, and saw the log into a beam. On a good day I could do five or six beams. Each beam then had to be air dried for at least twelve

CHAPTER EIGHTEEN **THE WAY OF THE FUTURE**

The first cottage at Halkett.

months before being taken to the plant to be treated. Most beams were cut to size to eliminate wastage, and all the trusses were cut and laid out on the ground with Roman numerals chiselled into them to identify them later. Just over 45 tonnes of timber were trailered back to the property after treatment to be dried again before being ready to be put up.

It was simple construction really. You bought a second-hand door or window, held it in the place you wanted it to go and put a big square beam on each side. As you worked along the wall you put another great heavy beam up above to tie the whole lot together. Drill holes and hammer steel pipes down through the whole lot to tie it all together in place, and before long you had the framework of a building. Working with the weight of the beams was a bit of an issue, but then so was building the pyramids. By using the simple techniques of levers and ropes, it was surprising what could be done, given time. Because it was to be a two-storey house, it all became a bit more difficult getting everything in place at that height, but it could be done. Two planks leaning against the house made a bit of a ramp, and the beam would be

With my water tower.

worked up end by end with muscle and lever, helped by ropes along the way until the top was reached. At one stage on the build we had a digger on site that lifted some of the larger beams into position for me. The driver estimated that the weight of the longest was about a tonne, which would probably not be far wrong as it was 300 millimetres square and about 6 metres long. Once the beams were in place, it wasn't hard to frame in between them, then put on an outside lining using some T & G timber that used to line the chillers at the recently closed Sockburn Freezing Works. One day, halfway through

CHAPTER EIGHTEEN **THE WAY OF THE FUTURE**

Building the main house.

the construction, I noticed a sign on the main drag with an arrow pointing down our road to 'PINEHENGE'. It was some days before I realised one of our friends was exhibiting their sense of humour and, with embarrassment, removed it. After four and a bit years of living in the cottage and $46,000 later, we crossed the driveway and moved into our new home.

The house has improved a lot over the intervening years, but the basic structure is immovable and sets it apart. It has featured in housing articles and supplements, lifestyle magazines and other periodicals, but for us it's the home that we built. We used what was available and what we could afford, and though the journey may have been harder and longer, the end results have little to do with money.

One day a real estate agent came into my Willowbank office and offered me all the buildings that comprised an animal boarding facility that was being cleared to make way for a subdivision. 'Don't have the money, mate,' I said. 'Just can't afford it.' He went away and in a week or two came back and said, 'Make an offer. You just may get it.' By then I had seen the buildings, and they were in very good condition. Basically, they consisted of half a Keith Hay home – the kitchen and surrounding rooms – with a large complex of outbuildings attached. 'A thousand dollars then,' I said, and much to my surprise, a few days later, I was told they were mine. I hired three university students for a few weeks and we jacked up the home and transported it to Halkett for another thousand dollars. This would be the start of an aviary complex. All the rest was dismantled into sections and taken out to be stored. All the former animal cages were lined with 25-millimetre thick finger-jointed timber panels. I sold the hundreds of mesh panels that made up the sides of the animal cages, thereby recouping most of my costs.

In many ways, my no longer living at Willowbank had to happen. The lifestyle, with the increased volume of people, wouldn't have suited me long term, and although the path is often not the one you would have chosen, the end result can sometimes actually be better.

For a while, the family came and went. Daughter Kirsty was travelling and teaching overseas, Kathy went into town where she started her own restaurant, and Willowbank just continued to grow, relatively unperturbed. I was lucky in that I had very good financial controllers and/or managers who took responsibility for the day-to-day running of the main building. One by one, however, the family came back.

Kathy had closed the doors of her restaurant, and with her new husband, stayed on at the Willowbank house for a few more years, until our son Mark and his wife Kelly moved in, before purchasing a property. When Mark left to go into business on his own, the new park manager, Paul Rushworth, moved in with his family and, after a few more years, Kirsty, her husband Dale Hedgcock and their children returned from Africa and took over the residence. They have extended it from the tiny house I first built to a lovely family home. Kirsty started a drama academy, which she ran for some time before selling it and taking over much of the Willowbank administration. Dale, who has an engineering background, worked off site for a couple of years before expressing an interest in also joining Willowbank. At his request, he began at the bottom, cleaning cages, and worked his way up to a senior management position.

With Dale also coming into the business, and Mark maintaining a close involvement in the advertising and promotional aspects, a new family unit was slowly becoming established, with loosely defined roles. We would all meet and try to plan and manage as cohesively as possible, but this didn't always work. For some years the restaurant had been causing concerns. We had entered into an arrangement with a management company, but they weren't interested in providing the service that we wanted and needed. I knew from personal experience that restaurants are tough to manage. Since none of the family wished to be involved, I suggested that we should be

CHAPTER EIGHTEEN **THE WAY OF THE FUTURE**

leasing it out to a top operator. Nobody shared my view and then at one of our management meetings in May 2009 we decided to close the restaurant temporarily over winter and reopen in August with a new format. I reluctantly accepted this as a temporary measure. August came and went and nothing was happening. When I asked why, I was told that no one had any intention of reopening the restaurant, but just wanted to maintain the cafeteria during the day. For me it was, and still is, a difficult decision to accept. All that work wasted. No more night tours, no inspirational point of difference, no stimulation in providing a New Zealand dining experience, and a loss of souvenir sales because a lot of tourists came in the evenings.

It was, however, the way of the future. Whether I liked it or not, they were the ones who were going to be taking Willowbank into that future, and they needed to have some control over their own destiny. There was little I could do if we wanted to keep some semblance of family unity. Then, a few months later, the massive September 2010 earthquake struck, and everybody's minds moved on to other things. We were very lucky at the park: although we suffered damage, it was negligible compared with what many others experienced. As a community gesture we opened for a couple of weeks without charge, in order to let families, especially, enjoy a peaceful visit that would provide some form of normality. A lot of people turned up. They were grateful for the gesture and their behaviour showed it. They would clean up their rubbish and tidy up their tables. Several even took their dirty plates into the kitchen. When we emptied our donation box near the counter, we found to our astonishment that it contained more money than we had taken for the same fortnight the year before. It was a humbling experience. On top of that the city council identified us as being of critical value to the community and gave us additional assistance to stay open.

One result of the February 2011 earthquake was that it wiped 80 per cent of the restaurants in town off the map. Surely, I thought, this had to be

Putting on the roof and walls of the house.

Above: The finished house from the drive.

a golden opportunity to consider reopening ours, but no, there was still no family interest whatever. Frustrated, I came up with another idea: I would start hangi meals and add those onto the Māori concert that we had most nights. Good friends Paul and Sandra Wilson owned a wildlife park in Queenstown. Paul was also a chef by trade, and had previously started a small cultural performance and hangi meal, but it didn't work out for them in that location. This meant I knew where there was a hangi cooker just sitting waiting to be picked up. I always enjoy a trip to Queenstown and this was to be no exception. Paul could also give me all the hints on menus that worked and I came away with enough information to start operating. Best of all he said, 'Don't worry about paying me now for the hangi. Just do it when you can afford it.'

So I took the hangi back, dug a hole and installed it. We did a trial run, invited forty-odd guests and had a party. No restaurant meant no waiting

CHAPTER EIGHTEEN **THE WAY OF THE FUTURE**

Above: Creating a fireplace.

Above right: The finished fireplace

staff, but we used the girls from Ko Tāne. They were wonderful. They had no training, but it didn't matter. The food came with a big smile and you felt pleased and grateful to be the recipient. The hangi meals were a great success, but Wildlife by Night was now a lost dream. Distasteful though it may be, you often have to accept change, and things like compliance and health and safety have contributed to a shift in how things are done. I still firmly believe, however, that some time in the future, a new pioneer will reignite the concept.

The days of straightening nails and struggling for recognition are now well gone. With a steadily increasing number of visitors a year, Willowbank is now by far the biggest wildlife facility in the South Island, and probably comes third in New Zealand behind Auckland and Wellington zoos. It's unique in that most other major zoos rely on council funding to survive, while we rely on business management and smart, innovative thinking. The park has won numerous accolades, one of the most recent being, in 2017, the top award in the tourism/retail/hospitality, medium/large enterprise category of the Champion Canterbury Business Awards. We were put ahead of both Mount Hutt Ski Field, which is the largest winter sports operation in the region, and the recently opened multi-million-dollar Christchurch Adventure Park. It has been a long journey from the ramshackle jumble of cages and paddocks that marked our first opening. As a reflection of the effort from so many people that have made Willowbank what it is, the land is being protected in order to maintain its environmental features, and so it can contribute to conservation into the future.

New generations are coming through, and there's a subtle change in both the way things get done and the results. Usually today if we have a building project we'll go out and buy new pieces of timber, fittings and other bits and pieces, but the result isn't always as good as when we had no money and had to create out of the materials that were available at the time. Sometimes some things just feel right, but that simplicity can be overlooked.

My home property, known as Willowbank Farm, has kept developing, if still rather uncompliantly. Its value for Willowbank itself is considerable. It allows the park to continue with its support of breeding endangered species, lets some of them travel between the two for R and R and also helps to maintain breeding groups of some minor and threatened breeds. For me, it has become the place where I can retain my hands-on 'animal fix', since at Willowbank staff do all the daily animal-related work, and I need to get involved only when required. Initially we bred a lot of birds but later decided to focus on a few specialty species such as some macaws and rare cockatoos, and on others that I simply enjoy and can also contribute to a form of conservation that few New Zealanders consider. Most houses in the past had a canary on the porch, and a budgerigar in the kitchen, but those birds, along with a large range of other avicultural species, are seldom seen today.

My interest in the conservation of rare and minor livestock genetics continued and soon we had a number of groups that we enjoyed working with and developing. Many of these breeds become rare because market forces change, but often it's how you view the product and who you market it to. For instance, livestock that's not wanted in New Zealand is often highly sought after overseas, and what may not sell in a supermarket is valued by

CHAPTER EIGHTEEN **THE WAY OF THE FUTURE**

Winner: Willowbank Wildlife Reserve Champion Tourism/Retail/Hospitality Medium/Large Enterprise Award.

Presented by Christchurch International Airport and Air New Zealand

Winning a tourism award was a high point.

the halal butcher in the next town. Many of the livestock breeds we deal with are far rarer than the rarest of our native species. Some people would question their value, but there's a massive movement worldwide to try and stem this extinction, and with good reason. Humans rely on this partnership with livestock, and for many countries losing their traditional breeds threatens their very communities and way of life. Throughout the world about twelve breeds a month are becoming extinct, and the rate is increasing. Globally the genetic pool is shrinking, and with it our ability to maintain our current forms of agriculture, and develop new ones.

In 2003 I was asked to become one of twelve directors of Rare Breeds International, which was founded in 1989. Sitting under the Food and Agriculture Organisation of the United Nations, it's the only body with a UN mandate to advise and coordinate livestock conservation programmes. This exposure gave me a much greater understanding of the value of the work. It's not just about saving livestock breeds, it's about saving lifestyles and community groups, while maintaining villages, providing working roles for all of the families and making niche products to sell. And this doesn't happen only in developing countries. Many regions in so-called developed countries rely on such items as specialty cheeses, meats, pates and so on to create an identifiable market that enhances the whole area and gives it a unique flavour. The role has given me an opportunity to participate in events and projects in Europe, Africa and Asia, all of which further reinforced the urgent need to conserve breeds. New Zealand thinks of itself as a modern-thinking agricultural country and so it was fascinating, in Vietnam for instance, to see the emphasis the government has put on research and development of old traditional breeds to suit a lifestyle.

In New Zealand, the Rare Breeds Conservation Society coordinates that work, and there's a strong and active group in Canterbury. Each year we hold a fundraising auction, which is a great day for like-minded people to buy and sell stock or just catch up with other breeders. There can be hundreds of lots of different animals and birds, and it's not uncommon for the auction to last

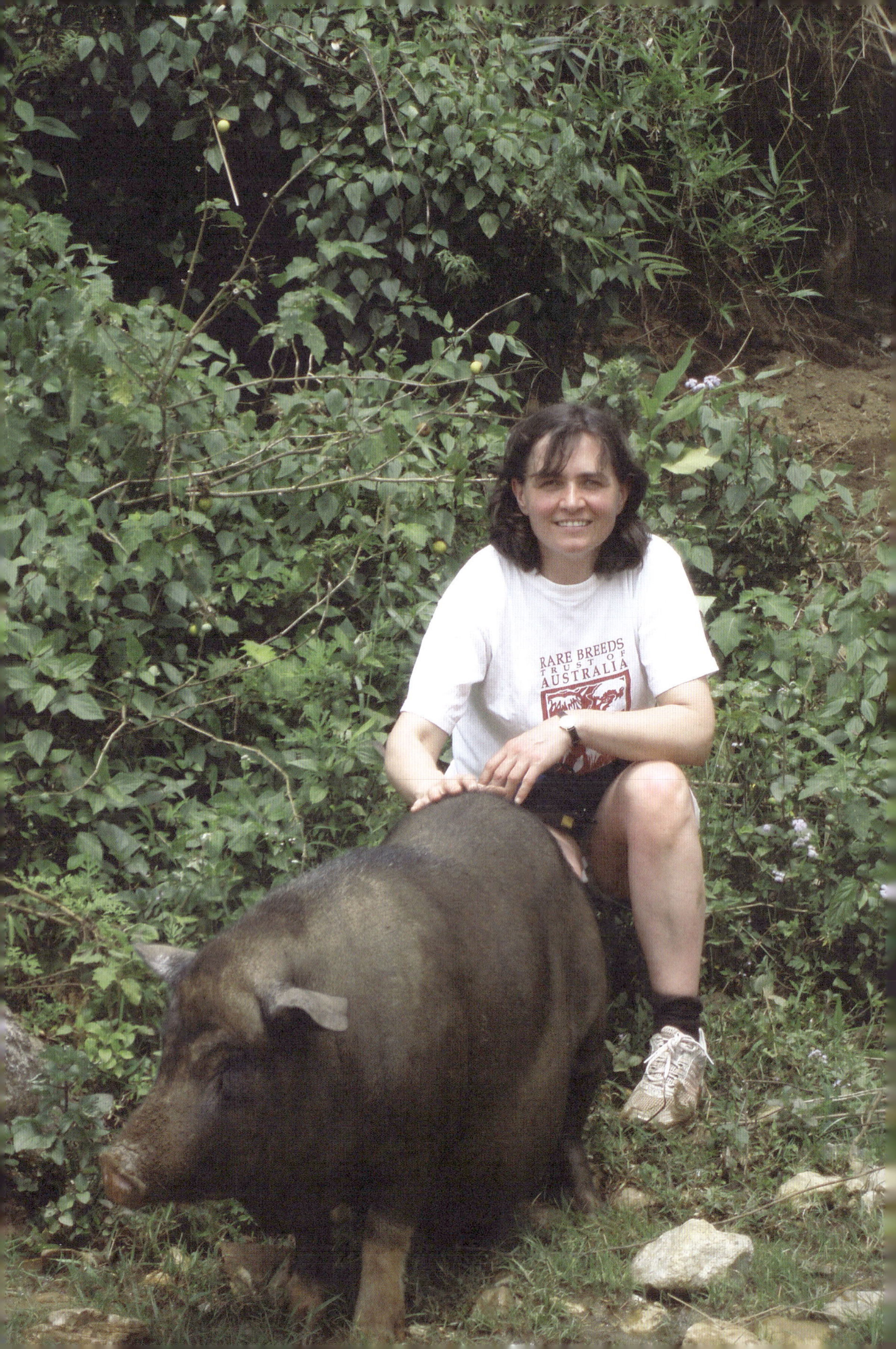
RARE BREEDS
TRUST OF
AUSTRALIA

CHAPTER EIGHTEEN **THE WAY OF THE FUTURE**

Rare Breeds fundraising auctions are popular and well-attended occasions.

over three hours. People travel the length and breadth of the South Island to attend, and North Islanders often make the journey. Anything can happen, and often does. One year we sold a yak: the animal was in Nelson and the purchaser was in Auckland. The event makes a bit of money that goes back into rare breed conservation but, probably more importantly, it brings people together and allows for genetics to be moved around. Cars and vans pull up, loaded to the gunwales with crates of chooks, ducks and various livestock, which they unload into the pens. They then buy an equal amount of livestock, if not more, and head off back home, having had a great day. Matings are arranged, new breeders are brought into the fold: it's conservation in action. The approach is much more like that taken by plant people, totally different from the management of native and exotic species.

The Zebu cattle I imported from Australia have been very slow to breed – a bit of inbreeding depression probably – but there's nothing quite like these delightful little highly endangered cattle, and we continue to get comments about them at Willowbank, especially from tourists. Many from India come especially to see them. The total opposite to these are the miniature white Galloway cattle. Fluffy and white with black points, they're soft and cuddly storybook cows, with quiet, gentle temperaments. Even after all these years, I still love putting my arms around their necks and giving them a cuddle, when no one's looking.

Opposite: Rare Breeds International Australian director Fiona Chambers with a Vietnamese pig.

287

RESCUE ONE NEW ZEALANDER'S CRUSADE TO SAVE ENDANGERED ANIMALS

A year-old Zebu.

I've had many sheep breeds over the years but am now focusing on some of the exotic breeds that have been brought into the country more recently and are unlikely to be reintroduced. In the late 1990s the government went out on a limb and imported some sheep breeds at the astronomical cost of approximately $24,000 per animal because of the stringent testing required, over five generations, for the degenerative neural disease, scrape. Fat-tailed Karakul sheep were one of these breeds, their main claim to fame the quite amazing fur-like coat of the newborn lambs. At its best it's called astrakhan: many grandmothers and celebrities had coats made of this. A good astrakhan coat may well cost in excess of US$100,000. Everyone will be familiar with

CHAPTER EIGHTEEN **THE WAY OF THE FUTURE**

the woolly hats that the Russians so often wear. These are usually also made of karakul, from lambs a few months old.

The karakuls arrived in New Zealand from South Africa, at a rough cost of around $24,000 per head when they left quarantine. Landcorp ran them for some years but the shepherds hated them, a feeling that was mutual. If the sheep saw a dog they would huddle in a group and not move. They were used to being herded and put away at night. Because they were so frustratingly hard to handle, I was rung and asked if I would like to buy the lot, which I did, though I then got three other people involved, to help with the purchase and to split the mob into different breeding groups. I embarked on an AI and embryo transplant programme, which dramatically improved the quality of the stock. We ended up exporting genetics to the United States and Brazil. The karakuls were a true success story and we liked them very much, but we had only a relatively small property and were running too many breeds. Reluctantly, after many years, we decided to pass the flock on to other breeders and sold the flock off, but not before we took a large number of embryos and several hundred straws of semen from five rams to go into the Rare Breeds Genebank. That's our safety net. It's comforting to know that if anything happens, or the other breeders lose interest, we, and others, can recreate the flock very easily.

The decision about the karakuls has allowed us to focus on some other breeds, including the Awassi, a fat-tailed milking breed imported by the government from Israel in the 1990s. As with the karakul, the government lost interest and ended up selling the entire flock to a wealthy Saudi Arabian man. Most were exported to Australia and the others were shifted down to Pleasant Point in Canterbury, where a lovely old couple, John and Karen Garrick from Timaru, obtained some stock from the farm manager, who was a friend of theirs. A few years later the rest were then moved back up north to Hawke's Bay and nobody thought anything of it. The Garricks were successful in breeding the animals, which looked quite different with their white bodies, brown heads and legs and large floppy ears, and because of that attracted some attention. There were numerous articles and photos in the local papers. Then one day they were visited by some dark-suited gentlemen with dark glasses, who stood on their doorstep and said they had no right to those sheep, the genetics were all owned by one other person, and if they continued, then they were personally at risk. At the end of that discussion John and Karen were left scared stiff and, knowing of my interest, asked if I wanted to purchase the animals, which I couldn't do quickly enough. The flock was a bit nondescript, but I took the best ones out and continued with

RESCUE ONE NEW ZEALANDER'S CRUSADE TO SAVE ENDANGERED ANIMALS

Jim McPhee and Greg McKay of XCell Breeding Services implanting embryos.

them. Years later I imported some more genetics and now have a small flock of good animals, which have become quite highly sought after, especially now that the interest in sheep milking has grown enormously. Having exported several animals and genetics to other countries, I've been waiting for the black-suited brigade to arrive with baseball bats to break some kneecaps, but so far they've left me alone.

One day I got a phone call from a man in Raglan, who wanted some Awassi sheep. Did I want some Damara sheep in exchange? I knew of the breed but had only seen one Damara before in New Zealand, a ram at Ag Research. I was fascinated: it looked much more like a goat than a sheep, with a shiny hair coat and a fat tail. So I agreed to a swap and a month or so later five Damaras came down on transport. I didn't know quite what to expect, but was very taken by them. The ewes in particular were very doe-like, and had a natural appeal, and they were all multi-coloured. These had been imported from Australia, but originally they come from Namibia, where they're run in the deserts as pastoral animals — they're browsers. Rich green grass didn't go down very well and tended to contribute to foot problems. Fortunately our property is quite dry, and the more it burnt off in the summer, the better they liked it and the fatter they became. Like goats, they hated the wet and cold and needed protection against the elements in the winter. They're gentle sheep, quite timid, and tend to huddle together for protection. Once you've established a relationship with them, however, they're easy to work with and will follow you anywhere if you're carrying a bucket of sheep nuts. Many have throat tassels, something I've never seen before in sheep. After a few years of getting some outside blood and selective breeding we now have some big strong animals, in comparison to what we started with, and we've exported rams to places like New Caledonia.

Sometimes they're too big and strong. If I'm going to keep male animals, I normally start tying them up from an early age, with a halter and a rope. After being tied up a few times they can be led, which makes a huge difference when handling them or taking them out to shows or displays. One day the next-door neighbour rang me to say that there was a strange animal in with his ewes, chasing them around. I went over and, sure enough, it was my big Damara ram. The ewes, which had been on the boundary, were just starting to cycle into an interesting condition. My ram had broken through three deer gates, plus the boundary fence, in order to try and impress them. Less impressed was the neighbour. The culprit had no intention of being caught. Climbing into the neighbour's ute, I chased him round the paddock a few times. Being overweight and unfit, the ram soon came to a stop and just stood there, enabling me to jump out and grab hold of his horns.

'Now what are you going to do?' asked the neighbour, looking reasonably admiring that the animal was still.

'Have you got any baling twine in the back of the truck?'

'Yep.'

'Well, pass me a bit and I'll make a halter and lead him home', which I did.

Lambing time came and among the neighbour's studs were a few odd-ball-looking brown lambs, leaving him to mutter that the only good they would be was if he threw them back over the fence. A few months later, however, and the stock agent came out to take the first draft off to be sold. He, too, was scratching his head wondering what they were, but they all went away with the top of that first draft, and I was confident enough to suggest that the neighbour should lease one of my rams for the next year to get some decent lambs on the ground.

Strangely enough, although the pure Damara is not an animal whose carcase you would rate very highly, the cross is. A Damara cross is recognised as a breed in its own right, called the Meatmaster. It seemed logical to try this, and so I have now also been breeding Meatmaster sheep for a number of years

A magnificent Damara ram.

and firmly believe they have a good future. They're extremely meaty and they have no wool, which means no shearing or crutching or tailing. About 40 per cent of a sheep's energy goes into growing wool, which is currently not worth having, so putting all that energy into the manufacture of valuable meat makes good commercial sense.

A number of years ago I was going around my Damara ewes and found a couple of tiny little ram twins. I looked at them without much enthusiasm and moved on to bigger and better lambs. A couple of months later I was still looking at these two animals, and no matter how often I looked at them they didn't seem to want to grow. A total waste of time, I thought, and then one day I suddenly realised that the problem was mine. It's all about how you look at something. These are the most valuable sheep I have *because* they're so small. When I researched the background of some of these African sheep, I found that there's a pygmy gene in some breeds. I therefore selected for that gene over a number of years, did some embryo work and ended up with a little multi-coloured, very naughty flock of miniature sheep that were hardy and did not require any shearing or intensive management. I called them African Pygmies. They're very much a favourite of mine and have a good future on lifestyle blocks, vineyards and in other niche circumstances. We also have a small flock of spectacular African four-horned sheep and equally spectacular

CHAPTER EIGHTEEN **THE WAY OF THE FUTURE**

Sue with a miniature Highland bull.

Valais sheep, which hail from Switzerland. With their long, lustrous, fluffy wool, sparkling white with black noses, feet and eye patches, they're like a cross between a cuddly toy and a panda bear. Definitely designer sheep.

This may seem a strange mix of livestock, and many people, especially our more conventional farming friends, shake their heads when they see them. Our return per animal, however, far exceeds anything other such farmers may get. A good quality product will always have a niche market, and it may not even be in New Zealand.

We have a variety of other animals at Willowbank Farm: horses, donkeys, dogs, of course, as well as ducks, geese and chooks. All are special breeds but we do like our chooks which are Cochins. One of the largest chickens in the world, the Cochin came initially from China, which was extremely advanced in that type of breeding. It had pretty much died out in New Zealand, but a breeder named Roger McCormick set about recreating it by extracting the Cochin gene from various breeds of fowl that had bits in them. Twenty-four years later I heard about his project and offered to be part of it. In essence, Cochins are like great big Pekin bantams, with broad chests and fluffy feet. They come in a range of colours and are very quiet and docile. The simple pleasures of a chook around your feet and an egg in the nest are pretty hard to beat, as is the pleasure of helping to conserve a rare breed.

Designer Valais sheep from Switzerland.

Our Sebastopol geese are enough to confuse anyone. We started with three ganders. Two became a couple and ostracised the other, who went on to become firmly attached to a white Galloway cow. The couple wished to be same-sex parents, and each breeding season would attempt to steal ducklings off the mallards, which led to bizarre scenes as the mother duck tried to entice her children back. Eventually I introduced a female goose, which had the effect of splitting off a pair, who went off and built a nest. The odd one left out then partnered up with a small white duck. It all becomes difficult trying to explain to visitors what's happening.

A dog has always been an essential part of my life, and I've owned and trained many breeds. My little fox terrier Tussle followed me onto the farm. Terrier means earth, and she loved any opportunity to expand on her basic hereditary calling, digging things out or just creating mayhem. Often you would see her heading down the driveway, pretending she was just cruising, but you could see by the way she looked over her shoulder, that, given an opportunity, she had other adventures on her mind. One Saturday night I arrived back early in the morning, buggered after a late night in the restaurant. As I crawled into bed and Sue whispered, 'Tussle's missing.' She had sneaked off during the evening and had not returned. It was a sombre breakfast and an empty day. That night we were putting the remaining two dogs away, when Sue said, 'I can hear a dog barking.'

Walking away from any outside noise, I stood and listened. Sure enough, there did seem to be a muffled bark coming from somewhere in the distance.

CHAPTER EIGHTEEN THE WAY OF THE FUTURE

Torch in hand, I followed the sounds into the neighbours' place, half a kilometre away. As I got closer, the realisation hit me. The neighbour had a deep offal pit, into which went any sheep or anything else that had died. Shining my torch into the depths, I could see little Tussle bouncing up and down on swollen carcases, with a belly like she was several months pregnant. After going back home for an extension ladder, I lowered myself into the spongy pit to grab the little bitch by the scruff of the neck and haul her up to the top. A swift kick up the backside saw her heading gratefully for home, and although for months afterwards there were longing looks in the direction of the pit, she never went there again.

The dog that now suits me best is the little mongrel farm dog. I say mongrel with tongue in cheek because they can be very highly bred and a good one will set you back several thousands of dollars. They're working dogs, and need to be kept that way. They have no breed standard as such, but there's always a chain on a kennel for a good honest working dog. Circumstances change. In the early days of Willowbank's development, I enjoyed the back-up of a good German shepherd. Now I couldn't do without the skills of my little collie heading dog, Fly. The stock are well aware if the dog isn't around and are only too pleased to play up because of it.

Handling animals is something I really enjoy – working with them, or as I call it, getting inside their heads. This applies whether you're dealing with a wild horse, teaching a dog how to behave, walking in with a big cat or understanding why a bird won't settle on a nest. No computers can teach that. You have to be able to think at the animal's level as best you can. I often find it hard working stock with people watching. It's such a personal thing: lose your focus and things can go badly wrong. Every bodily expression from both parties is important and needs to be understood. It can be mentally and physically exhausting, but the reward is that special relationship. Yes, it's a partnership, but you must always be the one controlling the outcome, while maintaining absolute trust.

One day, while watching a short animals clip on TV, I was astounded to hear the presenter say, 'You would almost think they felt emotion.' I remember clearly the day I brought a small cow called Olive back from Willowbank and put her back in with her bull friend Gulliver. They ran to each other and just stood nose to nose, nuzzling and lowing quietly with a strong intensity. Tears started to roll down Gulliver's face until they formed rivers in the dust on his cheeks and dripped onto the ground. Sue and I looked on with respect and awe before quietly slipping away.

With the number of kiwi at Willowbank, and the wide open enclosures they were in, it was often difficult to find one if it had moved camp and gone for a holiday under a log. Plus, if one did ever escape, it was good to have the means of finding it again. So I registered, and was accepted for, the DOC dog programme. This is very under-recognised within New Zealand, yet we lead the world in the use of dogs for conservation purposes and this initiative has trained handlers and their dogs from a number of other countries. The programme is strict, with only a limited number of handlers and dogs ever involved. Normally those handlers, at the upper level of conservation work, are as full of character as their canines. There are two types of conservation dogs. The first are the protected species dogs, who get rated for their ability to find a particular target species, such as kiwi. The other type are the predator control dogs. Some people think that this means a pack of animals hunting and chewing up nasty predators, but this isn't the case. In both instances the dogs 'indicate' when there's a target species and the handler then decides how to resolve the situation.

There are rat and mouse dogs, stoat dogs, cat dogs and even an ant dog. When the Auckland Regional Council had a problem with Argentine ants, a dog was trained up that could find one of these insects in an area the size of a tennis court, and even differentiate between ant species. Without conservation dogs, it's most unlikely that there would be any kākāpō left, as they would have been almost impossible to find and capture. And without them saving kiwi would be much more difficult and not nearly as successful. My little heading dog Fly, sadly no longer with us, was not only an essential tool for me as a farm dog; she was also fully accredited as a kiwi dog, and did a great deal in that role.

The home farm has continued to develop over the years, with everything we make put back into it. For me, however, it has to be a commercial operation, as opposed to a conservation facility like Willowbank. Every year new fences go up, paddocks are sown, buildings are erected or maintained. Some would regard us as alternative lifestylers, but we don't see ourselves that way. Certainly our power is still totally off grid. We've added considerably to it over the years and have little need to consider changing it. Because it does limit us in providing heat, much of that is generated by a large double-oven wood-burning stove, which also heats the water and most of the house. We have a lot of wood available and prefer a natural flame to artificial heat. It certainly means a bit of firewood cutting, but then neither of us has had to pay to join a gym class. The large vegetable garden is Sue's pride and joy: often everything on the table is home produced. There's a certain pleasure in being able to shut the gate with the knowledge that you can provide for yourselves.

CHAPTER EIGHTEEN **THE WAY OF THE FUTURE**

In Fiordland, setting off in search of moose.

These basic instincts are embedded in all of us; they just get plastered over with bling and ambition, and the lifestyle that society promotes and requires us to adhere to. The concept that more people brings more growth, which creates a better lifestyle, is something that I have difficulty comprehending.

To some extent our work in saving rare breeds, such as the Galápagos donkey expedition and capturing the wild pigs on the Auckland Islands, has had some global recognition.

Willowbank's role in helping to achieve these conservation goals has been significant and I would like to think that our role has extended well beyond that of keeping an animal in a cage. From small beginnings, the park has morphed into an organisation whose ripples have spread far. It should always be remembered that there's both an emotional and an ethical cost in keeping any living creature in a captive environment.

If you don't believe that something is possible, then you'll never believe the truth even when you see it. An acquaintance from DOC rang me one day to say that he had seen evidence of pigs in Fiordland, where there's never been any record of such animals. It took a while, but I couldn't help myself. I just had to find out if it was true. So far we've done four trips into Fiordland, at huge cost because it's the furthest point in New Zealand from civilisation. On the last trip we found that the pigs did exist. We found physical sign of where they had been and obtained some faecal material. From that DNA has been extracted and we are now waiting for further research to try and establish their relationship and possible origin. The current thought is that they may

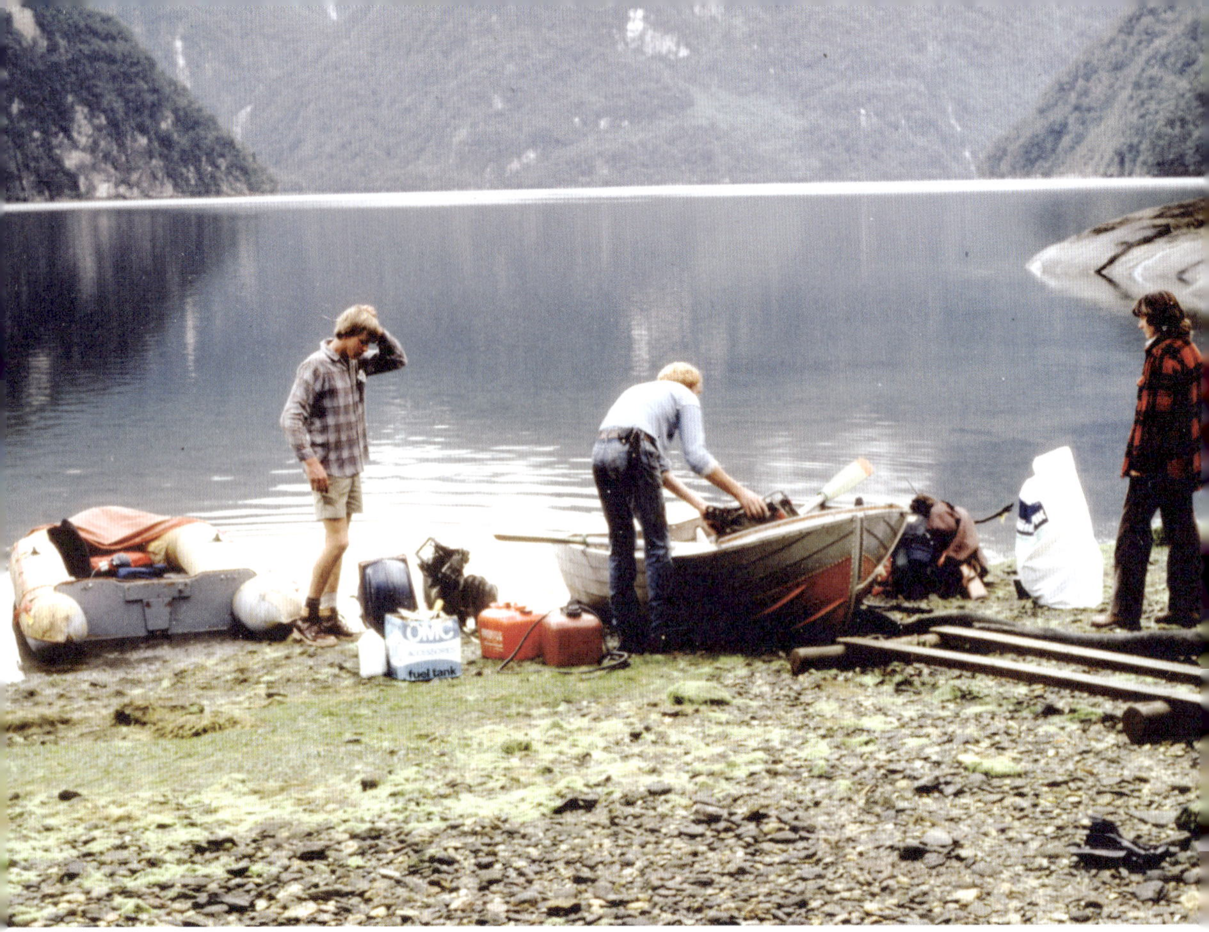
OMC
fuel tank

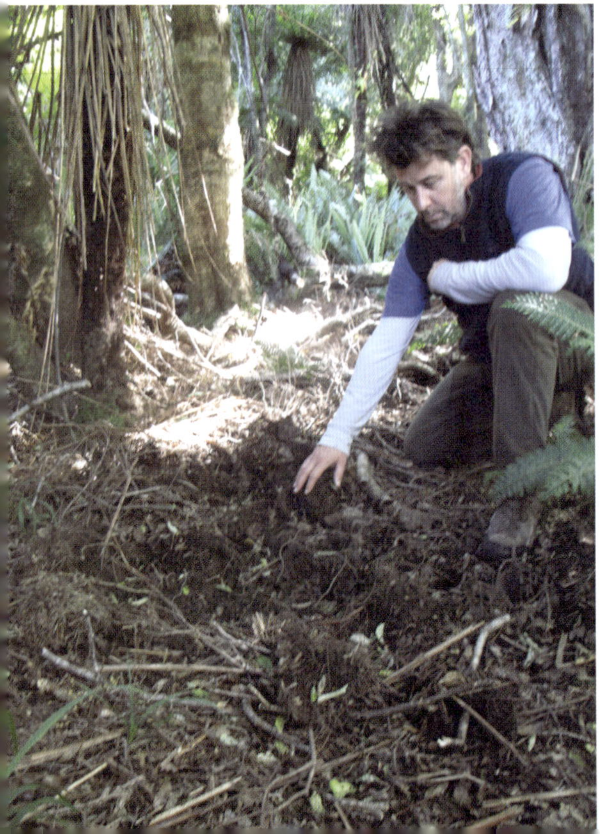

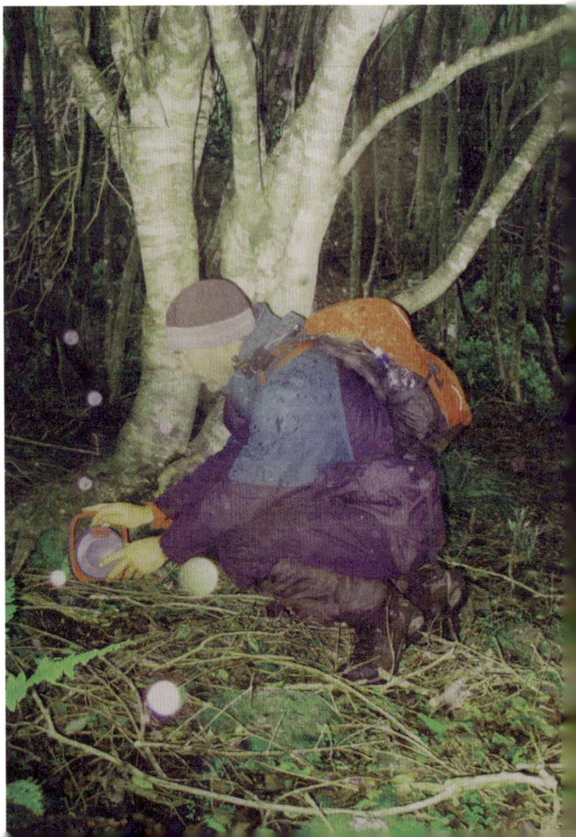

CHAPTER EIGHTEEN **THE WAY OF THE FUTURE**

date back to the sealers, as pig bones have been found in some sealers' caves in the same location. On our first trip, Sue and I, and Terry and Heather Nelley, were living in one of those caves in the middle of winter. Terry and Heather are very familiar with the North Island kōkako, and are quite convinced that they heard and later maybe saw one, so we've also been hunting for the elusive South Island kōkako on Stewart Island and in Fiordland, and have many more trips planned. New Zealand is truly an amazing place, with still many secrets to yield, from lost ruby mines and historical artefacts to breeds that no one knew existed and are waiting to be rediscovered. The childhood dream of a zoo of elephants and lions may have been displaced, but what we're doing now is surely going to be the way of the future.

Opposite: Loading the boats before departure.

Opposite far left: Mark with signs of pigs in Fiordland.

Opposite left: Dale sets up a sound system as part of a Fiordland kōkako search.

The sun was setting over Mount Ngauruhoe on a gorgeous blood-red autumn evening in a stunning wild and windswept landscape. I was travelling across the volcanic plateau with John Simister from Staglands Wildlife Park. We had done this trip often and little had changed except that the Land Rover was a bit more modern than it had been in the past. The long, flat roads lent themselves to contemplation and many memories of the past. We weren't collecting any animals on this trip, even though there were some boxes in the back just in case. Rather it was a yearly pilgrimage we used to make, travelling around the country visiting other wildlife establishments. We both found it stimulating to see what others were doing, and always came back with refreshed ideas and a desire to improve. Strangely enough, it wasn't the big spending concepts at some of the major zoos that impressed us, but often the simple ideas that a small operator may have dreamt up. It could be hand feeding fish and being able to feel their lips around your fingers or bringing a rabbit up to eye level with a child, so the pair can communicate with each other. It could be looking at conservation projects and hearing from the people trying to juggle their priorities. For us it was always about people, conservation and creating an experience, and only a little about money.

The road noise and constant scenery dulled me into a reflective state, until John broke the spell.

'I think we're an endangered species,' he said abruptly.

That got my interest. 'Why?'

'When we first started there were wildlife parks, zoos and farm parks opening all the time around New Zealand. How many are still there?'

That was a point to ponder, but it didn't take long to answer. Virtually none. The attrition rate was catastrophic. There used to be several small zoos in New Zealand and they have all gone. Farm parks open and close. Apart from some community- and council-based establishments, there was really very little.

'So, okay, what point are you making?' I asked John as we started on the long descent down to Lake Taupo.

'It's too bloody difficult now. We just went out and did it. People don't do that today, and if they try, they'll get bound up in so much red tape and compliance it will never work. People today have boxes to tick, while we just bulldozed on and did it. We've had the best of it. We don't have the personal make-up to join and be part of today's world.'

'So we're basically living in the past?' I countered.

'Yes, we're not part of the future.'

And in a way John was right. Almost inevitably, the people who started such institutions have run into conflict with the future. And the future, in many cases, hasn't been kind to them. This all felt a bit odd, as I had always assumed that I would be doing what I do for the rest of my life.

'It hasn't been a bad past,' I said. 'Sure, there have been some tough times,

Far left: Left to right, Simon Nelley, Terry Nelley and Dale Hedgcock, looking for kōkako.

Above: Me, at Richard Henry's camp. The ponga logs mark his kākāpō holding cages.

CHAPTER EIGHTEEN **THE WAY OF THE FUTURE**

In 2015 I received the insignia of a Member of the New Zealand Order of Merit for services to wildlife conservation from Governor General Sir Jerry Mateparae.

but we've managed to squeeze a fair bit in and have a bucketload of fun on the way. I'd rather live on memories than dreams any day.'

When people ask about retirement, my stock answer is that I've never worked a day in my life, so there's no way I can ever retire. My work is my life and I love it with a passion. My memories will inevitably become dreams, but I'll always be grateful for the people and animals who have become part of them.

Willowbank
your kiwi guarantee
www.willowbank.co.nz

Heritage New

Wild New Zealand

Safety Points:
- Stay on the pathways
- Be aware of waterways
- Read and follow all signs
- Supervise children feeding the animals
- Some animals cannot be fed for dietary reaso[ns]
- Willowbank is smoke free

Enjo[y]

WILD NEW ZEALAND

1. Eels
2. Swan
3. Deer
4. Pukeko
5. Geese
6. Emu
7. Wallaby
8. Chinese Geese
9. Monkeys
10. Turtles
11. Parrots
12. Lemurs
13. Otters
14. Siamang Gibbons

HERITAGE NEW ZEALAND

15. Peacock
16. Kunekune pig
17. Tortoises
18. Iguanas
19. Clydesdale
20. Chickens
21. Donkeys
22. Llama
23. Goats
24. Cattle
25. Sheep
26. Rabbits
27. Alpaca
28. Miniature Horses
29. Auckland Island Pigs

NATURAL NEW ZEALAND

30. Kakariki
31. Trout
32. Salmon
33. Weka
34. Black Swan
35. Kea
36. Wood Pigeon
37. Kunekune Pig
38. Blue Duck
39. Tuatara
40. Reptiles
41. Takahe
42. Kiwi
43. Kaka
44. White Heron
45. New Zealand Falcon
46. Ferret
47. Morepork
48. Possum

FACILITY

A. Entrance
B. Restaurant
C. Ko Tane – The Maori Cultural Experience
D. Cafe
E. Shop
F. Toilet
G. BBQ and Picnic area
H. Barn

ATTRACTIONS

I. Deer Stalkers Hut
J. Mai Mai
K. Bitch Box
L. Nursery / Eco Garden
M. Tractor Museum
N. Donkey Rides
O. Stock Yard
P. Hanks Hut
Q. Maori Village
R. Alpine Walk Through Aviary
S. Kiwi Breeding House
T. Tuatara World
U. Meeting House – Advocacy Kiwi
V. Nocturnal House
W. Natural Kiwi Breeding Area
X. Trout Viewing Window
Y. Rare Breeds Centre

Natural New Zealand